AMERICAN CICERO

American Cicero

Mario Cuomo and the Defense
of American Liberalism

Saladin Ambar

OXFORD
UNIVERSITY PRESS

OXFORD
UNIVERSITY PRESS

Oxford University Press is a department of the University of Oxford. It furthers
the University's objective of excellence in research, scholarship, and education
by publishing worldwide. Oxford is a registered trade mark of Oxford University
Press in the UK and certain other countries.

Published in the United States of America by Oxford University Press
198 Madison Avenue, New York, NY 10016, United States of America.

Library of Congress Cataloging-in-Publication Data
Names: Ambar, Saladin M., author.
Title: American Cicero: Mario Cuomo and the defense of American liberalism /
Saladin Ambar.
Description: New York, NY: Oxford University Press, 2018. |
Includes bibliographical references and index.
Identifiers: LCCN 2017015740 | ISBN 9780190658946 (hardcover: alk. paper) |
ISBN 9780190658960 (epub)
Subjects: LCSH: Cuomo, Mario M., 1932–2015. | Governors—New York
(State)—Biography. | New York (State)—Politics and government—1951– |
Liberals—United States—Biography. | Democratic Party (U.S.)—Biography.
Classification: LCC F125.3.C86 A83 2017 | DDC 974.7/043092 [B]—dc23
LC record available at https://lccn.loc.gov/2017015740

9 8 7 6 5 4 3 2 1

Printed by Sheridan Books, Inc., United States of America

In memory of Ida Thacker, nèe Ida Carmela Canale
and for her grandchildren,
Gabrielle, Luke, and Daniel

This Lord is very secretive, and I think no one but himself knows what he will do. His highest aides have often assured me that he never reveals his plans until he issues an order, and that is as late as possible, when the thing has to be done, and not otherwise.

—Niccolo Machiavelli, December 21, 1502

Contents

Preface

IT'S PROBABLY UNWISE to begin an introduction with a gripe, how-ever small. But, I confess, nearing the end of writing this book, I was experiencing a bit of authorial testiness. I was responding to what later proved to be (and was undoubtedly at the time) an astute observation from one of the anonymous editorial reviewers of my initial manuscript who had the unmitigated gall (whatever that is) to ask, in so many words: *What is this book all about?* Why do we need a book on Mario Cuomo? The trouble was, I had been living with New York's 52nd governor in my head for the past four years and thought the question somewhat supercilious. But once I took a moment to reflect (with a gentle nudge from Oxford University Press's ever-skillful editor, Dave McBride), it occurred to me that I had not been making my case for Cuomo strongly enough. My life had in its own way tracked along with Cuomo's political career. I lived in Forest Hills between the ages of five and six—a little black kid living with his mother and Italian American grandmother (to whom this book is dedicated). Little did I know at the time that a good number of Forest Hills residents were up in arms over, well, people like *me*, moving into their neighborhood. I also had no idea who Mario Cuomo was, or that he was charged with mitigating this dispute centered on race and class.

From there I moved to Flushing, a long walk from the auto chop shops near what was then Shea Stadium, where Cuomo got his first start in politics, defending the small business owners who the legendary (some might say infamous) Robert Moses was trying to force out for the 1964 World's Fair. It turned out that I came to know the neighborhoods—Corona, Willets Point, Forest Hills—where Cuomo made his name in politics in the always chip-on-its-shoulder Borough of Queens. But it wasn't these early experiences in Cuomo's career that mattered to me. It was later, during my teens, when I came to know Cuomo as the governor who got involved in the myriad racial conflagrations that defined my youth: Howard Beach, Bensonhurst, Crown Heights, and so on. I was part of that world in the 1980s of black youth who came of age when the old New York, the one before its gentrified makeover, was still untamed, a bit frightening, and altogether real. Cuomo stood out to me even then, as I began to journey into the world of Jesuit education at Georgetown University, as a statesman of some stature. He certainly wasn't in the mold of Ed Koch, or the other petit figures of the period's politics. Cuomo was, at least as far as white politicians went, *understanding*. I think in my own way, in beginning this book, I presumed that many had been along on this journey through Queens and New York politics too. And that gracious reviewer picked up on that misguided assumption, and so I had some further explaining to do.

To wit, I thought I'd include my emailed response to him or her in this space, hoping to give readers my instinctive burst of who Mario Cuomo was and is, and what he means for those interested in American politics these past few decades. I've left out as much of the academic-speak here as possible. You'll have your share to come in the main text. But, suffice it to say, I don't think you had to "be there" in the 1980s and early 1990s in New York to grasp Cuomo, though it helps. And, if you weren't there, then I hope this short response serves as a window into the book now in your hands—and into the larger world of American politics when its direction seemed to still be very much up in the air.

Fri, Apr 22, 2016 at 6:58 PM

Hi Dave,

I found some time this afternoon to respond to the reader. I thought I had been making myself clear, but apparently not as well as I imagined. In any case, it's a good thing to keep in mind going forward as I make necessary edits down the road. For now, here is my reply. Let me know if you'd like to discuss it or if you have any questions or suggestions.

All Best,

Din

Of all the liberal stalwarts in the period Sean Wilentz (2008) defines as the "Age of Reagan" (1974–2008), Mario Cuomo presented the most serious counter-argument to Reagan's brand of conservatism. This challenge exceeded the ones presented by the likes of those who had failed to tackle this nascent conservatism (George McGovern), represented the dying flame of liberalism's most successful days (Teddy Kennedy), or embodied its rich intellectual tradition (Patrick Moynihan). In this book, I am arguing that Mario Cuomo posited a New Deal–style liberalism to be sure, but one that was more ardently ethnic and without the deep compromises along racial lines endemic to that coalition. He also was no mere theoretician—governing from a state house; Cuomo was an executive leader who had to test his ideas against a legislature, one largely opposed to his ends. He governed from the largest stage in New York and was from his first election to the governorship a serious contender for the White House. And Cuomo had to earn the support of voters with his governing record, one he could not mask in the way senators can. *He was, in short, the most significant voice from the liberal wing of the Democratic Party who represented the most realistic chance of unseating Reagan or his successor.* I think this makes him, from a progressive point of view, the most important Democratic national figure in the last 30 years. He was no mere flash in the pan (Howard Dean) or end-of-career phenomenon

(Bernie Sanders). Cuomo governed in the heart of the Reagan Era (1982–1994), and he did so in terms unequivocally opposed to that agenda. You can find no admiring sentiments of his for Reagan as you do with Obama. Cuomo in this regard was more of a Franklin Delano Roosevelt (FDR), who exhibited open disdain for the opposing ideological stance of the Republican Party in his time. This is important because Obama, and now [Hillary] Clinton, are not making those kinds of arguments, and if [the presidential scholar] Stephen Skowronek is correct (and I think he is here), reconstructive presidents carry along with them rhetorical assaults on the fading regime; they do not buttress them with centrist language.

So, this is what I hope readers come away with. If they are interested in how Democrats took back the White House, they can read about Bill Clinton; if they are interested in the mastery of legislation or policy, they can read about the "American Burke" as a new biography of Moynihan sees the famed New York senator. But if readers are interested in learning about the best template for progressive governance in the Reagan era, one that best married New Deal liberalism with civic republicanism and an emphasis on the working class—and an open appreciation for and connection with black and white ethnic voters—they should read what I have to say about Mario Cuomo. The ability to marry these two segments within the Democratic Party—by progressives—has been the party's greatest challenge at least since 1972. Sanders, McGovern, and perhaps Elizabeth Warren—they have sterling liberal credentials and sadly, a limited appeal to black voters. Cuomo, the record as governor says to me, offers a poetic model—but also a practical one—for thinking about progressivism's future within the party, and how to bring these two factions together.

And this is where "fudging" may rear its head. Cuomo's story was also one of serious failings. His progressive vision was short-circuited in profound ways. It was Cuomo who built an archipelago of prisons for mostly black and brown people in New York. It was Cuomo who pushed for and got enormous tax cuts as governor that ultimately contributed to the state's budgetary crisis.

It was Cuomo who promised large programs (such as his massive New York City rescue plan in 1991) that came to naught. Cuomo tried to govern from the left, and he suffered serious setbacks for it, a good number of his own doing. So, yes, my claims require qualification. I think intelligent readers can discern the importance of such qualifications in writing about a career in politics that ran the better part of two decades. But I also think they will be able to see the forest for the trees. And that bigger picture shows Cuomo in speech and in action, pushing liberalism to its limits in its twilight hours.

I do think there has been great debate (including in this 2016 Democratic election cycle) over the value of rhetoric. Clinton routinely chastises Sanders (as she did Obama) for being all talk and vision and lacking a practical grounding in real-world politics. It is an old saw, one that Cuomo faced in his years as governor. Cuomo's voice resonated all the same with Democratic voters in 1984 when his convention speech thrust him into the national spotlight. In both 1987 and 1991, he was, in every poll I've looked at, the clear favorite for his party's nomination the following year. I think with Cuomo, such support went beyond nostalgic passes at the New Deal Era. No, I think George F. Will was right in noting that Cuomo's brand of liberalism was about what government can do, but also what communities could do, what religious faith could do, what a world of diverse voices could do. Will said famously that Cuomo believed in government but also in cops. He might've gotten it better had he said priests. But Cuomo's prison building certainly earned that remark.

I see Cuomo as more Social Gospel progressive than I do Great Society man. I see him in direct line with the Hudson Progressive tradition of "goo-goo" liberals who believed in government but did so with a sort of religious zeal. And often, in the name of religion (if not "Armageddon," a la Teddy Roosevelt). I do think there is a thesis here, but as with most theses, there are secondary (and often other) stories to tell. There is wreckage and failure, and missteps, and flat-out weak moments to Cuomo's leadership as governor of

New York. Some of these failings were all Cuomo's own; others were structural and related to a changing economy; and others— perhaps the largest failings—had to do with the simple fact that voters were no longer nearly as liberal as they had been. Cuomo was governing on the fringes of his party's ideological heyday. Time was running out.

In the end, I hope to strike a balance somewhere between hagiography, where Cuomo is simply the liberal lion, and the alternative of footnoting his legacy, where Cuomo is just another northeastern liberal whom history passed by. I think it is not only fair but accurate to say that Mario Cuomo has been the most significant liberal politician to challenge Reaganism in the past 30 years. I think it is also fair and accurate to say that even in his challenge to Reagan, Cuomo's legacy was that of the perhaps heroic, but nevertheless losing, side. At least for a time. A Bryan figure, if you will, before Teddy Roosevelt, Woodrow Wilson, and ultimately, Franklin Delano Roosevelt took progressivism to its long-hoped for heights. Wilderness years may lack a certain definitiveness, but they also produce interesting figures and, I think, inspiring stories and personalities. Mario Cuomo's is one. I believe people will be glad to read about him, not necessarily because I am the author, but because if they are under 40, they will have heard of him only in passing, and I believe they will find him compelling; or, if they are over 40, they will likely recall him with some degree of fondness. For most readers outside the academy who are interested in this book, that level of fondness for him will increase with their age. That has been my experience in researching and talking about this work. [End of email]

Part of the pleasure of writing this book has been my association with a number of people and institutions who've extended their professional and personal kindness in ways I can never repay. I ought to begin with my research assistant and translator during my time in Italy in 2012 and 2013, Àngels Miralda. Àngels put aside her time at the Royal College of Art and her PhD studies to return to Italy, where she had attended John Cabot University in Rome, in order to help me navigate the beautiful but daunting linguistic terrain of southern Italy. Àngels's fluency, intelligence, and charm helped win over any number of policemen, archivists, townspeople, and Cuomo relatives while we were in Italy. She also had a keen eye for the direction of the project from the beginning and helped me focus on the importance of unearthing Cuomo's familial origins and ties to Italy. I am eternally grateful for her help—especially for helping me navigate the less than sublime roads of Stabia.

Another serendipitous benefit of working with Àngels was her introducing me to the wonderful scholars Vanda Wilcox of John Cabot University and Nick Dines of Middlesex University in London. Over a lovely dinner in Rome, Vanda and Nick provided important insights into the period of fascist Italy, early 20th-century migration history and patterns, and perspectives on organized crime in and around Naples. Great scholars lead you to others, and my early bibliography began to form around that dinner table back in 2012. If only I could have carried Vanda and Nick along these past years. Others in Italy, where this research began, are owed a great debt of thanks—and these include Gigi Mauro, Nocera Superiore's registrar, Rosaria (Rosy) Cuomo, and the extended Cuomo family who greeted me in Nocera. Mario Cuomo's cousin (on his mother's side), Giordano Maddalena, was my anchor in Tramonti; her hospitality and warmth know no bounds. She provided important accounts of the land in which Cuomo's mother grew up, and later, in Nocera, where his father lived. In Nocera, the Cuomo family crest was presented to me—an indication that the Cuomos were hardly an impoverished clan from the hills of southern Italy. Cuomo comes from a proud and successful ancestry—one that perhaps belies a touch of nostalgia for the Italian version of the Horatio Alger story. I'd also like to thank Rita Cuofano, who ran the agro-tourist hotel I stayed in while in Tramonti, along with the City of Tramonti, for its hospitality.

Back stateside, there are innumerable people to thank so I'll be necessarily brief: Blythe E. Roveland-Brenton, the archivist at St. John's University's Library; Keith Swaney at the New York State Archives; my colleague and director of the Gipson Institute at

Lehigh University, Monica Najar, whose generous grant provided early assistance; my friend and longtime supporter, Ruth Mandel, director of the Eagleton Institute of Politics at Rutgers University, whose Center on the American Governor provided critical and early support for this research; Lehigh University, whose numerous grants these past years also sustained my work; I also owe many thanks to my colleagues at Lehigh whose insights, support, and kindness have always been exceptional. I should also like to extend a hearty thanks to those who agreed to be interviewed by me, including Gerald Benjamin, the Reverend Dr. Calvin Butts III, Dr. Nicholas D'Arienzo, Elizabeth Drew, Joseph Grandmaison, Joseph Mattone, Ray Scheppach, and Peter Quinn. David McBride at Oxford University Press continues to impress me both as a person and as an editor. This is my second book with Oxford and Dave has always found the time to be supportive, encouraging, and incisive. I'd also like to thank my agent, Geri Thoma at Writers House. Every author needs at least one believer. I'd like to think I have more than one, but Geri believes enough for everybody. Finally, I'd like to thank my wife Carmen who exceeds all others in encouragement and support. Every book is as much hers as mine. And then there are three nine-year-olds I know: Gabby, Luke, and Daniel. Their love is my every horizon.

Bethlehem, PA
June 2, 2016

AMERICAN CICERO

Prologue: Tarmac

SOMETIME DURING THE late morning of December 20, 1991, Mario Cuomo was told he had to make a decision. He was going to have to make an announcement by 2:00 pm saying whether he was going to take his aides and reporters with him from Albany aboard two chartered planes, and fly directly to Concord, New Hampshire, for the purpose of entering the race for the presidency as a Democratic Party candidate. The planes had arrived in Albany early that morning. The initial plan had been to fly the governor and his staff to Manchester, where they would then make their way to the state capitol in Concord.[1] The logistics of filing for the New Hampshire primary dictated the peculiar set pieces of the day: two planes waiting on the tarmac at the Albany airport; a quickly assembled staging for an afternoon press conference; and the former New Hampshire Democratic Party chairman, Joe Grandmaison, sitting in the lobby of the Ramada Inn across the street from the capitol, by a pay telephone awaiting word from the governor's man in Albany, John Marino, then chairman of the New York State Democratic Party.

Grandmaison had been a longtime player in New Hampshire politics. He went as far back as George McGovern's campaign in 1972 and was there for Michael Dukakis's first gubernatorial run in Massachusetts.[2] Marino had asked him, "What would it take to get you to support Cuomo?" "Well, I'm a liberal, hell," Grandmaison said, "if there was a meeting with six people at it, I'd expect to be one of them." Marino told him, "Let me check with Andrew [Cuomo]. He said 'fine.' So I was to file his paperwork."[3] That paperwork was to include a $1,000 certified check to cover the state's filing fee. Grandmaison was there in the event a New Hampshire snowstorm prevented the governor from arriving. "It happened to be a very nice day," he recalled.[4] Cuomo had until 5:00 pm to meet the filing deadline, but by 2:00 pm, Vincent Tese, New York's state commissioner of economic development, had spoken with the governor, and he "sounded 'depressed.'"[5] The impasse between Republican leaders in the legislature and Cuomo were even now, at the eleventh hour, dogging Mario Cuomo's presidential ambitions.

Meanwhile, Grandmaison had assembled some 200 volunteers at the State House for a Cuomo announcement by mid-afternoon.[6] "The cameras were just incredible," Grandmaison recalled.[7] For his part, Cuomo remained in varying accounts either "holed-up" or "secluded" in the governor's home; the *New York Times* invoked images of papal succession, describing reporters waiting for "white smoke" from the executive mansion throughout the day.[8] Cuomo was busy in part, preparing "two statements, one announcing his candidacy and the other explaining why he wasn't running, and previewed them for his aides."[9] At issue was an $8.75 million gap in the New York State budget and a looming $3.6 billion deficit for the coming year. Finally, at 3:00 pm, Grandmaison got the call from John Marino, and by 3:37 pm, there was Cuomo at the State House in Albany announcing that he would not seek the presidency in 1992. "It seems to me," he said, "I cannot turn my attention to New Hampshire while this threat hangs over the heads of the New Yorkers that I've sworn to put first."[10]

To date, there is but one book by a historian or political scientist about Mario Cuomo. The longest serving Democratic governor in the most powerful American state in the 20th century has a presidential candidacy–fueled biography to his credit—one that turned out to be overly hopeful.[11] There are few biographies or scholarly treatments of defeated presidential candidates; there are even fewer about those who elected not to run at all. Why should the case be any different with respect to Mario Cuomo? This book, it must be said from the start, has little concern with what has driven the bulk of political discourse over the past 25 years concerning Cuomo: namely, what he did not become. Indeed, so much has been said and written about what Mario Cuomo was not that an entire generation of Americans has had little to no exposure to what, in fact, he was. There is no denying that the intrigue surrounding Cuomo's decision not to run for the White House remains a veritable feast of innuendo and speculation for lovers of politics and American political history. Indeed, I went to Italy for two summers in part to consider those rumors. Yet Cuomo was far more than a passing or enigmatic figure in American life. He is, as I argue, one of the most important political actors in the last quarter of the 20th century and may well be the most critically important Democratic politician of his time not to become president. To understand why, we must understand a fundamental shift in both American and Democratic Party politics some 30 years ago.

As I've written elsewhere, the bookends of the 20th century can best be understood as two periods dominated by the resurgence of American governors in national politics.[12] The first era was led by progressive governors who posited a stronger role for government in what had previously been viewed as the private affairs of American citizens. Governors from the industrial Northeast— Hudson progressives—had been especially important in this business. These figures included Theodore Roosevelt, Woodrow Wilson, Charles Evans Hughes, Alfred Smith, and Franklin Delano Roosevelt. The progressive brand of politics in many ways shaped the first 75 years of the 1900s, building into the American social contract a new, more economically motivated commitment by the government to the American people. But this commitment did not go unchallenged, and by the mid-1960s, the tide had begun to turn, with 10 Republican governors elected to office in 1966, and a growing conservative movement in the Sunbelt states to overturn the legacy of their progressive forebears. Out of these states, national leaders emerged touting the conservative mantra of limited government; they were not all Republicans. Both Jimmy Carter and Bill Clinton rose to prominence in American politics in large part because of their executive leadership in southern states where the Sunbelt philosophy of limited government had taken hold. Their two presidencies surrounded the two terms of Ronald Reagan, who, like his Democratic cohorts, came from the governorship of a state eager to distance itself from the public policies of the progressive Northeast. The liberalism of experimentation in the states—the so-called laboratories of democracy touted by Louis Brandeis in another time, was now being recast as unfit for a republic long tired of doing too much for too many. Experimentation was better left to the private sector, free to go about its business in the more pro-corporate South and West. And in 1984, when Mario Cuomo took the podium in San Francisco to reject this changing tide in one of the most memorable Democratic Convention speeches ever delivered, every Democrat was not enthusiastic. Responding to Colorado's Democratic governor Richard Lamm's effusive praise for Cuomo's stirring defense of liberalism that July evening, Bill Clinton was dismissive. "Come on, what did it really say about the issues we're trying to raise?"[13]

And so, in the mid-1980s, one of the crucial battles in American politics was under way—a pair of contending declarations about the nature of good government driven by two distinctive and appealing Democratic governors. Mario Cuomo's politics reflected the New Deal New York he was born into, the one his family emigrated to from the Campania region of Italy. It was a milieu of white, ethnic, urban, Catholic, liberal, and reform-minded politics dedicated to making government accountable to citizens on the basis of what it did rather than what it did not do. Bill Clinton's Arkansas, on the contrary, was predisposed to the postwar Sunbelt politics that was fueling demographic movement to the American Southwest. This milieu was white, Protestant (and increasingly evangelical), suburban, pro-business, and fiercely opposed to the perceived overreach of the federal government in the affairs of ordinary people. One of the great reasons to revisit the political thought and career of Mario Cuomo is not to pine for the would-be confrontation with Reaganism he might have had had he run for the White House in 1992; the first consideration of Mario Cuomo's legacy must be the fallout for his party and the nation in his inability to confront Clintonism and the politics of triangulation successfully in the hinge years of 1984 and 1985.

With this first consideration in mind, there is a second point to be ventured. Who other than Mario Cuomo offered the most effective and potentially devastating critique of conservative politics as articulated by Ronald Reagan? Liberal stalwarts such as Teddy Kennedy or Pat Moynihan emerged out of the Senate—leaders of policy and intellectual heft but devoid of executive leadership experience. The ultimate reach of their politics was also at varying points proscribed by their inability to be perceived as presidential in their own right. Their realm was one of deliberation and the skill to erect progressive policy over time (or in some instances to withhold it). Reaganism was powerful in large measure because it was the politics of executive leadership. Michael Dukakis ran as a governor in 1988 but his aura was more suited to the rewards of the more technocratic Senate than the brawling stage of presidential politics. Cuomo's assaults on Reagan and conservatism in 1984, 1988, and again in 1992 resonated because they came from a person who had led; from a man who could readily be seen as a president in his own right. In these pages, I argue that whatever his temperamental flaws or political weaknesses, Mario Cuomo was, and remains, the best alternative progressive voice to the politics of Sunbelt conservatism in the past 30 years.

Finally, over a political career that ranged from 1964 to 1994, Cuomo governed in the twilight of progressivism's power, and yet his voice rose above the din of those aspirants to the progressive mantle. His combination of governing a "City" in speech, and in reality, gives him a classical burnish that contemporary republicanism is sorely missing. The philosopher-king may well be a fool's conception in the world of practical politics, but Cuomo's is the best vision of a perhaps world-weary model. Cuomo governed. His speeches were not merely the cadences of "poetry" he so often associated with campaigning. Indeed, his greatest and most influential rhetorical flourishes came while in power, not while seeking it. Does anyone remember what Cuomo said in the 1977 mayoral race or in his campaigns for governor? Cuomo's profoundest reflections are those unrelated to the dynamics of personal power. Perhaps this is more telling than we may know. If there is an American Cicero from our era of politics—the one who challenged Caesarism and a dim view of the poor and neglected—it is Cuomo. For it was Cicero's Philippics that sought to bring down Antony; his words—and record as governor of Cilicia—made his attacks all the more powerful. Perhaps the Philippics must be seen as a losing proposition in the eyes of history. They cost Cicero his hands, his tongue, and his life. But the model of oppositional politics to the vainglory of individualism had been laid down. This book is about Mario Cuomo's defense of liberalism in America—not necessarily its successes or its victories. And yet there is a wisdom in defense all the same. In this regard, this is a work in American political thought as much as it is in presidential or executive politics in the states. It is, once again, reflective of the long-standing crucial debates in the American republic concerning the best way to live, the good republic.

The book is divided into four parts. In Part One, I cover the Politics of Cuomo's rise to power in New York—the near 20-year climb in Queens that speaks to the ways in which New York City and New York State mirrored the changes taking place nationally. Cuomo's forays into the dynamics of urban power politics—beginning with an early conflict with Robert Moses and other, more pedestrian, stories of racial housing discrimination, before larger issues of progressive governance—are analyzed and given attention as hallmarks of his ultimate leadership style and values. The period focuses on the years 1974–1983, but begins with the confrontation with Moses in 1964.

In Part Two, I assess the Poetry of Cuomo's politics through a close examination of what may arguably be the two greatest speeches by an American politician in such a short window of time: Cuomo's Democratic Convention speech in San Francisco and his address on religion at Notre Dame some 60 days later in the summer of 1984. These two speeches are indispensable contributions to progressive political rhetoric in the second half of the 20th century, and they reflect not only the depth of Cuomo's political thought but, in many respects, are the best lodestar for considering a more resolute and progressive politics of the future. When those talks were behind him, Cuomo demurred. "I'm not a terrific candidate," he said. "I gave two good speeches."[14]

In Part Three, I focus on the Albany years and the heart of Cuomo's governorship, from 1985 to 1990. These "Prose" years of governing in the Reagan years and during New York's powerful economic struggles offer a window into the limitations of political theory and rhetoric. And yet the two prove not to be mutually exclusive as Cuomo's record is hardly without signature progressive successes, though it is his shortcomings that have come to highlight the difference between his theory and praxis. In Albany, Cuomo provides an intriguing look at the last of the great Hudson progressive governors and the significance of that world and its demise.

Last, in Part Four, I cover Cuomo's final years in Albany, including his decision not to seek the presidency in 1992. These years (1991–1994) are devoted to the Democratic Party and the unraveling of liberalism's leadership within the party in Washington, and Cuomo's last, and ultimately unsuccessful campaign for the governorship in 1994. I put this last campaign in historical perspective and contextualize it within the broader conservative movement's unprecedented victories in 1994.

Before closing, in the Epilogue, I cover my trips to Tramonti and Nocera Superiore, Italy, the hometowns of Cuomo's mother and father and the political, cultural, and economic history that informed Cuomo's upbringing in the Queens, New York, of his birth and his youth. I take a final look at Cuomo's cultural legacy through the eyes of the immigrant experience at the dawn of the New Deal era in America, and I weigh the whispers of Cuomo's "real" reason for not seeking the presidency, as I walk through my interviews and archival visits in Campania. While this book is not a political biography, I hope it will serve as a parallel track for understanding the progressive Democratic Party and presidential political history of liberalism over the course of its waning years of influence. I hope to illuminate how the political thought and career of Mario Cuomo offers a credible window into future considerations of liberal politics going forward. A generation after Cuomo's time in office, it is clear to me at least, that America had in fact produced a contemporary Cicero—a pragmatic and yet philosophic executive of the first order. The fact that he didn't seek the presidency—or more rightly, sought it and turned away—suggests more about our longings than it may about Cuomo.

Those longings came into the governor's office in Albany in the form of letters in the months leading up to the presidential elections of 1988 and 1992, like so many missives seeking to influence the heart of their target.

"Mr. Governor, you have a gift . . ."

"The purpose of this letter is to plead with you . . ."

"I am a survivor of the 1906 Earthquake . . ."

"It is your duty to run . . ."

"I'm 69 and have voted straight Republican since the early 1940s . . ."

"Don't stand from the challenge . . ."

"I believe you are the only viable Democratic candidate . . ."

"I cried in 1984 because you touched my soul . . ."

And, finally: "Dear Governor Cuomo: Run goddamn it!"[15]

When I was winding down my interview with Joe Grandmaison, I asked him about Cuomo's legacy today. He had been less wistful about a potential Cuomo candidacy in hindsight than I thought he might be. And yet, I was struck by his final thoughts.

"It's difficult to go back then," he said. "It was more difficult to have a conversation with the voters. He was such a major presence. He was poetic in speech. He made you feel good, *dammit*."

And then came a bit of history.

"I remember giving the declaration of candidacy to someone to take back to Albany—it's the kind of thing you wish you had kept on to. But it wasn't mine to keep."[16]

Part One

Politics

QUEENS, 1974–1983

IN MAY OF 1977, New York's Italian language daily *Il Progresso* was busy covering the rise of two prominent Hudson-area progressives.[1] Jim Florio of New Jersey, already a congressman, was eyeing a run for governor. Meanwhile, across the river, Mario Cuomo, New York's secretary of state, was officially a candidate for mayor of New York City.[2] Both men would go on to lose their respective races that year, though by the close of the next decade each would become governor, with Cuomo elected New York's 52nd executive in 1982 and Florio the Garden State's 49th governor in 1989. And while both men governed during the waning period of ethnic-based politics within the Democratic Party, it was Cuomo who would ultimately symbolize the closing chapter in the progressive brand of governance that had flourished within the party since the New Deal. By 1994, something fundamental had changed—both within the region and throughout the United States, as the conservative politics of the Sunbelt worked its way into the central ethos of the Democratic Party and much of its leadership. But in the mid-1970s, the urban landscape of ethnic, labor, and liberal politics was still very much at the heart of the world of ascending Florios and Cuomos.

The fatal flaw of "identity politics" that had plagued the Democratic Party since the resounding defeat of George McGovern in 1972 had not yet wound its course through New York—although Mario Cuomo often spoke to its antagonisms as an Italian American in nearly racialized terms.[3] His prickly rejoinders about his ethnic heritage proved to be premature on one level but altogether prescient in recognizing the corporate politics of a party increasingly attuned to fending off accusations of racial pandering rather than meeting the needs of its myriad ethnic constituents. The rise and fall of Florio—a tale of anti-bossism's burnish marred by "liberal" tax policies, mirrors that of Cuomo's progressive narrative. In Cuomo's instance, it was early career success through the forging of an uneven but largely successful compromise in Queens—among chop-shop and auto repair owners in Willets Point, working-class whites in Corona, and blacks and Jews in Forest Hills. His undoing, like that of Florio's, was association with a kind of caricature of the left—in Cuomo's case, opposition to the death penalty. In this light, Cuomo's political history reads as a continuation of liberalism's undoing during the Reagan era. Indeed, his lingering defining moment is often presented as a non-event: his decision not to seek the presidency in 1992. All of which begs the question of what can be learned about American politics in the late 20th century by examining the political career and thought of Mario Cuomo?

To begin, Cuomo's rise in New York politics was in part because he was what in political discourse at present is often called a "white ethnic." The term in many ways occludes the very real point that Italian Americans had for a time been frequently seen as "nonwhites." This was certainly true at the time when Cuomo's father, Andrea, came back to the United States (where he was born) in 1926 after a brief return to Italy. The racialist patina of American politics was still present for Italians in the 1980s, when that group's high school dropout rates began to be distinguished from that of African Americans and Puerto Ricans and mirror the rate of other whites. New York Senator Daniel Patrick Moynihan spoke to such residual sentiments in a private letter to Cuomo when he said that the then "chairman of the State Power Authority sees you as a somewhat overcompensating son of Italian immigrants."[4] The fact that Cuomo's personal ascent paralleled the successes and challenges of the Democratic Party's efforts to keep intact the white ethnic component of the New Deal coalition is essential to understanding both Cuomo's political thought and conservative inroads into urban and industrial America.

In addition, the conservative shift within the Democratic Party was emblematic of Cuomo's unsuccessful 1977 campaign for mayor and in his proxy rhetorical battles with Bill Clinton in 1984 and 1985. These transitional years saw Clinton's executive leadership and politics exercise an increasing hold on the party, and with the creation of the Democratic Leadership Council, the Arkansas governor helped orchestrate a movement away from the older, more traditional party politics forged during the New Deal. In hindsight, Ed Koch's victory against Cuomo likewise suggested that even in New York City, hard-bitten liberalism was vulnerable. And yet Cuomo governed during the presidency of Ronald Reagan and his successor George H. W. Bush. As the longest serving Democratic governor of New York State, Cuomo's record reflected the idealism of liberalism while pragmatically working with a legislature frequently at odds with his policies. As such, Cuomo's governorship represents an important counter-narrative to the rise of conservatism in the 1980s, concessions to its allure notwithstanding. No politician on the American left governed for as long and in such opposition to conservative thought as Cuomo did during the Reagan era, nor did any proffer an alternative politics with such fervor and plausibility.

In the end, the words of Cuomo carry great weight in suggesting his relevance beyond New York State politics. Cuomo's language was unabashedly liberal, to be sure, but it also was classically republican in its rejection of the magic of the private sector. Cuomo's was a community-based liberalism tied very closely to his Catholicism and his intellectual development. While not fusing the secular and the sacred, Cuomo held them aloft as veritable twins for garnering support for the ideal of the "public good." In this way, Cuomo's politics harken back to the Progressives— a reimagining of local politics that were imbued with a sense of responsibility—and indeed, an unapologetic insistence that the state owed far more to its citizens than merely standing aside.

The Southern Question: From Italy to New York

Andrea Cuomo returned to the United States in 1926, the year the Italian intellectual Antonio Gramsci published his work, "The Southern Question," a socialist discourse on the challenges uniting the entirety of the Italian peninsula against Fascism. Southern Italy had long been viewed as something of a netherworld politically. John Dickie, professor of Italian Studies, has noted the stereotypes well: "the South as a place of illiteracy, superstition, and magic; of corruption, brigandage, and cannibalism; of pastoral beauty and tranquility admixed with dirt and disease; a cradle of Italian and European civilization that is vaguely, dangerously, alluringly African or Oriental."[5] The historian Matthew Jacobson sees Italians as occupying a "middle ground" in the American racial order as late as 1925. His assessment of the racial identity of Joe Christmas, a character in William Faulkner's *Light in August* (1932), is instructive: "I thought maybe you were just another wop or something," Christmas, who is black, is told.[6] The racial contingency of Italians had not been lost on Cuomo, who as late as 2010, still spoke, albeit with humor, about how discussions of his "big hands" and surname were proxies for racial hostility.[7] In 1974, Cuomo commissioned a poll that found a potential run for statewide office would yield a 6 percent drop-off in support based on his presumed "mafia connections" —on the basis of his name alone.[8] These political realities were rooted in the pseudo-science of race emergent in the late 19th century. As Daniel J. Tichenor's work instructs, the idea that Europe was the sole vestige of common "whiteness" is false. Europeans, it was argued, were actually made up of "three races: a Nordic race, a Teutonic race, and a Mediterranean, the 'darkest' and most primitive of these races," a view owing to William Z. Ripley's 1898 treatise, *The Races of Europe.*[9]

Cuomo's father Andrea, who was born in Brooklyn in 1901, was the son of Donato and Maria Cuomo. Like a sizable number of early Italian immigrants, Donato returned to Italy in 1904. By the early 1920s, Andrea left his father's hometown of Nocera Superiore for Tramonti, where he worked on the farm of the Giordano family. In 1925, he married Immaculata Giordano and would return to the United States—this time to New Jersey—two years later. When Mario Matthew Cuomo was born in Brooklyn in 1932, he was part of a long wave of Italian immigrants to America; in his case, his father's cousin Rosario, paved the way after service in the Italian army in the First World War. While the mid-1920s was a period in which Benito Mussolini and the fascists established open dictatorial rule and the virtual elimination of political opposition, there is no Cuomo family narrative of "fleeing fascism" as such.[10] Economic opportunity seemed to be by far the greater motivation. The region of Campania was almost exclusively agricultural, and while Naples was the port of exit for the Cuomo family, it was a distant urban enclave, one that marked a sort of beginning to the "chaotic" South. As Patrick Moynihan noted in his influential sociological study *Beyond the Melting Pot,* "Of 2,300,000 Italian immigrants to the United States between 1899 and 1910, 1,900,000 were South Italians."[11] Indeed, as Donna Gabaccia's work points out, from Campania alone the annual rate of emigration jumped from a meager 0.6 percent in the years 1876–1894, to a formidable 10.9 percent in 1895–1914.[12]

This largely uneducated and unskilled workforce became a significant part of the expanding population of New York and part of a growing transnational story of the Italian diaspora in the Americas. And by 1931, the Cuomos moved into South Jamaica, Queens, where Andrea ran a small grocery store, one now part of the lore of Cuomo's upbringing and story. It was the "bleeding feet" of Andrea that became a symbol of Cuomo's childhood—and more important, the sacrificial and communal brand of progressivism Cuomo extolled at the Democratic National Convention in 1984.[13]

In its marathon-like profile of Cuomo in 1984, the *New Yorker* described Cuomo's South Jamaica neighborhood as a mix of "Italians, Germans, Irish, blacks, and Poles."[14] The Borough of Queens had long been a kind of hinterland of political action; working-class and upper-middle-class families made up a sizable portion of the borough in the period before suburban sprawl, before the advent of white flight. Cuomo's politics were thus decidedly born out of a community whose self-identification was in many respects oppositional to Manhattan and the wealth, prestige, and elitism it represented. By the time of the 1939 World's Fair, Queens represented 14 percent of New York's population, with German and Italian residents its two largest groups.[15] Comparatively speaking, Italians were late in coming to support Franklin Roosevelt and the New Deal, with FDR taking into account the sentiments of Italian Americans for Mussolini during the Spanish Civil War. As his biographer Frank Freidel noted, Roosevelt "had firm reasons for being quiet about Italian Fascism."[16] It was Roosevelt, after all, who had come to power in New York as governor, through his strong association with ethnic newspapers throughout New York State. While there remained a lingering conservatism among many Italian Americans, in time they would come to be strong supporters of New Deal policies and New Deal liberalism.[17]

New York City experienced a remarkable period of growth and support from the federal government in the 1930s. As the historian Mason Williams has written:

A crucial moment . . . came in the 1930s. During that turbulent decade, Franklin Roosevelt and his Democratic Party chose to channel the resources of the federal government through the agencies of America's cities and counties. Fiorello La Guardia's coalition of reformers, Republicans, social democrats, and leftists rebuilt New York's local state, chasing the functionaries of the city's fabled Tammany Hall political machine from power and implanting a cohort of technical experts committed to expanding the scope of the public sector.[18]

With about 7 out of 10 New Yorkers having at least one parent born in another country according to the 1930 Census,[19] the immigrant communities of Cuomo's youth were the beneficiaries of many of these public works—and they developed a growing identification with the Democratic Party. When Ronald Reagan defeated Jimmy Carter in the 1980 presidential election, he took 60 percent of the Italian vote in New Jersey and 57 percent in New York, representing a remarkable dissection of a key constituency of the Democratic Party from its geo-political roots.[20]

By carving into liberalism's key constituencies of white ethnic and labor voters, much of the Democratic Party's traditional support—rooted in religion, group identity, and community—were exchanged for the presumed idyll of the suburbs and the "tax-free office parks of the exurbs."[21] The integration that bedeviled American Italians was different from that of southern Italians seeking economic union with the north; and yet Cuomo's identification with ethnicity—and its relation to race—serves as a template of sorts for understanding the ways in which liberalism's growth in the decades preceding Reaganism flourished in part, under a complex and multifaceted ethnic banner.

St. John's to Willets Point

The "Little Indians" of St. John's Preparatory School in 1946 included only a few Italian Americans. The families of this distinct minority were, in part, Cannavenos, Napilatanos, Crispianos, Zitos, Fasullos, Garaventes, Cardones—and one Cuomo. "Most of the kids were of the Irish elite," Cuomo recalled. "You see, in those years, to be a Catholic was to be an Irish Catholic. Italians were something else, something not as good."[22] The *Prep Shadows'* 1949 yearbook contains a short note about Mario Cuomo, including a photograph of his baseball playing days ("The game was also highlighted by a sparkling catch by Mario Cuomo"). There are no hints of oratorical prowess or other prospective distinctions. By his college years, however, he had moved on to more distinction, including, in the *Vincentian*, a reference to his time on the Student Council and Debate Council. He shared space in the publication with someone who by all accounts was a brilliant black classmate and friend, Alex Farrelly. Hailing from the Virgin Islands, Farrelly, like Cuomo, was part of the International Relations Club. Farrelly would later join Cuomo in law school at St. John's, where few women made up part of the class in 1954. The sole woman faculty member was Bella Dodd, a lecturer in law. These were the faces of diversity in an otherwise austerely white and male world.

In time, Cuomo began to separate himself from his classmates in law school, where he would put to use his "versatile and keen mind." The Brooklyn-based St. John's world was decidedly Manichean, as was customary for its times. "Fight World Communism with Christ's Love," ran missionary ads in the *Vincentian*. Along these lines, it was also "Good to Give Your Blood, [but] Better to Give Christ's Blood." And there were principled stands as St. John's fencers quit their association over incidents of racial prejudice that were "against Catholic principles."[23] The education that led Cuomo on to law school was one that encouraged debate and sound reasoning. As his biographer, Robert McElvaine notes, "St. John's [required] that all students take a full complement of religion and philosophy courses."[24] The Order of St. Vincent de Paul—the Vincentians— also stoked a strong sense of interconnectedness and community obligation in its followers. The missionary vision emphasized personal virtue and collective responsibilities. Yet Cuomo wrestled with his Catholicism even as he became richly tied to its intellectual traditions and spiritual message.[25]

"He was a very unusual young man," according to his longtime friend, Nicholas D'Arienzo. With that remark, D'Arienzo got up during our interview and walked into an adjoining room, where he soon pulled out an old yearbook. Dr. D'Arienzo, now a retired pediatrician (and formerly the pediatrician of the Cuomo family), welcomed me to his Park Avenue apartment to talk about his former St. John's classmate. *"The Divine Milieu . . .* Pierre Teilhard de Chardin, that was his man," he said, as he thumbed through an old *Prep Shadows* yearbook.[26] The year is 1953, and D'Arienzo is now reminiscing about his St. John's community. "To the sports-minded, [Cuomo] appealed to them; to the intellectuals, he appealed to them. He was a man's man. He was good company." Like others, D'Arienzo comes back to the ethical and legal training of Cuomo—in short, his sense of moral grounding. D'Arienzo met Cuomo on the first day of college in 1949; both needed a biology course—D'Arienzo for "medicine and Cuomo, to get it out of the way." Cuomo's "unusual" quality had to do with a near ascetic appreciation for education, one founded in Catholic teaching. D'Arienzo was not alone in emphasizing the Vincentians along with Teilhard de Chardin as critical influences on Cuomo. St. John's University was a heady place in those days—Joe Mattone, perhaps Cuomo's best and longest friend from that era, recalls taking 22 mandatory credits of philosophy in undergraduate work, including intense study of Paul J. Glenn's text on *Dialectics*.[27]

According to McElvaine, Cuomo first read *The Divine Milieu* in 1960 or 1961, when "it provided striking confirmation for the direction in which his own thoughts had been moving for several years."[28] The journalist Kenneth L. Woodward has written that "the first time I met Mario Cuomo, the first words out of his mouth were 'Teilhard de Chardin.'"[29] Teilhard, a French philosopher and Jesuit priest, was not the first to attempt to reconcile reason and faith among believers. But his teaching was particularly salient in the early to mid-20th century when technological advances and the scale of human catastrophe had superseded anything previously known in history. Eschewing the division between spirit and material nature, Teilhard reasoned that the soul was in fact, part of the natural (and evolutionary) world. "In each of us," he wrote in *The Divine Milieu*, "through matter, the whole history of the world is in part reflected. And however autonomous our soul, it is indebted to an inheritance worked upon from all sides—before ever it came into being—by the totality of the energies of the earth."[30] As he told his biographer, Cuomo understood through Teilhard that "God did not intend this world only as a test of our purity but, rather, as an expression of his love. That we are meant to live actively, intensely, totally in this world and, in so doing, to make it better for all whom we can touch, no matter how remotely."[31] For any number of politicians such theoretical constructions would seem either implausible or naively self-serving. In Cuomo's politics, they made up the underpinning of his later philippics against Reagan and the popular religious conservatism of his time; nor would such reflections be divorced from the world of practical politics.

The point of Teilhardian thought was to bring the moral sense of individuals into practical line with the world as it actually is. For Cuomo, this meant a life in public service of some kind. He may have demurred about earlier considerations for the priesthood by suggesting that upon meeting his future wife Matilda, he abrogated all thoughts of celibacy; fair enough—but there is equally compelling if less earthy evidence that Cuomo was not merely interested in the Heavenly City, as Augustine put it. He was likewise interested in the earthly city, the realm of politics. Having to abandon a now well-known stint with the Pittsburgh Pirates' minor league team after being struck in the head by a fast ball, Cuomo entered law school, ultimately finishing tied for first in his class.[32] But in the mid-1950s that didn't matter. Cuomo's "law school dean, Harold F. McNiece gently suggested he change his name to something without a vowel at the end."[33] It had become apparent that Cuomo "couldn't get an interview with a Wall Street firm" because of his ethnicity.[34] It was a stinging introduction into the world of New York legal society. "He didn't wear the white tennis shoes," Joe Mattone, said, employing a metaphor nearly hallowed in the Cuomo *bildungsroman* that has become his personal narrative.[35]

It was that slight and his boredom with work at a private firm that led Cuomo to his first foray into New York City politics. After some time clerking at the New York State Court of Appeals (the highest court in New York's system), he moved on to the private Brooklyn firm of Corner, Weisbrod, Froeb, and Charles—and then he took on a teaching position at St. John's Law School. In 1963, the same year he joined the law school's faculty, he was "elected president of the Catholic Lawyers Guild of Brooklyn" at age 30.[36] Cuomo enjoyed the position as an adjunct professor and didn't give it up completely until 1973.[37] It is hard not to read similarities into Barack Obama's ascent into politics through Cuomo's early career story. In fact, Cuomo's role in his first public dispute, one that put him in the *New York Times* for the first time, in 1964, had much to do with "community organizing."

There is no mention of Mario Cuomo nor his imbroglio with Robert Moses in 1964 in Robert Caro's massive work *The Power Broker*.[38] For Moses, the impasse over his desire to clear the area around Willets Point near what was then Shea Stadium for the World's Fair, represents a footnote (and not even that in Caro's classic biography) in an otherwise unparalleled political career. Yet, for Cuomo, his fight and ultimate victory over Moses—who has been rightly deemed perhaps the most powerful (if not reviled) figure in 20th-century New York politics—was the pivotal event in launching his career in public service. "It started a whole chain of events that got me into public life," Cuomo would say more than 40 years later.[39] His first appearance in a New York newspaper was in an August 1964 article in the *New York Times* which reported: "The city moved yesterday to use its own funds to convert a controversial tract containing junkyards near the World's Fair into an addition for Flushing Meadow Park."[40]

This innocuous beginning in the public record ("the association though its lawyer, Mario Cuomo, reaffirmed yesterday its intention to continue the fight against the park") reflected Cuomo's early penchant for siding with the underdog while seeking compromise in seemingly intractable disputes. Moses viewed the Willets Point area, strewn with scrap metal shops and long identified with what one urban studies expert has called "probably the worst physical conditions of any city site," as an enormous blight on his prospective construction near the World's Fair site in Queens.[41] As Cuomo biographer, Robert McElvaine notes, the scrap-metal dealers "hired an attorney named Michael Castaldi" initially to "fight the condemnation in court."[42] But Cuomo was soon brought in to take over, as Castaldi had been named a judge. Cuomo, a largely unknown quantity, was to match legal wits with Samuel I. Rosenman who formerly served as an aide to President Franklin Roosevelt.[43] Cuomo was also going up against New York's Mayor Robert F. Wagner, who was supporting Moses's efforts to "establish a chain of six city parks" in the area.[44] Years later, Cuomo recalled, "I told [Mr. Moses], 'Look, we'll do the following, we'll put up Lombardy poplars around the place, we'll put up a colored fence.' . . . Moses said, 'That's very imaginative of you, but no.' He was not used to not having his way."[45] Ultimately, Cuomo defeated Moses in New York's Court of Appeals, preserving the Willets Point space for the dozens of local auto repair shop and scrap metal owners and workers. It was a rare defeat for Moses, but a minor skirmish for him, ultimately. For Cuomo, it represented a new possibility. "Fighting politicians," his friend and fellow law clerk Fabian Palomino said, "he learned that government had a lot of power. It could do a bit of good."[46]

Race, Class, and Housing in Queens

In the mid-1960s, Mario Cuomo got involved in the hornet's nest of New York's triangulation of antagonisms: race, class, and housing. The meeting point was the largely Italian Corona neighborhood of Queens, where the city was interested in razing many of its residents' homes in order to build a new high school and athletic field. But this was only part of it. The high school and athletic field were ultimately selected as a compromise, when New York's Board of Estimate faced massive opposition in the neighborhood for its plans to build low-income housing on a four-and-a-half acre plot there. Cuomo is said to have "insisted that the problem is more one of class than race"—a clash between working and nonworking people.[47] All the same, African Americans were to represent the overwhelming number of new residents in the community, and the initial rebuff to the board "altered its plans" and led to its

seeking out another site.[48] Thus, the small idyllic, "simple" neighborhood of "bocce courts" described by Cuomo years later, was itself
not immune to harboring its own racialized views of the "other."[49]
Cuomo would later argue that those who showed up to protest the
board were outside agitators from nearby Lefrak City rather than
"the people of Corona."[50] Perhaps—but there is little indication that
members of either community were eager to welcome blacks into
their neighborhood in 1966. As Richard Sennett put it squarely in
his classic work on the period, *The Fall of Public Man*, "[Corona]
waged a bitter struggle with the city, first to prevent a low-income
housing project from being built, and then to scale down the size of
a school the city proposed."[51] While Cuomo's fight to preserve the
homes of so many working-class Queens residents has been rightly
credited to the more altruistic side of his character (Cuomo was
barely paid for representing Willets Point or Corona), the vortex of
race and class had familiar results for the African American community. As sociologists Douglas S. Massey and Nancy Denton com-
mented, "Although liberal planners often tried to locate the projects
away from ghetto areas, white politicians and citizens mobilized to
block the construction of projects within their neighborhoods . . . .
[A]s a result, projects were typically built on cleared land within or
adjacent to existing black neighborhoods."[52]

The 69 threatened homeowners—the so-called Corona 69—
were nevertheless faced with the stark reality that their homes
were slated for demolition. Word had made its way from the not
too distant Willets Point community that Cuomo was someone
who could resolve these sorts of disputes. "You oughta get this guy
Cuomo," said Nicholas Piazza, head of the Corona Taxpayers' Civic
Association.[53] Before long, Cuomo took up the association's case,
ultimately defeating the city. "Mayor [John] Lindsay announced
that the city would return the property to 31 of the homeowners
and move the homes of the 28 others to a new site just a block
away."[54] Lindsey also cast the compromise in ethnic terms, observ-
ing, "A very small and very special Italian-American community
by their special determination to stay together and build a sense

of pride in neighborhood symbolizes that part of New York that we must take special efforts to preserve."[55] By the time he was running for lieutenant governor in 1974, Cuomo was being described as "not only Italian and Catholic" but also "tall, physically attractive," and "articulate."[56] In 1977, when he ran for mayor, he was dubbed by one politician as "the class Italian in the race."[57] These were considered compliments.

In a sense, Cuomo as an Italian, served an almost medieval function in the city's politics. He was neither black nor a Jew, and therefore he could serve as an intermediary in disputes between these communities. He likewise was not a member of the white, Anglo-Saxon Protestant (WASP) establishment and could therefore lay legitimate claim to being an outsider to clubhouse politics. Jews and African Americans might be wary, but they had reason to believe Cuomo shared more in common with them than other city politicians not tied directly to their identity. The resolution of the Corona conflict added luster to Cuomo's growing image as a mediator. The famed journalist Jimmy Breslin chronicled the Corona story firsthand and was among the earliest newspaper writers in New York to see Cuomo as more than a passing figure in the city's politics. Breslin and Cuomo soon became friends, with Breslin writing the preface to Cuomo's *Forest Hills Diary*—a chronicle of the next community battle Cuomo would preside over. In his review of that book, another influential journalist Murray Kempton wrote of Breslin's fascination with Cuomo: "Breslin has the journalist's bent for tragedies with vaguely hopeful endings; he sees Cuomo, not unpersuasively, as that solitary just man whose 'lonely, excruciating work' might redeem the city."[58] Robert McElvaine called the Corona compromise a "remarkable accomplishment" in that it "was the first time that an already accomplished New York City condemnation had been turned around." And he was right to note, "It is unlikely that [Cuomo] could have achieved his success without Breslin's intervention."[59]

The Cuomo victory was unlikely, to be sure; low-income blacks were "staved off" within a lower-middle class community of white ethnics who were lacking in political clout. But that did not resolve the plight of so many African Americans seeking low-income housing in a city with increasingly limited stores of either such housing or white residents willing to accept them. "On the face of it," Cuomo wrote in his 1974 *Diary*, "Neither Corona nor Forest Hills would have seemed to be logical receptacles for the placing of large numbers of low-income blacks, although one might have guessed that the presumably more liberal Forest Hills community would have been better disposed to the objective, if not the implementation, of a scatter-site program."[60] Yet, as early as 1971, when excavation work began on 108th Street, residents protested at the site, "some of them throwing rocks, smashing the windows of the construction trailers."[61] Mayor Lindsay's first name became "Adolf" in a popular chant, as the largely Jewish community voiced its unease over the possible relocation of so many blacks (a presumed "criminal" element) into their community.[62] Forest Hills' state senator, Emanuel Gold, voiced his displeasure with members of the community. "My ancestors did not break loose from the ghettos of Europe," he said, "to have me lead the charge here in New York City to keep others in ghettos."[63] Harlem's *Amsterdam News* put the perspective of many of the city's blacks in its headline: "The Queens Theme: 'Niggers Get Out!'"[64]

By 1971, the year Mayor John Lindsay appointed Cuomo to investigate and propose a solution to the Forest Hills crisis, it was apparent that the backlash against the black civil rights movement was hardly a southern phenomenon. And it also wasn't limited to "parochial" Bostonians opposed to busing. Whites in New York City, the great "melting pot" that exemplified so much of the mosaic that Mario Cuomo would later speak of so often, was now encountering its own form of racial conflagration around the issue of housing. As Clarence Taylor has written, "While New York City remained strongly Democratic, whites in the boroughs outside of Manhattan could no longer be counted on to vote the party line, especially for candidates who carried a left-of-center agenda. Many in the outer boroughs blamed Lindsay for caring more about the needs of blacks and Latinos while ignoring them."[65] While Cuomo saw a glimmer of political opportunity in serving as mediator, he was also aware of the potential damage taking on the dispute might do to his career. At a dinner Cuomo and Lindsay attended in Corona, dozens of Forest Hills residents showed up to protest, leaving Cuomo with a slap across the face—literally; both he and Mayor Lindsay could have faced far worse as police were called to the scene.[66] Meanwhile, the city's largest black newspaper, the *Amsterdam News* was unequivocal in its editorial:

> There is no reason to seek a compromise with those who fear that white, middle-class residents of Forest Hills will leave with an influx of minority or poor residents. The housing needs of minority communities are much too critical to pander to the prejudices of such persons. Mayor Lindsay . . . should stand fast on the Forest Hills Project. Mediator Cuomo should report to both sides that the Black community will tolerate no compromise.[67]

In fact, it was Cuomo's compromise that ultimately settled the fight, if not the antagonisms in Forest Hills. In what *Newsday* called a "Solomon-like solution," Cuomo called for cutting the proposed housing project in half, "suggesting that the development be changed from three 24-story buildings with 840 apartments to three 12-story buildings with 432 apartments."[68]

Paul Sandman, president of the Forest Hills Neighbors association, "said that Lindsay's decision" to back Cuomo's plan "took the heat off the controversy" while not resolving the enmity embedded in a relationship between two communities who knew little of each other.[69] Both anticipating future unrest and reflecting upon past conflicts, Cuomo was poignant in his *Diary* near the end of the process. "We cannot wall off the ghetto," he wrote, "and not expect it to explode. If we step back from the problem today and return to the callous neglect of twenty years ago, we may squelch a few assaults and wind up with race riots. I'm afraid politicians will fear that any talk of uplifting and relieving the ghetto problem will be regarded as a relenting on the necessity for more 'law and order.' We've come perhaps, full circle."[70]

Politically speaking, Cuomo's resolution lacked the kind of brio associated with clear-cut victories. And yet Forest Hills elevated him as a political figure. It also demonstrated his early penchant to observe progressive principles while acknowledging the more conservative voices within the liberal Democratic coalition. Cuomo understood that white ethnics harbored their own prejudices as well as their own grievances; recognizing both while seeking social justice was no easy matter—particularly in the urban North where urbanity and cosmopolitanism mask traditional fears, hatreds, and unfulfilled longings. As he wrote in his final report on his work on Forest Hills, "If the concern of the Forest Hills community with the project as now planned, and the erosion of the present character of the community which it now threatens, could be allayed by intelligent disputation, that would have occurred already."[71] Education alone wouldn't resolve the problem of race, class, and segregated housing in New York City or anywhere else. More of the human spirit was needed. And then, Cuomo closed out his report with a quote from Edmund Burke. "All government—indeed, every human benefit and enjoyment, every virtue and every prudent act—is founded on compromise."[72]

Electoral Politics

In the midst of the Corona crisis, Cuomo was presented with his first offer to enter electoral politics. Hugh Carey, then a congressman testing the waters for a mayoral run in 1969, asked if Cuomo would join him on the ticket as his comptroller. Cuomo thought about it and said no.[73] Cuomo had written speeches for Carey, who was also a St. John's Law alumnus.[74] Jimmy Breslin recalled in his preface to Cuomo's *Forest Hills Diary* Carey's lamentations over failing to persuade Cuomo. "I got a genius nobody knows about,"

Carey said. "He's a law professor at St. John's. Brilliant sonofa-bitch. Mario Cuomo. I begged him to run with me. Nobody knows him. The first time they ever hear of him, they'll be right there in his hands. But I just couldn't talk him into running."[75]

Cuomo was again offered a prospective run for office in 1973— this time for mayor. Cuomo formed an exploratory committee, raised money, and "had breakfast meetings with hundreds of sup-porters."[76] Joe Mattone, who would later help pay for the plane that was to take Cuomo to New Hampshire and into the presidential race in 1992, helped raise the meager dollars that proved insuffi-cient to sustain a run in 1973.[77] But the abortive race was not with-out its moments for Cuomo. In a passionate and off-the-cuff speech delivered at supporter Matty Troy's club in Queens Village in front of a number of key Democratic Party leaders in the city (including the rising Ed Koch), Cuomo spoke to the whites in the audience as few politicians had spoken to them before.[78] The speech remains unimaginable in today's politics, not the least for its political incor-rectness, honesty, and forthright assessment of white self-interest in the vein of Alexis de Tocqueville—self-interest "properly under-stood." It remains a marvel worthy of more than passing attention:

> You've got all these blacks and Puerto Ricans down in South
> Jamaica where I was born and raised. You think they're *all*
> bad because they're the ones who are coming up here mug-
> ging and raping you and breaking into your houses. And you're
> saying, "We don't want them in our neighborhoods. We don't
> want them anywhere near us. Leave them where they are.
> They should all die." Well, the net result of that attitude is
> their poverty will get worse and they'll produce more muggers
> and rapists. The truth is *we can't get far enough away from
> them to be safe.* Okay, the liberals come and tell you that it's
> our moral obligation to help those people because we oppressed
> them—the blacks anyway—for 400 years. That's what John
> Lindsay told you, right? However, here in Queens, how can
> I tell my father that? My father who for so many years had a

grocery store in South Jamaica. In that store he never pun-
ished a black or hurt a black or enslaved a black. If you tell him
about his "'moral obligation," he won't know what you're talking about. Here's what you have to say to my father. Whether
you love them or not, whether you have an obligation to them
or not, is between you and God. When you go to confession
on a Saturday, talk to the priest about it. But unless you do
something about where they are now, how they live now, they
will continue to come into your neighborhoods and mug and
rape. Where are you going to next? Wyandanch? Then where?
Montauk? You know what's going to happen? In time, they'll
be three miles away from Montauk and your daughter is going
to get caught because next is the water and it's all over. You
can't run forever. You have to find ways to break up segregated
neighborhoods. And most of all, you have to find ways to get
them jobs. Real Jobs. And that, in part, means electing people
who will really do that. Remember, we have to do this because
we love ourselves, not because we love them. In the end, the
only thing that works is self-interest.[79]

Cuomo later told Nat Hentoff of the *Village Voice* (which reprinted
much of this speech before Cuomo's 1977 run for mayor), other
politicians "don't talk about what's coming, because they're afraid.
They're afraid of stirring up the fears of those who, if told the city's
going black and Puerto Rican, see a city full of muggers and rap-
ists. And they're afraid that if they said what I said in Queens,
they'll be misunderstood by yet another constituency."[80]

If Cuomo degenerated into stereotyping it was assuredly on both
sides ("You're saying . . . 'Leave them where they are. They should
all die'"). While not fully delegitimizing white fears of black violence and crime, Cuomo also offered no consolation to white racism. He likewise had the temerity to speak in a fashion directed at
what his constituents (one might say "his people") thought at that
time, in those circumstances. And he did it also toward a particular end—to help them move toward a primal, if inelegant sense of

tolerance. Cuomo was speaking to white flight in New York as few liberal politicians were addressing it around the country. Queens, after all, had only 18 of New York City's 46 housing projects.[81] But one more was seen as one too many. Cuomo's speech may not have been "courageous," but it was frank in the best, classical sense of the word: denoting *parrhesia*—honest speech that educates, even as it offends.[82]

For all of its brutal honesty, Cuomo's speech fell on deaf ears. It was Koch's more sympathetic ode to "law and order" that held sway that evening.[83] Troy ultimately refused to support Cuomo, telling him, "You tell the people what they want to hear, then when you get in office you do what's right."[84] Ironically, Cuomo would tell a similar, though more off-color story years later, when his mother suggested he publicly support the death penalty before ultimately signaling (with a profane hand-under-the-chin gesture) he change his mind when elected.[85] Meanwhile, Forest Hills raised Koch's profile, setting him up well for the 1977 mayoral race.[86] Cuomo was now in a precarious position. As *Newsday* reporter Dick Zander pointed out heading into the 1974 gubernatorial campaign season in New York, "Perhaps if Cuomo had been a little less of an individual; perhaps if he in the past [had] not rejected suggestions that he run for lesser offices; perhaps if he had played humble before important county leaders such as Troy, he would be the official choice of his party of the No. 2 spot [lieutenant governor]."[87]

What *Newsday* missed was Cuomo's friendship with Carey, which helped put Cuomo in the running for lieutenant governor as Carey was making his bid for governor in 1974. Cuomo would face stiff competition in the Democratic primary, however, as it was filled with others with "ethnic appeal"—including state senator Mary Anne Krupsak (who was Polish) and Assemblyman Antonio Olivieri of Manhattan.[88] A virtual unknown upstate, and running in but his first campaign—something he had an immediate distaste for—Cuomo lost to Krupsak, garnering 32 percent of the vote to her 44 percent.[89] The hope had been that Cuomo might add ethnic balance to the ticket with Carey in November. "You can't tell

Irish, Italians, and upstate WASPs that they're not good enough to be on the ticket," said former Democratic candidate Adam Walinsky, who lost in 1970, "and then ask them to vote for you."[90] Cuomo displayed perhaps too much cheek at one point on the campaign trail. "I'm really Jewish," he joked, "but I changed my name for business reasons."[91] Meanwhile, Krupsak, who became the first female lieutenant governor in the state's history, campaigned successfully on the slogan, "She's not just one of the boys."[92] It was also more than a passing footnote that Cuomo campaigned as the only statewide Catholic candidate in the Democratic primary who was "wholeheartedly against abortion."[93] The *Village Voice* endorsed him anyway.

The newly elected Carey soon offered Cuomo a cabinet position in his government. Cuomo would become New York's secretary of state, a position with very few formal powers but amended for Cuomo to include a new responsibility—"general ombudsman." The position's responsibilities would include oversight of "public disclosures of finances and interests of state governmental officials" and "investigating complaints about state government."[94] Ever astute, Cuomo saw in the position an opportunity to "build himself up" politically in the state as Jerry Brown had done with a similar position in California. Brown was elected governor in 1974.[95] Cuomo was not quite the "non-political, articulate 'do-gooder' type" other politicians were making him out to be.[96] He had serious ambitions, something that became evident when he later rejected Carey's offer to head the state Democratic Party two years later. Cuomo may have "been the caliber of man" Carey was looking for in the post, but it was a position many sights below Cuomo's growing interest in elective office.[97] As he would say about another potential office he would pass on, "I didn't get into politics for blind ascendancy for who knows where."[98]

Even in his new position as secretary of state, Cuomo was having to overcome his status as a relative outsider and newcomer to state politics. Just months before his appointment, *Newsday* was incorrectly referring to him as "the son of Sicilian immigrants"

(Cuomo's father was born in Brooklyn before repatriating to Italy, and his mother was born in Tramonti, Italy).[99] Underscoring such descriptors, Cuomo was also still very much locked into the persona of an "ethnic" candidate (headlines like "Carey's Appeal Gets Italian Dressing" didn't help).[100] In time, Cuomo did build a resume as a reformer, using his position to take on lobbyists in Albany accustomed to "freebies" such as clubhouse passes to racing tracks and other "gifts." Cuomo "raised some eyebrows" by even declaring the acceptance of a lunch or a drink to be odious.[101] Not every state official was pleased. "We get four or five [cocktail] invitations like that every night we're here," said Assemblyman George A. Murphy. Unimpressed, Cuomo deadpanned, "Then a law like this would save you a lot of time."[102] Cuomo's lobbying bill ultimately died in the legislature in the 1975 session, but it did add to his credentials as a reform politician.[103]

Much of Cuomo's time in his new office was also spent on budgetary issues as New York State dealt with a nearly unprecedented fiscal crisis in 1975. This was the period when New York faced "the imminent threat of bankruptcy" and when Governor Carey "used a broad array of extraordinary powers" to keep New York afloat.[104] It was also a time that in many ways came to be identified with the now classic *Daily News* headline, "Ford to City: Drop Dead." For his part, Cuomo reduced the State Department budget by 40 percent, developing a record that helped counter the "image of big-spending liberal Democrats that had become entrenched in the minds of many voters, particularly upstaters."[105] In a time of growing racial divisions, Cuomo also used his oversight powers to revoke the license of a real estate company that refused to rent to African Americans.[106] Meanwhile, Ed Koch positioned himself to run for mayor in 1977, ostensibly to save the city from "incompetent" leadership at all levels—a sort of code word, controversial even then—invoked against Health and Hospitals Corporation president, Dr. John L. Holloman Jr., who was black.[107] Between cuts to the city's services, the growing sense of lawlessness, and a fiscal crisis of the first order, New York had become a veritable focal point for testing liberalism's staying power in the twilight of the New Deal coalition's epoch. While Koch, and later others, worked to exploit that rupture, Cuomo sought to harness what remained, seeking progressive resolutions, however on the defensive he was compelled to be, given the city (and nation's) changing political realities. As Governor Carey put it at the time, "The days of wine and roses are over."[108]

Despite later pulling his support in the general election, Hugh Carey backed Cuomo for mayor in 1977. The decision to enter the race was one Cuomo is said to have agonized over.[109] Looking back on his entry into the race, Cuomo was frank about his weaknesses as a candidate. "I was stiff. I was tentative. I was called Hamlet, and that was about right," he said.[110] Once he decided reluctantly to enter, Cuomo hoped to take advantage of the ethnic fault lines in the city's politics. Italians made up roughly one-fifth of the population in New York City at the time—but the Jewish vote was twice that in the primaries, where many Italians abstained, waiting until the general, or "real election."[111] The ethnic breakdown was also largely geographical: of the nine candidates, six were from Manhattan, and five of them were Jewish (Percy Sutton, of Harlem was African American). Abe Beame, seeking reelection as mayor, was from Brooklyn. The other "outer-boroughers" were Representative Herman Badillo of the Bronx, who was Puerto Rican, and Cuomo, from Queens.[112] John Lindsay had been the only mayor elected as a "white Anglo-Saxon Protestant" since 1905.[113] While Cuomo sought to draw outside celebrities such as Sylvester Stallone and Frank Sinatra into his campaign, he was nevertheless stung by the aforementioned description of him in the *Daily News* as "the class Italian" in the race.[114] And there was the odd suggestion of a sort of ethnic swapping of votes as Cuomo was alleged to have entered into an agreement to support Bronx Borough president Robert Abrams in the following year's race for state attorney general. Not much came out it except Abrams's memorable rejoinder, "You mean a quid pro Cuomo?"[115]

Cuomo was, in fact, late to the race and, as the *New Yorker* described him, "had no real clubhouse affiliations."[116] He was also only able to get in the race, according to Manhattan state senator Roy Goodman, because of Carey's arm-twisting of his Liberal Party allies to support Cuomo. "They found a godfather," Goodman crudely put it, "who made them an offer they couldn't refuse."[117] Carey's support was a two-edged sword—Cuomo was derided almost instantly as Carey's "puppet." Koch employed a more colorful if not racist image to describe Cuomo's relationship with the governor: "He's like Idi Amin," Koch said of Carey, "They bring him in on a chair and carry him around the room."[118] In a sign of the direction of future national politics, Rupert Murdoch's conservative *New York Post* endorsed Koch late in the summer, arguing that Cuomo, a strong opponent of the death penalty, "has not shown the toughness we think the job of Mayor demands."[119] The summer of 1977 was defined by the search for the serial killer, David Berkowitz, the so-called Son of Sam, and a blackout that led to much unrest throughout the city. The *New Yorker* was correct in noting that the "preoccupation with the death penalty has been a curious one since a New York mayor plays no formal role in the enactment of laws that call for capital punishment," but many voters found such arguments immaterial. Undaunted, Cuomo said he was willing to lose the race because of his opposition to the death penalty because "I believe with all my heart that capital punishment is not a remedy."[120]

Along with his support for the death penalty and outer-borough status, Cuomo was dogged by his connections to Carey. The word "stooge" was used more than once to describe him in the press, and it ran counter to his earlier image as an outsider to clubhouse politics. Cuomo did well to finish second to Koch in the primary, but his poor showing in Manhattan was indicative of his troubles to come in the November runoff. In a twist of irony, Koch declared his opposition to "low-income housing projects in middle-class areas" in his first debate with Cuomo on PBS channel 13, while on the same day the *Amsterdam News* announced its endorsement of him.[121] "We find [Koch] to be more open, responsive and more willing to listen than his opponent," declared the city's historic black newspaper

in an editorial that would prove shocking in hindsight.[122] Cuomo
had come off as shrill in his debates with Koch, but as his biographer put it, "Without Manhattan, the blacks, or the Hispanics,
Cuomo wasn't likely to win anyway."[123] Cuomo also lost Carey's
support. "Commitment," one of Carey's aides said, after the governor announced he was backing Koch for mayor, "is a two-way
street." Cuomo, he said, "ran a lousy campaign."[124]

Meanwhile, the run-off between Koch and Cuomo became
increasingly bitter. *Newsday* and other newspapers began reporting that fliers were appearing bearing the slogan "Vote for Cuomo,
Not the homo,"[125] a vulgar allusion to Koch's presumed status as
closeted gay man. "There will always be someone who will bring
that question up," Koch said, as he was accused of using his close
friendship with Bess Myerson, a former Miss America, to shield
his sexuality during the campaign.[126] Cuomo denied involvement,
and in his campaign diary of 1982, he wrote that in fact, "I had
thrown a policeman out of my campaign office in 1977 because he
was making allegations concerning Koch's sexual orientation."[127]
The truth probably lies somewhere in-between both candidates'
memories. As Jonathan Soffer has written in his biography of
Koch, there is evidence that Cuomo's Brooklyn campaign manager
Michael Dowd was in fact investigating Koch's private sex life.[128]
Cuomo's son Andrew, now New York's governor, was accused of
putting up the notorious signs as his father's campaign manager, but there has never been any direct evidence linking him
to what Andrew Cuomo biographer, Michael Snayerson, refers to
as "a matter of fading memories and speculation."[129] Yet Mario
Cuomo's biographer makes the case that "the raising of questions
about Koch's life-style was in fact part of the strategy to attack
Manhattan."[130] The Cuomos to this day have denied the posters
ever existed and pointed out, years later, that "people were going
around saying [Cuomo] was connected with the Mafia."[131] The
truth about the offensive posters may never be known, but in the
late summer of 1977, Mario Cuomo was a desperate candidate,
trailing by as much as 15 points in one poll.[132]

In the end, Koch won a relatively easy victory, garnering 50 percent of the vote and winning four out of the city's five boroughs (Cuomo even lost Queens, garnering only Staten Island).[133] Koch voters were also roughly one-quarter black or Hispanic, while Cuomo rated only 14 percent among this pivotal group of the electorate. Cuomo the outsider, anti-clubhouse politician, had little to show for such presumed qualities. As the *New York Times* reported, the results of the general election were strikingly similar to the primary, with "Cuomo winning Catholic, mostly Italian American districts, and Mr. Koch running strongly in Jewish, black, and Puerto Rican districts."[134] But there were bright spots. Cuomo won 41 percent of the vote on the Liberal Party ticket in the most Democratic city in the nation (the *Times* headline said it well: "*Democrat* is Mayor"). Despite not having won an election, Cuomo had built a name for himself. More important, he was to the left of Koch and now perhaps the best-known liberal ethnic politician in the state. And while his bromides against Koch were at times petty, they bore little resemblance to what he was capable of rhetorically. Late election night, November 8, 1977, as Cuomo answered questions from the press, his remaining supporters could be heard shouting, "Cuomo for governor."[135]

Becoming Governor

"I like him," Mario Cuomo had been quoted as saying of Governor Hugh Carey just before the mayoral election, "but I don't really respect him."[136] Such lines put Cuomo in a seemingly precarious position having to now reenter politics as Carey's secretary of state once again. But within a year, it was Carey who needed Cuomo, as Mary Anne Krupsak, his lieutenant governor, decided to challenge him in the 1978 primary.[137] By Carey's calculus, Cuomo would help with Italian, upstate, and suburban voters; despite his reticence to do so, he reached out to Cuomo.[138] In but another example of ethnic reductionism common to the city's politics at the time, one Carey critic deadpanned, "We thought the people were electing

Pat O'Brien but we ended up with Charles de Gaulle."[139] Cuomo had to decide whether to accept the offer only three days before the Democratic convention in Albany. There really was no decision to make—if Carey wanted him, he needed to accept for the good of the party and his own political future. Within short order Cuomo had drafted a 38-page document extolling the virtues of the Carey governorship.[140] As Robert McElvaine, put it, Cuomo had morphed into not only Carey's running mate but also his campaign manager.[141]

Cuomo was ultimately seen as a boost to Carey in the November election against Republican State Assembly minority leader, Perry Duryea. Carey carried 68 percent of New York City's vote, and 46 percent of the upstate and suburban vote, figures that Cuomo would match four years later.[142] "I didn't see a whole lot of him," said Cuomo of Carey, "once I became lieutenant governor. It was quickly apparent that I was not invited to staff meetings."[143] Cuomo busied himself over the next few years in his role as ombudsman for the state and in numerous speaking engagements. Presiding over the Senate was but another of the more mundane tasks that Cuomo found insufferable in his position.[144] Carey was likewise floundering in his second term. By late 1980, Cuomo's diary entries were marked by indicators of Carey's growing political weakness and personal challenges with Cuomo: "The Governor continues to get himself into difficulties" (November 15, 1980); "A typical week in my dealings with the Governor: he hasn't attempted to contact me in over six weeks" (December 5, 1980).[145] This was also a period marked by Cuomo's support of President Jimmy Carter, when he was being challenged by Ted Kennedy for the Democratic nomination. Cuomo had given his word to Carter to support him and was his New York campaign leader during the New York primary—an indication of how far Carter had fallen from favor among the state's political elite.[146]

By early 1981, Cuomo established an advisory group to consider a campaign for the governorship in 1982. The thought wasn't to challenge Carey if he sought reelection, but it was also not ruled out.[147] By December 1981, Cuomo had decided to run against Carey (moving from his earlier position, "If Carey doesn't run, I will definitely run");[148] it was a moot point, as Carey would announce in January that he would not seek a third term.[149] Cuomo's diary entry on the day of Carey's announcement began with a pithy but telling statement: "Carey announced he's not running. He didn't invite me to the announcement. He told me about it formally, in a phone call afterward."[150] On March 16, Cuomo formally declared his candidacy for the Democratic nomination for governor.[151] It was clear at the outset that it would be a race between Cuomo and the current mayor of New York, Ed Koch, a rematch of sorts, of their 1977 race. But unlike that campaign, Cuomo was fighting on a larger field of battle, the entirety of New York State. Cuomo immediately attacked Koch on this front during his announcement. "There will be no relief from New York City's fiscal despair," Cuomo said, "if the two-thirds of the population that vote in November and live outside the city's limits are given reason to feel alienated."[152]

Koch did himself no favors. In a November interview with *Playboy* after his reelection in 1981, Koch took his New York City parochialism to new heights. Describing suburban life, the mayor was unflattering, to put it kindly. "Sterile. It's nothing. It's wasting your life."[153] Adding insult to injury, he said, "Anyone who suggests I run for governor is no friend of mine . . . . [I]t requires living in Albany, which is small-town life at its worst."[154] For all of his movement to the right in recent years, Koch was hard-pressed to give up his bona fides as the quintessential New Yorker. But the interview damaged him, leading to what his media strategist David Garth called "the biggest, fastest, plunge" he had ever seen in politics.[155] Koch would eke out a victory over Cuomo in New York City in the September Democratic primary, but he barely made any dent in the 12-point lead in the polls Cuomo had built upstate.[156] This was despite Koch's having nearly tripled Cuomo in fundraising by the summer.[157]

By the time the primary was nearly upon the candidates, Koch had finally attacked President Ronald Reagan at an elderly citizens meeting in Queens, a sure sign that he was late in making the connection to New York's economic challenges and the new regime in Washington, which Cuomo had begun to assault.[158] Reflecting on his second race against Koch in his diary, Cuomo noted, "Conceptually, it was a little different," as "Koch had moved much further to the right in the interval, capping his transition with his 1980 speech at the Democratic National Convention in Baltimore, in which he attacked 'traditional Democratic philosophy.' He had also been perceived as sympathetic to Reagan."[159] With this larger question of Reagan's ascendancy looming, Cuomo was philosophical on the night of his primary victory over Koch. "I have said from the beginning I thought this campaign would be a struggle for the soul of the Democratic Party," Cuomo said.[160]

With Koch defeated, and Reagan in his second year in office, Cuomo began to shift his attention to national political issues and the nation's growing conservative agenda. Unlike others of his generation of governors, Cuomo seemed to lack policy focus. "I never remember Cuomo tied to an issue," recalls Ray Scheppach, former executive director of the National Governor's Association. "If I looked at Bill Clinton and Mario Cuomo—and say, 29 to 30 other governors at that time, Cuomo didn't have a relationship with anybody."[161] This reflection offers a window into a deep flaw in Cuomo's political acumen, if not his ambition. But what it fails to uncover is his significant rhetorical record against Reaganism. Cuomo's issue, if he can be said to have had one, was his opposition to the ethos of small government and religious conservatism as articulated by Reagan. That grand perspective may have cost him the type of "hook" policy initiative that candidates could build a national record on: education, or crime, or taxes, and so forth. But in speaking to the forest rather than the trees, Cuomo grew in stature. His defeat of Koch in the Democratic primary in 1982 was the beginning of this broader politics. "Now we move into a new struggle," Cuomo said at the time, "a struggle to keep at the top of our state government and to bring back to our national government a politics built on a body of beliefs that have been shared by a generation of Democrats. It's a politics that's worked."[162]

Cuomo would have more mundane concerns in the fall of 1982. He was to face Republican businessman Lewis Lehrman in the general election, and he was in desperate need of money. "We had no money at the end of the primary," Cuomo recalled in his diary. "The lack of money kept us off television for more than a week, during which the Lehrman television campaign was pervasive and relentless."[163] But unlike his previous campaign against Koch, Cuomo's team was able to rally and raise large sums of money for the campaign. By late October, Cuomo was writing in his diary "We have more money than we can spend—much more! I . . . believe we have a moral obligation to tell people we will accept no more contributions."[164] But of course, by that time, the race was nearly over. But not before Cuomo successfully tied Lehrman to Reagan. "My opponent . . . not only likes Reaganomics," he said, "he wants to go farther."[165] The recession at the time was taking its toll on Reagan politically, and Lehrman ultimately did not invite the president to New York to campaign for him.[166] Cuomo was unrelenting. "He said he would make Reaganomics the New York experience." Cuomo said, "I will say, 'God forbid!'"[167]

Described as an "intellectual populist" at one point during the campaign, Cuomo kept up a tiring pace of campaigning across the state.[168] The *New York Times'* endorsement was in its own way, a backhanded homage to Cuomo's ability to identify successfully with liberalism. "Mario Cuomo offers no imaginative new agenda," the *Times* said. "But he does forcefully advocate the humane values of the old one. He is the child of immigrants who knows the concerns of New York City's neighborhoods. He reviles the death penalty because it is impractical and immoral. He attacks Reaganomics because he knows what it costs in unemployment and deprivation: 'We can both control government spending and still afford wheelchairs for those who need them.'"[169]

In addition to Lehrman's troubles tied to the New York and national economies, Cuomo was also benefiting in the polls from an emerging gap among women voters. In late October, the *New York Times* reported that "Lieut. Gov. Cuomo [was] barely trailing, 44 to 47 percent, among men who were likely voters in his race with Lewis Lehrman, the Republican candidate for Governor. But he led, 52 percent to 44 percent, among women and 48 percent to 41 percent overall."[170] And Cuomo was already well positioned to hold the familiar New Deal coalition together for the election. As E. J. Dionne Jr. wrote about him in a lengthy piece just before the election in the *New York Times*, "The ethnic mix of the Cuomo campaign and the labor muscle behind it have an old-fashioned liberal look to them, and Mr. Cuomo's campaign speeches also have an old-fashioned sound."[171] Cuomo was staking his claim for the office in an ideological proxy war against Reagan.

In what the *New Yorker* described as a battle between "The New Right vs. The Old Left," Cuomo defeated Lehrman by about 4 percent (51 to 47).[172] It was not a sweeping victory, but it was the culmination of what was an improbable rise in politics. And it was accomplished against a newly emboldened politics from the right that seemed channeled directly from the Deep South. "Mario brought us twenty-two thousand rapes," Lehrman declared at one point in his debates with Cuomo.[173] The line conjured up not only Dixie, of course, but also Forest Hills, and the attacks on Cuomo, and his concessions to the "savages." As Robert McElvaine put it, "While many other Democrats were trying to accommodate themselves to the conservative era, Cuomo refused to apologize for his party's commitment to the poor and the role of government in dealing with social problems."[174] Around 12:30 in the morning, the night of his victory, Cuomo jotted down some lines for his first speech as governor-elect. In the very heart of it stood out one line: "We were criticized for relying on old-fashioned principles."[175]

Conclusion: Of Power and Philippics

The 1982 national midterm elections proved highly favorable for Democrats. The party picked up seven governorships and made big gains in the House. In the end, even Koch was compelled to "tack to the left" and attack Reagan.[176] The then struggling president would make up much of the subtext of Cuomo's Inaugural Address on New Year's Day, 1983. Despite his advisers feeling as though "it was too similar to his campaign speeches," Cuomo made some revisions, but he kept to the underlying themes that brought him victory.[177] The speech was an immediate success, drawing praise from all quarters—even Richard Nixon sent Cuomo a congratulatory note.[178] In hindsight, it represents the beginning of a certain form of speech, not unique to Cuomo, but uncommon for the period.

Mario Cuomo's political arrival coincided with Ronald Reagan's on the national level, and over the better part of the next decade, his speeches would be marked by elements of his First Inaugural as governor. It was his first great speech, and indeed, it was his first philippic against Reagan. Put in contemporary terms, it was Cuomo's rhetorical assault on not only the person of Reagan as a political leader—a modern Antony (or better still, Caesar)—but more pointedly, an assault on a certain approach to government. Like Cicero, the great Roman orator (and regional governor) of the first century bc, Cuomo proved unrelenting in his condemnation of the imperial politics of his day.[179] Few politicians sustained their arguments over the 1980s as Cuomo did. The opening salvo, and what proved to be the template for other such speeches, was the Inaugural. Cicero, so revered by America's founders for his republicanism and aversion to empire, launched some 14 philippics against Mark Antony. Cuomo did not have as many great speeches truly dedicated to his overarching political adversary— but he had perhaps half as many, and they account for much of what defines the alternative language imposed against Reaganism over the years.

Flanked by his family, with his wife Matilda, and his son, Andrew (who directed his campaign) directly behind the rostrum, Mario Cuomo took the oath of office making him New York's 52nd governor. After receiving a strong ovation, Cuomo began by thanking his wife, Hugh Carey, and Erastus Corning, the mayor of Albany. And then Cuomo opened by making the philosophical connections of his election to larger questions of the direction of the country. In short, clipped sentences, and with an unmistakably refined but nonetheless New York accent ("surer" became shoor-ah, "firmer," firm-ah), Cuomo launched into the meaning of his victory:

> "I would be less than intelligent," he said, "if I didn't recognize that the outcome was not so much a personal vindication as it was the judgment of the people of New York as to the body of principles and programs which we advanced as the reason and justification for my candidacy." And then after a short list of his plans for "jobs" and "justice," twin pillars of his campaign, he spoke to the rising tide of conservatism in the country. "Part of [our] program will be our message to Washington. We will say to our president and present administration that we have no intention of using Washington as a scapegoat for all of our failures and difficulties, or as an excuse for not doing for ourselves, as a state, everything we can." But then, Cuomo pivoted to a more frontal assault. "On the other hand, we will not allow the national administration to escape responsibility for its policies. We will continue to point out what we believe, respectfully, is the massive inequity of the new redistribution of national wealth—a redistribution that moves our nation's resources from the vulnerable Northeast and Midwest to the affluent or at least less troubled parts of the nation."[180]

Describing Reagan's measures without mentioning him by name, Cuomo labeled them forms of "cruelty" and "economic recklessness."[181] He then went on to elaborate on "the soul" of his administration, a "philosophy of government" that could be described as "progressive pragmatism." The history of New York's government, he said "has proven that government can be a positive force for good. It still can be."[182] In one sense, Cuomo's use of "progressive pragmatism" was a by-product of the many sufferings of the term "liberalism." But it was in some ways, historically accurate. Cuomo sought to hearken back to the early part of the century, when progressives and pragmatists theorized about government anew. He was, in effect, linking himself with old-line Hudson progressives going back to FDR, Al Smith, Charles Evans Hughes, Woodrow Wilson, and Theodore Roosevelt. The new levels of economic inequality—the basis for his most powerful philippic against Reagan to be delivered the following year—fed Cuomo's passion for a form of executive-led progressivism as much as it did those governors of New York and New Jersey at the turn of the 20th century. This speech would mark the beginning of the last stage of that long line of reform governors, steeped in the belief of government's positive good, going as far back as Teddy Roosevelt and Cleveland, and perhaps all the way back to Samuel Tilden who brought down Boss Tweed.

For Cuomo, progressive pragmatism meant "government's basic purpose is to allow those blessed with talent to go as far as they can—on their own merits," while being obliged to "assist those who, for whatever reason, have been left out by fate: the homeless, the infirm, the destitute."[183] Turning Ronald Reagan's theory of government on its head ("government is not the solution to our problem, government is the problem"), Cuomo sought a restoration of a former one: "Of course, we should have *only* the government we need," he said, "But we must insist on *all* the government we need."[184] On two occasions Cuomo referenced the growing criticism of Reaganomics as a form of Social Darwinism. "Survival of the fittest may be a good working description of the process of evolution," he said, "but a government of humans should elevate itself to a higher order, one which tries to fill the cruel gaps left by chance or by a wisdom we don't understand."[185] And then, the coup de grace: "I would rather have laws written by Rabbi Hillel or Pope John Paul II than by Darwin."[186] Like the progressives of old, Cuomo was claiming a moral obligation to resolve social inequity; he was attempting to revive a Social Gospel that was increasingly being reconfigured by Republicans—toward private ends. "We can, and we will," Cuomo said again, "refuse to settle for survival, and certainly not just survival of the fittest."[187]

Toward the latter part of his speech, Cuomo built upon the idea that New York State was, in fact, a family. It would be a recurring theme in speeches to come, but for now, it had the character of being a locally prescribed doctrine. In lines that nearly echoed John Winthrop, Cuomo said, "We must be the family of New York, feeling one another's pain, sharing one another's blessings, reasonably, equitably, honestly, fairly, without respect to geography or race or political affiliation."[188] Cuomo used the word "family" or families" five times—and he wisely packed them near the end of the speech, right after telling the story of his own family's immigrant struggles. And he would end the speech on that note, reaching out metaphorically to his deceased father, Andrea. "And Pop, wherever you are, and I think I know, for all the *cerimonia*, and the big house and the pomp and circumstance, please don't let me forget."[189]

The ovation was thunderous. Some of the most hardened politicians were said to be in tears.[190] Assemblyman Arthur O. Eve from Buffalo, a key black leader charged with recommending minorities for Cuomo to hire, called the address "the greatest speech ever made by a Governor in this state."[191] Two weeks after the speech, the *Amsterdam News* was reporting that the National Association for the Advancement of Colored People (NAACP) had placed Cuomo on the "top of the list of newly-elected governors" around the country it planned to meet with.[192] Chief Judge Charles Desmond, who swore Cuomo in, is said to have told him it was the best inauguration he had ever seen—and he had been "going to them since Al Smith's."[193] For his part, Cuomo was less effusive in his diary. "It proved to be a personal and emotional speech, and that's what works best on such occasions."[194] He spent far more space writing about the new bathtub in the governor's mansion the following day.

Mario Cuomo was now among the most powerful liberal voices in the country. But his governorship was just beginning. He would have to find time and space to tackle the more mundane aspects of governing. And yet, he'd soon be drawn into national politics. Over the course of the next year and a half, he'd grow even more in stature, becoming the most sought after Democrat in the country. But there was something small lurking in the inaugural address, something perhaps telling of Cuomo's deeper ambitions. It was a line that drew the lengthiest applause, but one that in hindsight may have proven more telling about Cuomo's future than could possibly have been known at the time. He was deeply proud, it appeared, to be the son who from his parents' "little grocery store in South Jamaica" moved on to "occupy the highest seat in the greatest state of the greatest nation in the only world we know."[195] It seemed like it might be enough.

Part Two

———

Poetry

"HE'S PROVED HE'S an immortal," said Arthur Kremer, chairman of New York's Ways and Means Committee. "The next two hundred and sixty-five days will show whether he's human like the rest of us."[1] Halfway through his first year in office, Cuomo continued to bask in the afterglow of his successful inaugural address. He also had begun to achieve a number of public victories and policy achievements. Within just over a week of taking office, Cuomo helped resolve without bloodshed a 53-hour hostage crisis at the state's correctional facility in Ossining, 30 miles north of New York City. He also successfully pushed through his first ($18.6 billion) budget on time—a rare occurrence in New York politics. A year later, Cuomo would crow: "In the face of the most massive budget deficit in our state's history . . . we were nevertheless able to balance the budget without abandoning our weak."[2] Hearkening back to an old Hudson progressive tradition of blurring the boundaries between executive and legislative functions, Cuomo "went into the Assembly chamber in late March as groggy legislators finished passing the budget shortly before 2 AM."[3] His reward was a new-found sense of comity—some called it "an ecumenical spirit"—with

lawmakers in Albany.[4] Before the session was over, Cuomo would also see the passage of a partial state takeover of local Medicaid costs.[5] Within the year, he also gained support for a $1.25 billion bond issue, the largest ever approved by the state's voters.[6]

These, along with other moves, earned him tremendous early support. He had kept his coalition intact—and he earned high marks for his appointment of minorities and women to positions within his administration, winning plaudits from the *Amsterdam News* for having "a very successful first year in meeting the needs of what [Cuomo] calls 'the family of New York,' including the state's Black and Hispanic citizens."[7] But here, and in other areas, there were signs that the so-called Cuomolot as some were describing his administration, was not all that it appeared to be.

By early 1984, Cuomo was being criticized in some quarters for being "too hands-on" a governor. "My rhetorical question is why does he have Andrew that close and no one else," said William Bianchi, an early campaign supporter, referring to Cuomo's son's powerful influence in the administration.[8] Likewise, there was the growing sense that "Cuomo believes he can govern by words alone."[9] Chastising Cuomo for attempting too much in his second budget a year later, Assembly Speaker Stanley Fink said, "When you raise the level of expectations of people I think it becomes incumbent to sort of zero in on the ones we're going to do."[10] More important, members of his own party were furious with him for imposing what they viewed as severe austerity measures on the state government, including staff reductions in New York's public universities— something that represented an about-face in previous negotiations with legislators. The move was seen as a preemptive effort against Republican proposals for tax cuts.[11] By his own admission, Cuomo was also trying to set Wall Street and New York's conservative business community at ease.[12] In his defense, Cuomo argued that the projected $1.8 billion deficit in the state's budget "made it easy to provide an agenda. It's called survival."[13] Perhaps the uprising at Sing Sing left an early and indelible effect on Cuomo in thinking not only about his budget but also about crime. "I want to be able to say, 'We're doing half expenditure cuts, half revenue increases . . . . If we're going to do cuts, every agency has to be cut. There's not going to be somebody safeguarded—well, except for prisons."[14]

Over the next 12 years, Cuomo would add more prison beds to the state than had been done by all previous governors in New York history combined.[15] Cuomo's opposition to the death penalty—and in 1984, his proposal to place non-violent offenders under house arrest—were seen as weak bulwarks against the growing tide for anti-crime legislation.[16] While *Newsday* called his house arrest plan "unmanageable," Cuomo pitched it along with other more liberal measures directed against recidivism while trying also to appear fiscally responsible and strong on crime. "New York," he said at the time, "is more fiscally sound and prudently managed than the federal government."[17] The Reverend Calvin Butts III, pastor of Abyssinia Baptist Church in Harlem, was one of New York's most influential African American figures during Cuomo's tenure as governor, and I asked him what he thought now, many years later, of Cuomo's role in helping build America's currently massive prison-industrial system. "I was in countless meetings," Butts recalled, "oftentimes with the governor there, or with his major surrogates there. When you are a parent and you see your child destroyed due to the use of drugs sold to them by somebody who looks just like them; when you see young girls in heroin dens selling their bodies; when you see that kids are dying—I'll tell you, not many people were stopping to have a 'let me look at the system' approach."[18]

In the twilight of liberalism's dominance, Cuomo was attempting to govern with the limited prescriptions available to him. In time, he would call this "progressive pragmatism." It was, most assuredly, a concession to different times. Robert Begnoche, director of the Pilgrim Psychiatric Center whose staff was cut by nearly a quarter, spoke for any number of liberals when he said one year after Cuomo's inaugural, "We hear the rhetoric and we look around. The two don't really go together."[19]

Beyond Cuomo's attempt to reduce overcrowding in state prisons through his parole program, there were other, more successful progressive policy positions. He spoke out against Congress's restrictive Simpson-Mazzoli immigration bill, vetoed the legislature's death penalty bill, backed new funding to treat AIDS patients, won the largest increase in school funding in the state's history, and proposed new and less predatory tuition loans for college students. And he sought to further consolidate authority in the executive office in what was already one of the nation's most powerful governorships. In all of these efforts, Cuomo was acting very much in the tradition of progressive governors in the state's history, who used the executive office to further social welfare policies that often put them at odds with members of their own party. On a national level, Cuomo's first year in office earned him considerable attention. Despite the end of honeymoon relations with Democrats in Albany, Cuomo's accessibility (he restored informal cocktail parties at the governor's mansion last held by Governor Alfred E. Smith) helped him build a strong record heading into his party's national convention in July.[20]

Already, by the spring of 1984, Democratic candidate for president, Gary Hart, was making no pretense of borrowing from Cuomo's rhetoric. "I believe we must offer the people of this nation a theme much like that offered by the incumbent governor of New York," the Colorado senator said in March. And then he added, "I'd like to talk about the family of America."[21] As *Newsday* reported at the time, it was "almost enough to make one forget that Cuomo had endorsed Walter Mondale," who was probing Cuomo's interest as a possible running mate.[22] The conservative syndicated columnist George Will weighed Cuomo's appeal from the right. "Cuomo combines Rooseveltian liberalism and social conservatism," he wrote. "He demonstrates for Democrats something that, until 25 years ago, few doubted; it is fine to be enthusiastic about both the welfare state and policemen."[23] Cuomo's then-counselor Tim Russert put it in broader terms from the left: "There really is a philosophical struggle here," he argued. "Will progressivism allow the New Right to capture the notion of family and voluntarism?"[24] Before Russert became a household name as the host of the long-running NBC

Sunday morning news program, *Meet the Press*, he had been an influential Democratic Party operative. Born in Buffalo, Russert rose through the ranks to become New York senator Daniel Patrick Moynihan's counsel and chief of staff, before being plucked to join Cuomo as his counsel in 1983. Their Catholic faith, non-elite legal educations, and strong ties to working-class families, connected the two men.

Despite Cuomo's compelling profile, Mondale should have been somewhat wary. Cuomo had pledged in his first year that he would not leave the state "except to handle matters of urgent concern to his constituents."[25] He had also pledged to serve a full four years if elected governor. "At the time," Cuomo said, "no one really cared."[26] But Cuomo was not about to break this vow to voters, and when enticed, he held firm. But with this spurring of a possible vice presidential nomination, Cuomo opened the door to possibly being the party's keynote speaker at the convention. It would be easy. "I'd just do my inaugural again," he said.[27]

"A Tale of Two Cities"

When Cuomo became governor in January 1983, the national unemployment rate was at its recession peak of 10.8 percent.[28] Before the Great Recession began in 2008, the early 1980s marked the nation's deepest economic downturn in the postwar era. There was much talk of the possibility of another Great Depression, and in March Cuomo noted that "the analogy to today, though certainly not perfect, is most disconcerting."[29] Slowly, the unemployment rate would tick down, to 8.3 percent by year's end and to 7.2 percent by the presidential election.[30] While the Reagan administration pushed the narrative of recovery—"Morning Again in America" became the upbeat message that summer—Democrats tapped into the residual and festering economic anxiety in the electorate. On June 21, Cuomo was officially named the keynote speaker at the Democratic National Convention (DNC), becoming the first New Yorker to deliver the address since the progressive Martin

H. Glynn had made the speech to renominate Woodrow Wilson in 1916. It seems that Cuomo accepted the task during the same conversation with Walter Mondale in which he deflected the overture to run as Mondale's vice presidential nominee. "I never made a promise not to be keynote speaker," Cuomo said, recalling his earlier pledge to serve out his term as governor.[31]

Mondale's interest in Cuomo was plain. He coveted the "Cuomo majority" (blacks, Hispanics, white liberals, and union members) that helped Cuomo defeat Koch in the gubernatorial race in 1982.[32] And Mondale was particularly keen on winning not only New York's electoral votes but also the Italian vote, "a constituency worth cultivating."[33] Mondale also rightly thought that Cuomo would be an excellent spokesperson for the struggling middle class. Yet, in hindsight, despite the historic nature of the pick, Mondale's selection of Geraldine Ferraro as his running mate left Democrats with a northern-ethnic and industrial-centered ticket—an old hand played amid dwindling New Deal coalition strength.[34] Conversely, the Reagan-Bush ticket reflected more proximate political realities. As Nicholas Lemann said in his post-election assessment:

> The Sun Belt is only one region, but it has cultural, economic, and social class implications that reach into various groups of voters nationally. The eastern establishment, which grew up in reaction to the late nineteenth century Gilded Age of unbridled business competition . . . engendered, by virtue of its power, considerable resentment—to a much greater extent than its own members probably suspected.[35]

White ethnics were now leaving the Democratic Party—Jews would be the only such demographic to vote in the majority for Mondale. And Cuomo (and more specifically, Italians) still suffered from a latent anti-ethnic bias. William Sexton of *Newsday* would incur Cuomo's opprobrium perhaps more than others for an early 1984 article in which he used pseudo-sociological arguments to paint Cuomo as an unfit leader. "Loyalty to the in-group," Sexton wrote, "unshakeable confidence in one's own perceptions and refusal to delegate authority are not helpful to the exercise of power beyond the [Italian] family."[36] For all the jocularity and at times racist sentiments expressed about the Italian vote, Reagan's team was pleased that Mondale did not pick the running mate they feared most: Cuomo.[37] But their fear had less to do with ethnic concerns and more with Cuomo's ability to re-forge the fraying New Deal coalition—in short, to reinvigorate liberalism. As the *National Review* acerbically stated, "One of Walter Mondale's supporters has described Mondale's liberalism, in a classic cornball phrase, as 'hotter than high-school love.' This is not a correct tonal description of Walter Mondale, who acts more like the school principal, but it exactly fits Mario Cuomo."[38]

Entering the 1984 convention, Democrats were facing a host of difficulties beyond balancing the ticket. Jesse Jackson had run an outsider's campaign that compelled the party to address issues of race and inclusion in its nominating process, which rankled elites within the party and further identified Democrats with "interest group" politics; Senator Gary Hart reflected an anti-union and libertarian streak that became identified with the "yuppies" who were relatively new in American politics; for his part, Mondale garnered traditional union support and upheld the banner of New Deal social welfare programs; and there was also organizational fracturing as Mondale launched an abortive attempt to remove Charles Manatt from the role of chairman of the Democratic National Committee. To make matters worse, as Elizabeth Drew reported for the *New Yorker* in her sweeping coverage of the convention, there was considerable shock in the Mondale camp over a "Gallup poll published on July 1st [which] showed Mondale losing to Reagan by nineteen points."[39] That poll was later backed up by a New York Times-CBS poll showing the margin at an only slightly less grim fifteen points.[40] As if these woes weren't ample enough, Latinos were "saying that they might abstain on the first ballot, because they [didn't] feel Mondale [was] strong enough in his denunciation of the Simpson-Mazzoli immigration bill."[41] As Drew reported from the convention on the day of Cuomo's address, the open question was "whether the Democratic Party can ever amount to more than a loose and uneasy collection of its interest groups."[42]

All of these concerns made it apparent that Cuomo was going to have to go considerably further than simply repeating his inaugural address, effective as it was. Jimmy Breslin anticipated that Cuomo was up to the task. "I've more or less heard that speech at least a few times," he wrote in his column in the *Daily News*, "in places like the Corona Volunteer Ambulance headquarters in Queens . . . . Now, in a Democratic National Convention, and on nationwide television I can think of no way that it will not create the same explosion Walter Mondale . . . [was] talking about yesterday."[43] One week before his address, Cuomo was asked about the Republican Party's efforts to brand itself the pro-religion party. "If you really want to be happy," Cuomo began, "you have to do for other people. That's religion. That's the Democratic Party. But I don't want to give anything away because I have to write the keynote speech tomorrow."[44]

The houselights in the Moscone Center were still down when Mario Cuomo walked to the podium. The darkness was intentional, and Tim Russert and Andrew Cuomo saw to it that a single spotlight carried Cuomo to the stage, as an introductory biographical video of Cuomo concluded. The idea was to rivet the television cameras on the governor rather than engaging in the perfunctory panning of the crowd for reactions from the delegates. Often, in the past, these were shots of people in "midyawn, dozing, wandering" as Andrew Cuomo recalled.[45] While the cameras did cut away on occasion for crowd reaction (including shots of the largely stoical Andrew, who at one point had to be prompted to smile by an elbow to the ribs from Russert, euphoric over the apparent success of the speech), Cuomo largely held the focus of the networks' cameramen.[46]

Cuomo used that attention to immediately target Reagan and the divide he believed was gripping the nation. After introducing himself "on behalf of the Empire State and the family of New York" (the first of what would be 11 references to family), Cuomo spoke to the economic crisis facing the nation. "Ten days ago," he began,

"President Reagan admitted that although some people in this country seemed to be doing well nowadays, others were unhappy, even worried, about themselves, their families, and their futures."[47] From the seemingly innocuous line about the "family of New York" to this entreaty to reconsider the darker side of "morning in America," Cuomo signaled his effort to wrest from conservatives the idea of family and economic prosperity so enshrined in Reagan as an individual, and in his party, which had appropriated these themes in his nearly four years in office. From here, Cuomo pivoted to the heart of his talk; this was his blistering critique of Reagan's appropriation of John Winthrop's 1630 speech referencing a "City upon a Hill." For Cuomo, conservatives were not engaged in what Winthrop had described as "A Modell of Christian Charity."

> The president said that he didn't understand that fear. He said, "Why this country is a shining city on a hill." But the hard truth is not everyone is sharing in this city's splendor and glory. A shining city is perhaps all the president sees from the portico of the White House and the veranda of his ranch where everyone seems to be doing well. But there's another city, there's another part of the shining city, the part where some people can't pay their mortgages and most young people can't afford one, where students can't afford the education they need and middle-class parents watch the dreams they hold for their children evaporate.

In these few early lines Cuomo revealed a subtle strategy to disentangle Reaganism from the man—to levy an assault on conservatism while leaving the president, still popular with the American people, intact. Reagan, from this vantage point wasn't a bad or ill-intentioned man; in a sense, he was worse—he was clueless. Ensconced on his "veranda" or from his privileged position looking out from the White House "portico," Reagan was simply out of touch with reality. Seldom has the word "maybe" been used to such slicing effect, but Cuomo's next rhetorical jabs had the effect of diminishing Reagan's leadership and sense of compassion by conveying to his audience the underlying meaning of the word: disappointment.

> Maybe if you visited some more places . . .
> Maybe if you went to Appalachia . . .
> Maybe if you stopped into a shelter in Chicago . . .

And then, in a rising cadence, one that carried above the growing sounds of voices and applause around him in the hall:

> . . . maybe Mr. President, if you asked a woman who'd been denied the help she needed to feed her children because you said we needed the money for a tax break for a millionaire, for a missile we couldn't afford to use!

Cuomo had set up these lines with stark images: "elderly people who tremble in the basements," "people who sleep in the gutter, where the glitter doesn't show," and "young people who give their lives away to drug dealers every day." And this was followed by what has come to be known in speechwriting as "the master sentence"—the sentence that unlocks the meaning of the speech in its entirety.[48] "In fact, Mr. President, this is a nation," Cuomo began to rising applause, "Mr. President you ought to know, that this nation is more of a 'Tale of Two Cities' than it is just a 'shining city on a hill.'" By the time Cuomo had gotten to his litany of seven "maybes" the crowd was completely in his hands. Elizabeth Drew, recalling more than 30 years later the speech she had covered, noted that "the Convention hung on his words."[49] Ironically, Drew wrote from the convention that Cuomo "establishes an intimacy with the audience. It is something close to what Reagan does, but with more warmth. With Reagan, one is aware of the acting skills; Cuomo seems to know exactly what he is doing, but, perhaps because the skills are less honed, he seems more natural."[50] David Axelrod reflected on Cuomo's address 20 years later, when at another Democratic National Convention, a young, relatively unknown speaker reminded him of this earlier "rousing, career-making keynote in San Francisco."[51]

Cuomo chose his words carefully in describing Reagan. They were meant to convey a level of artificiality associated with upper-crust indifference. Reagan was in turn "polished," a lead actor in a game of "showmanship," full of "glitter" and "smoke and mirrors." That the Republican Party was not held more accountable, "that its disastrous quality is not more fully understood by the American people," Cuomo suggested, "I can only attribute to the President's amiability and the failure of some to separate the salesman from the product." In his diary the next morning, Reagan would record his displeasure. "I read the speeches of Jimmy Carter & Gov. Cuomo. I couldn't believe the outright falsehoods & pure demagoguery of both. But I won't reply—yet."[52] In a perhaps more telling reflection, a young and upcoming Bill Clinton, newly reelected governor in Arkansas, would tell an effusive Colorado governor and fellow Democrat, Richard Lamm, after the speech, "Come on, what did it really say about the issues we're trying to raise?"[53] In Clinton's nearly 1,000-page memoir, there is no mention of Cuomo during his time at the 1984 convention. Cuomo was sowing a brand of liberalism not only at odds with conservatives but also with increasingly powerful members of his own party.

Of course, President Reagan had more reason to take umbrage with Cuomo; as noted earlier, the speech was indeed a kind of philippic against him. "President Reagan told us from the beginning that he believed in a kind of social Darwinism," Cuomo continued. "Survival of the fittest." Cuomo then attempted to link Reagan with Herbert Hoover (as nearly every Democratic politician has to a sitting Republican president, before and since). "The Republicans called it trickle-down when Hoover tried it. Now they call it supply-side." From here, Cuomo moved to remind his nationwide audience of the party's diversity—and its historic links to Franklin Roosevelt ("Ever since Franklin Roosevelt lifted himself from his wheelchair to lift this nation from its knees"). It was at this point that the cameras cut to Andrew Cuomo, calm, somewhat grim-faced, silently walking his father through the speech as he spoke of the party's commitment to "Blacks and Hispanics, people of every ethnic group, and Native Americans—all those struggling to build their families and claim some small share of America." Later, Cuomo would ridicule the Republican Party's relative homogeneity with a scathing line:

> We're proud of this diversity. We're grateful we don't have to manufacture its appearance the way Republicans will next month in Dallas, by propping up mannequin delegates on the convention floor.

Cuomo delivered such lines with a kind of measured passion. The speech was punctuated by intermittent hand benedictions, firm and almost mannerist gestures that gave his tone and appearance an almost spiritual quality. Elizabeth Drew caught it well, calling Cuomo "papal" and "rabbinical." "His hands are used expressively," she wrote, "he times his pauses carefully."[54] One strains to find a similar style of public speaking—then, or now. Reagan's manner was unique for his time, but as has been written, it was a close cousin to the style of Franklin Delano Roosevelt, whom he borrowed from heavily. Likewise, Democrats from Gary Hart to Bill Clinton to John Kerry have sought to emulate the style and delivery of John F. Kennedy. Part of the reason for the staying power of Cuomo's speech (delivered in a year in which the Democratic candidate was walloped) has to do with its crystalline message of 20th-century Democratic Party liberalism; the other reason is its underlying moral content—and its inimitable presentation. The great American political theorist Wilson Carey McWilliams was correct in saying that "conservatives are haunted by *A Tale of Two Cities*."[55] But in the age of Reagan, they were far less so. Much of Cuomo's task was in reminding the American people why Dickens's text was, in fact, such a nightmare. Poverty in and of itself is devastating; beside plenty, it becomes a horror. In a speech interrupted some 52 times, Cuomo received one of his strongest reactions for a simple statement that spoke to this reality: "Thou shalt not sin against equality," he said, to sustained applause.[56]

While making the moral case against Reaganism, Cuomo would also appeal to logic and reason—the speech is in its own right a testament to Cuomo's lawyerly skills. But before making his case, Cuomo devoted careful attention to the fragile nature of the Democratic coalition going forward. He made an urgent appeal to party unity, even as he recognized such unity was difficult to come by given not only the racial and ethnic diversity among Democrats but also the ideological diversity among progressives, who frequently pride themselves in rejecting unanimity—at times for its own sake. "We must convince [the American people] that we don't have to settle for two cities, that we can have one city, indivisible, shining for all of its people," Cuomo said. But then a warning: "We will have no chance to do that if what comes out of this convention is a babel of arguing voices; if that's what's heard throughout the campaign, dissonant sounds from all sides—we will have no chance to tell our message. To succeed we will have to surrender some small parts of our individual interests, to build a platform that we can all stand on at once, and comfortably, proudly singing out." Cuomo had more to say at the end of this line, but the audience, perhaps sensing the deep fissures of which Cuomo spoke, drowned him out before he could finish. Writing four days after the address, conservative columnist for the *New York Times*, William Safire, rebuked Cuomo's effort as pointless. "The party of F.D.R.," he wrote, "put together a coalition of big-machines, organized labor, Northern intellectuals and a solid South. In a Depression that worked. Now the party of Mondale is trying to fuse a following of old liberals, new women, blacks, the poor, labor and Southern politicians."[57]

"New Democrats"—conservative politically, and largely rooted in the South—were already drawing up plans at the convention for a new kind of Democratic Party, as Louisiana representative Gillis Long's hotel room became the headquarters for disaffected Democratic senators, governors, and House members. The party had in a word become "McGovernized" and plans were afoot to forge an "unofficial party organization."[58] As Cuomo spoke of unifying the party against threats to Social Security and peace, his words took on a sense of urgency not yet fully understood. "The different people we represent," he said, "have many points of view. Sometimes they compete and then we have debates, even arguments. That's what our primaries were about. But now the primaries are over and it is time to lock arms and move into this campaign together." If Mario Cuomo's 1984 Democratic National Convention speech was the last great rhetorical cudgel against conservatism, then perhaps Bill Clinton's little-known talk at that same convention was the first shot fired in an intraparty conflict less visible than the one Cuomo was aiming toward. In a speech delivered just before the address of President Carter, who preceded Cuomo, Clinton attempted to recast the party in a more conservative light. "Harry Truman would be mad tonight," Clinton said, "mad because the Democratic Party to which Americans have always turned for constructive change is now seen by millions of Americans who have no memory of Harry Truman as the Party of the past. Even when they agree with us, they see us as trying to preserve the gains of the past in Social Security, environmental protection and civil rights."[59] It was a curious remark for a Democrat to make—as though these central commitments were somehow negotiable. But they were soon buried in the avalanche of other, more pressing news coming out of San Francisco.

Cuomo had more immediate concerns. He had within the first 15 minutes drawn his audience in by contrasting the "two cities" America had become, while simultaneously reminding them of the Democratic Party's tradition of economic justice for the downtrodden. Nearly one-third of the way into his remarks, the Moscone Center had shifted from the mute and respectful atmosphere of a cathedral to a rollicking old-time gathering of believers. Reminding his audience of Reagan's "Are you better off now than you were four years ago" line that helped him get elected in 1980, Cuomo turned the question on its head. "The president has asked us to judge him on whether or not he's fulfilled the promises he made four years ago," he said. "I accept that. Just consider what he said and what he's done." With that invitation, Cuomo went after Reagan's record: inflation was indeed down, but only because of the national recession; unemployment had peaked at its worst rate since the Great Depression; there were "more hungry, more poor—most of them women—and a nearly 200 billion dollar deficit."

In a speech remembered almost entirely for the attention paid to domestic concerns, Cuomo then pivoted to foreign policy, where some of his most scathing critiques can be found. He declared (with his index finger chopping the air to make his point) American foreign policy under Reagan a failure, with "the largest defense budget in history"—one that brought with it "the loss of 279 young Americans in Lebanon in pursuit of a plan and a policy that no one can find or describe." He went further, drawing surprised gasps and a loud chorus of "oohs" along with enormous applause, calling the administration to task for giving money "to Latin American governments that murder nuns, and then we lie about it." This brought many to their feet—others just stared, mouthing something, unsure, it seemed, of what quite to do. Cuomo then paused, careful not to step over his applause. He then excoriated the Reagan human rights record, again mentioning the loss of lives in Lebanon—a fertile subject for attack: "We have pounded our chests and made bold speeches," he said, "But we lost 279 young Americans in Lebanon and we live behind sandbags in Washington. How can anyone say that we are safer, stronger, or better?" Few if any of the next day's headlines mentioned foreign policy, but Cuomo's attack on the botched militarism of the Republican Party put him and Democrats in a unique position, if only for a moment. They were on the attack on national security while still reflecting the party's anti-war politics in the post-Vietnam years.

Moving toward his close, Cuomo, who had mentioned Reagan by name only twice, went back at the president in a moment that bordered on mockery. In asking "Where would another four years take us?" Cuomo responded with only more questions—ones he understood his audience would know the answer to. "Ladies and gentleman, please, think of this—the nation must think of this. What kind of Supreme Court will we have?" This led to one of the biggest interruptions of applause of the entire evening, with people screaming, out of their seats for some 45 seconds. First imploring the crowd to quiet down, Cuomo followed up with more. "Please—we must ask ourselves," he continued, "what kind of court and country will be fashioned by the man who believes in having government mandate people's religion and morality? The man who believes that trees pollute the environment. That the laws against discrimination go too far. The man who threatens Social Security and Medicaid and help for the disabled." The line about "trees polluting the environment" had been honed over the course of months leading up to the convention and had been reported in New York newspapers. But Cuomo delivered it in San Francisco with newfound relish and it hit its mark with the crowd. Reagan's less than stellar environmental record made him open to such lampoons; he had said while campaigning for governor in 1966 that "a tree is a tree—how many more do you need to look at?"[60] Reagan nevertheless won that election, the first in a series of "Teflon" moments in his political career. Democrats would find him similarly impervious to such assaults in 1984. But it wasn't for lack of trying. Having done enough to pierce Reagan, Cuomo then moved to nobler pursuits. "This election will measure the record of the past four years," he said. "But more than that, it will answer the question of what kind of people we want to be."

> We Democrats still have a dream. We *still* believe in this nation's future.
>
> And this is our answer to the question—our credo:
>
> We believe in *only* the government we need, but we insist on *all* the government we need. We believe in a government that is characterized by fairness and reasonableness, a reasonableness that goes beyond labels, that doesn't distort or promise to do things that we know we can't do. A government strong enough to use the words "love" and "compassion" and smart enough to convert our noblest aspirations into practical realities.

And later, hearkening back to the saint for whom the city he was in was named, Cuomo brought his progressive faith to the fore once again. "We would rather have laws written by the patron saint of this great city, he said, "the man called the 'world's most sincere Democrat'—Saint Francis of Assisi—than laws written by Darwin."

There were seven of these "we believes" that began a series of poetic stanzas that seemed to enrapture the audience, as Cuomo spoke, hands clasped, almost imploring a new kind of politics in the form of a confessional. And he concluded on the subject that began his talk—"We believe we must be the family of America, recognizing that at the heart of the matter we are bound to one another . . . that failure anywhere to provide what reasonably we might, to avoid pain, is *our* failure." Cuomo, was in effect, delving into the text of John Winthrop, who said aboard the Puritan vessel, the *Arbella*, in 1630, "We must delight in each other; make other's conditions our own; rejoice together, mourn together, labor and suffer together."[61] These were the preconditions for making America a "City upon a Hill." Reaganism stripped the message of obligations, leaving American exceptionalism as a natural phenomenon or blessing, rather than a byproduct of God's bestowal of recognition premised upon an adherence and commitment to shared suffering and sacrifice.

Speaking of the "struggle to live with dignity" as the real story of the shining city, Cuomo concluded with perhaps the master stroke of the evening. Emphasizing the personal as political, he spoke of his father. It was the picture of Andrea, the "small man" with "thick calluses" filled with "simple eloquence" that Cuomo painted before the throng, still listening intently, many in tears. "I saw him once literally bleed from the bottoms of his feet," Cuomo recalled, "a man who came here uneducated, alone, unable to speak the language, who taught me all I needed to know about faith and hard work by the simple eloquence of his example." It was reminiscent of his conclusion to the inaugural, now, it seemed, so long ago. He had elevated himself tremendously, over these last 40 minutes. He had stolen fire back from the gods of conservatism, if only for one night—the fire of family, and faith, and patriotism. And then in the end, he concluded the personal portion of his remarks—before the perfunctory thank yous and calls to support Mondale and the party in November. He once again went back to the little grocery store in Queens, where Andrea had built his family, where one of his children went from "the other side of the tracks in South Jamaica where he was born, to occupy the highest seat in the greatest state of the greatest nation in the only world we know." And then came the applause. They would have let him go on. They wanted more.

"What happened?" Cuomo mouthed to his staffers and others as he climbed down the stairs of the platform after the speech.[62] Cuomo would play down the speech for years, but his immediate reaction suggests he understood something quite unique had just taken place. *Newsday*'s Murray Kempton was among the most effusive. "For a little less time than it takes a subway to get from Far Rockaway to Manhattan," he wrote, "Mario Cuomo had taken all the broken promises and put them together shining and renewed, and he had restored the Democratic Party to virginity."[63] Elizabeth Drew's real-time notes were no less laudatory: "He has conducted a psychological as well as spiritual exercise, and one can sense that a change has come over the hall."[64] James Reston of the *New York Times* continued along these lines, calling the convention "a revival meeting in more ways than one, vaguely religious at times." Deploring the "woeful decline of public political speech among the Democrats in recent years . . . in a masterful address, Gov. Cuomo gave them a key and just the right note."[65] Harlem's *Amsterdam News* was equally buoyant, calling Cuomo's remarks "a lawyer's brief for America."[66] As Calvin Butts remembered it, "I witnessed his ability to move an audience [there]. I was a delegate for Jesse Jackson at the time, and I knew, as great a speaker as Jesse was, he was going to have a hard time meeting or surpassing Mario Cuomo."[67] For many who watched that night, Butts's assessment proved prophetic.

Yet Cuomo had his detractors. The *New York Daily News* in its "Morning After" editorial (published three days after the speech), was one of the few local newspapers to throw a bit of cold water on

Cuomo's moment in the sun. "There's a big difference between the rhetoric of a convention," the piece ran, "and the realities of the statehouse. In San Francisco, Cuomo was a leader of the opposition, denouncing the federal government. In New York he is the government, and knows the limits of the state's power to help the needy."[68] This was a pivot from the paper's first reaction, which heralded Cuomo for demonstrating that "eloquence is still possible and politicians can still lead in an era of media consultants, packaged candidates and soft-core principles. Here at last is a man who knows what he wants to say and how to say it."[69]

Conservatives were naturally less charitable. In a back-handed compliment, William Safire wrote in the *Times* that Cuomo gave "the best-delivered keynote address since the days of Alben Barkley—devoid only of humor." Cuomo, he said, "almost succeeded in giving compassion a good name."[70] John Buckley, a spokesman for the Reagan campaign, called the speech "a well-crafted litany of cheap shots and half-truths."[71] While noting that Cuomo and Reagan "are the two greatest communicators in America today," Robert Reno, from his "Business View" column at *Newsday*, ultimately called Cuomo's speech "standard bleeding heart doctrine."[72] Meanwhile, George Will gave Cuomo "C for substance, A for delivery," in his nationally syndicated column. "Cuomo did what a keynote speaker is supposed to do," wrote Will, noting that "style being ten times more important than content on such occasions, he convinced the conventioneers that they are the children of light, destined to push back the darkness."[73]

Immediately after the speech, and ever thereafter, Cuomo attributed its success to the readiness of the crowd. Planning a cabinet shake-up the day after his return to New York, Cuomo told reporters that the audience had "devastated" the speakers before him, including Ed Koch and Jimmy Carter. "But when I stood there," he said, "they were all looking at me silently. It wasn't that I captured them. They were ready."[74] Cuomo did not stick around to bask in the sunshine of the moment. He took an all-night flight back east and left his party to heal further. Jackson, Hart, and

Mondale were convening into the night, smoothing over party differences, with Jackson telling reporters "there would be creative tension during the next forty-eight hours."[75] Jackson's speech the next night went some distance in relieving those tensions, as he delivered a powerful address before the convention. "I would rather have Roosevelt in a wheelchair than Reagan on a horse," he thundered to great applause.[76] Things seemed to be coming together. Perhaps Reagan's 18-point lead in the polls was a mirage. Maybe Cuomo had lit a fire that would carry on to Jackson, to Mondale, to the entire nation. Cuomo had done his part—and then some. But he was now to turn to the business of governing. He did have another speech of import to deliver, looming ahead on his calendar. It would come a mere 60 days after his address at the convention. His speechwriter Peter Quinn was not pleased about the subject, "Religious Belief and Public Morality." It was to be delivered at Notre Dame in September, and it seemed to Quinn to be fraught with great potential for political pitfalls. "I don't care if it takes an hour and forty five minutes," Cuomo told him. "I want to say what I have to say."[77]

"As a Catholic"

On June 24, New York's Roman Catholic archbishop, John J. O'Connor, made a provocative statement at a televised news conference that caught Mario Cuomo's attention. "I don't see how a Catholic in good conscience," he said, "can vote for a candidate who explicitly supports abortion."[78] In the same breath, the archbishop declined to respond to a reporter's query as to whether or not Cuomo should be excommunicated for his pro-choice position as governor.[79] Cuomo saw the battle over faith in the public arena—particularly the question of abortion—as part of a larger struggle over the appropriation of religious values by the Republican Party and conservatives. Without any equivocation, Cuomo targeted the president. "You have a President," said Cuomo, "who has wrapped himself in religiosity. Reagan has used religion aggressively as a weapon, as a tool. He has held himself out as offering the American people a religious value that will be the foundation for the Government. You have Reagan moving into what was a vacuum and brandishing religious values."[80] In this context, the speech at Notre Dame would serve as a third philippic, after his inaugural address and the convention speech in San Francisco, against Reagan—though Cuomo would not mention the president's name in the hour-long speech.

Within a week, *Newsday* was reporting that Cuomo would visit Notre Dame to "lecture on the proper relationship between religion and government."[81] Cuomo had already been at odds with the New York State Catholic Conference for its rejection of the Equal Rights Amendment (ERA) Cuomo hoped to pass. The conference opposed it unless it had an amendment clarifying that the ERA would not "guarantee the right to an abortion."[82] It was this sort of linkage of public policy to religious doctrine that troubled Cuomo. "What happens when an atheist wins," Cuomo argued. "Then what do I do? Then they're going to start drawing and quartering me."[83] But it wasn't the atheists in this instance, so frustrating Cuomo; it was the leadership of his own church.

Underlying the frustrations was politics. Ed Koch, who had long supported abortion and gay rights, nevertheless enjoyed a cozy relationship with the archbishop, dining with him about six times a year.[84] O'Connor's more selective bromides against Democratic politicians' spiritual shortcomings clearly irked Cuomo. Republicans meanwhile took on the mantle of faith in 1980, helping Reagan win over a sizable portion of working-class white voters who were formerly Democrats. As the political scientist Theodore Lowi explained at the time, "For example, although Carter was a truly observant born-again Christian, his faith played almost no political or policy role in his campaign or presidency . . . . Ironically, although Reagan is a far less observant born-again Christian, religion played a much greater role in his campaign and in his first term as president."[85] Cuomo saw these maneuvers as the politicization of faith in ways that were incompatible with his sense of constitutional law—and indeed, his own conscience. Meanwhile, Reagan had gotten into a bit of trouble during the summer campaign in 1984 for seeming to renounce the separation between church and state, calling the connection between religion and politics "necessarily related." Under some fire, he recast his statement: "The correct version is there is a wall of separation but some antireligionists are trying to break down that wall."[86]

After Cuomo's address at the Democratic Convention, the imbroglio with O'Connor and the religious right—the self-proclaimed Moral Majority—only heated up, even as the archbishop backed away from some of his previous statements. "I was naturally surprised to read statements in the *New York Times* this morning," explained O'Connor, "that some readers might construe as being attributed to me by Governor Cuomo, particularly since I have never had what I would consider to be a substantial discussion with the Governor."[87] O'Connor went on to say that "as Archbishop of New York, it is neither my responsibility nor my desire to evaluate the qualifications of any individual of any political party for any public office, or of any individual holding public office."[88] Sensing he had won the skirmish, if not the war, Cuomo declared victory. "I'm pleased with the Archbishop's response," he said, noting he was "delighted to have the clarification today where he is saying in effect we're not going to tell anybody to vote for anybody."[89]

Democrats seemed to have stalled for a time the question of their party's capitulation on matters of faith. Even the conservative *New York Times* columnist William Safire thought Republicans had overshot the bow. "If Mr. Reagan campaigns for ending the welfare state at home and turning back totalitarianism abroad, he will build a majority party; but if he sees the burning issues as abortion, school prayer and parochial school tuition subsidies, his second term will be a failing struggle to impose a religious government on people who prefer to practice their religions freely."[90] Speaking before B'nai B'rith in early September, Democratic nominee Walter Mondale chastised Reagan for forgetting his proper constitutional role. "The Queen of England, where state religion is established, is called the 'Defender of the Faith,'" he said. "But the

President of the United States is the defender of the Constitution—which defends all faiths."[91]

While all of this was transpiring, Cuomo had been working on his Notre Dame speech, one that according to his biographer, underwent 17 drafts over the course of five weeks.[92] Perhaps Cuomo, like Quinn, sensed the difficulties of the situation. The historian Garry Wills noted that Cuomo's task was more difficult than the one that confronted John F. Kennedy when he sought the White House in 1960. Kennedy merely had to convince his Protestant audience in Houston that he sought no special place for his religion in the public arena; this was in keeping with American political and cultural mores at the time. Cuomo was confronting a potentially hostile crowd—from his own church—and facing this "exposed position," he had to demonstrate his faith's relevance to him personally while seeking to explain its restrained position in his executive politics.[93] And, of course, this speech was designed not to arouse—there are no applause lines to be found in it after some initial levity by Cuomo before his prepared remarks. On the contrary, one can barely identify a smile in the audience, looking on soberly, as Cuomo methodically builds his case. There would be no teleprompter for Cuomo, nor would he have the kind of control over the aesthetic environment that Russert and Andrew had forged in San Francisco. Cuomo was, in fact, as much on foreign turf as he was at home at Notre Dame, the citadel of American Catholicism. And he was there because many in the church were unhappy with him. They were unhappy with his positions, and they wanted answers.

In an otherwise serious talk, Cuomo began by paying tribute to his venue with humor, citing a litany of great "Fighting Irish" football players' surnames over the years—all of them Italian. Noting that former New York governor Al Smith faced a dilemma of where to sit at the Army-Notre Dame game as a Catholic whose home team he was representing, Cuomo declared his "loyalties will remain undivided" so long as he was not asked to sit with the renowned Notre Dame professor and theologian, Father McBrien (who had invited Cuomo), at a St. John's basketball game. And that was it. Like a professor engaging a trying subject, Cuomo went on for nearly an hour, carefully delivering his words, rifling periodically through his papers on the lectern, and with no fear of stepping over his applause lines to worry about. With sweat accumulating on his brow throughout the evening and with no political banners to be seen, this was a moment closer to Cuomo's person than the one experienced at the Moscone Center 60 days before. A small detail marked the distinction between the two talks. In San Francisco Cuomo did not use his reading glasses. He wore them in South Bend.

Cuomo began his lecture by raising several questions that would become his audience's focus: "Must politics and religion in America divide our loyalties? Does the 'separation between church and state' imply separation between religion and politics? Between morality and government? And are these different propositions? Even more specifically, what is the relationship of my Catholicism to my politics? Where does the one end and the other begin? Or are the two divided at all? And if they're not, should they be?" These were formidable questions to tackle, to be sure. And Cuomo would take them on, one by one, as he had told Peter Quinn he would. It wouldn't last the hour and 45 minutes he suggested he'd be willing to take, but with questions and answers to follow—a number of them filled with their own sparks—it came close. One telltale sign of the speech's importance to Cuomo was how closely he hewed to his prepared remarks, delivering them faithfully, with few ad-lib departures.[94]

Of course, to get a line "wrong" at the Democratic National Convention could subject him to being lampooned; in this setting, however, Cuomo was concerned about something much deeper. Again, where Kennedy spoke to assuage the nation's fears over his presumed overdependence on his faith, Cuomo sought to correct the notion that he had somehow jettisoned his.

Citing the "recent discussion in my own state," Cuomo attempted to clarify the "confusion" over whether the National Conference of Catholic Bishops supported the taking of sides "for or against political

candidates."[95] Clearly, they had not, said Cuomo—and this new clarification by the bishops (even with regard to abortion, mentioned for
the first time five minutes into his talk), was but one step in getting to
the heart of the matter as he saw it. Careful to note that it would not
be a "sin if they did," Cuomo made a higher-order argument. While
it was certainly within their right to do so ("God doesn't insist on
political neutrality"), Cuomo argued that in the end, "it is not wise for
prelates and politicians to be tied too closely together." Here, Cuomo
moved to address his audience as governor, someone who is forced
"to wrestle with the problems you've come here to study and debate."
After a short humorous aside about an old Tammany Hall politician
named "Fishhooks," who stole his way to power, Cuomo reminded his
audience that his position was a necessarily limiting one; he was, after
all, "Elected to serve Jews and Muslims, atheists and Protestants, as
well as Catholics"—and that being so gave him greater responsibilities than if he were merely acting in his private interests.

It is this divide, Cuomo argued, the one between the personal
and the public that had to be carefully scrutinized. "The Catholic
public official lives the political truth most Catholics through most
of American history have accepted and insisted on," he said. "The
truth is to assure our freedom we must allow others the same freedom, even if it occasionally produces conduct by *them* which *we*
would hold to be sinful." This is the type of concession to both political reality and human nature made by John Locke in his *Letter
Concerning Toleration*—"The care of the salvation of men's souls
cannot belong to the magistrate," Locke wrote in 1689.[96] Cuomo
merely reiterates this truth, even in the case where the magistrate
is herself, a believer. Perhaps, especially in that case. Even as "an
old-fashioned Catholic baptized and raised in the pre-Vatican II
Church," Cuomo wanted to convey that the social conservatism
of his faith and upbringing did not preclude him from defending
the liberal Lockean roots of toleration, in part, because they were
equally protective of the church as they are of secular society. "We
know," he said, "that the price of seeking to force our belief on others is that they might someday force their belief on us."

Cuomo brought his audience along into more subtle terrain, arguing that an "insistence on freedom is easier to accept as a general proposition than in its application to specific situations." It could not have been lost on him how severe yet instructional some of his examples must have sounded to an audience made up of largely young people, however defined by their faith. The notion that we "should not sever sex from an openness to the creation of life," may well have been established bedrock Catholic teaching, but the prospect of it becoming the basis for public policy as a matter of faith with regard to the use of contraceptives was indeed much to digest. In this regard, Cuomo exercised astute judgment in parceling out a variety of positions of the church as a form of buffer against weighing in isolation the sin of abortion and the question of its legitimacy in the public arena.

> And surely I can, if I I am so inclined, demand some kind of law against abortion not because my bishops say it is wrong, but because I think that the whole community, regardless of its religious beliefs, should agree on the importance of protecting life . . . . No law prevents us from advocating any of these things: I am free to do so. So are the bishops. So is Reverend Falwell. In fact, the Constitution guarantees my right to try. And theirs. And his. But *should* I?

By siding with his critics in acknowledging the moral wrong—indeed, sin—he believes abortion to be, Cuomo effectively disarms or at least blunts one of their chief arguments against him: that he is but another secularist. Or, at worst, an "opportune" Catholic. But no, Cuomo is in agreement with his church's position. And he is clear on his right to advocate it (while not using his executive function against the law). But Cuomo makes a Catholic's argument against such advocacy by a public official. It won't work, and it is ultimately counterproductive to both the church and its desired outcomes. In the first of several such refrains, Cuomo responds, "As a Catholic, I respect the teaching authority of the bishops. But must I agree with everything in the bishops' pastoral letter on peace and fight to include it in party platforms?" Here, the pastoral letter on peace is but one substitute for abortion. At what point should a public official withdraw his or her public advocacy of the church's position—not only on the question of abortion, but on any number of such issues? "Must I," Cuomo continues, "having heard the pope renew the church's ban on birth control devices, veto the funding of contraceptive programs for non-Catholics or dissenting Catholics in my state?" Armed now with these rhetorical questions, Cuomo promises to go deeper. "Let me try some answers."

Citing the example of the civil rights movement's support and leadership from the black church, Cuomo said, "The arguments start when religious values are used to support positions which would impose on other people restrictions they find unacceptable." The support for ending second-class citizenship for blacks was built ultimately by consensus, an essential component in shaping the values of a pluralistic society. "The community," Cuomo said, "must decide if what is being proposed would be better left to private discretion than public policy." This point of Cuomo's was at the heart of his battle with Reagan over the proper role of religion in public life. Just three weeks prior to Cuomo's Notre Dame address, Reagan spoke forcefully on the subject. "The truth is," he said, "politics and morality are inseparable, and as morality's foundation is religion, religion and politics are necessarily related. We need religion as a guide."[97] Calling his opponents on the matter "intolerant of religion," Reagan alluded to Cuomo's fight with O'Connor on the question, stating that the guidance of church leaders on political issues was "a good and necessary thing." For Reagan, knowing "how a church and its members feel on a public issue expands the parameters of debate."[98] It did not go unnoticed by reporters that Reagan was engaging New York's governor in a bit of a debate on religion. When Reagan's White House spokesman Larry Speakes was asked if the president was referring to Mr. Cuomo, Speakes responded, "You'll have to draw your own conclusions."[99]

While this philippic of Cuomo's did not mention the president either, those in attendance and reading it in the many published versions in the following day's newspapers could "draw their own conclusions" about Cuomo's target as well. "This 'Christian nation' argument," Cuomo said, "should concern—even frighten—two groups: non-Christians and thinking Christians." And then Cuomo brought his point a step closer to home: "The American people need no course in philosophy or political science or church history to know that God should not be made into a celestial party chairman." Unlike at the Democratic Convention, such lines did not draw whoops and hollers from the crowd. They sat intently, almost stoically. For his part, Cuomo spoke with force, but also in a somewhat courtly manner, adjusting his glasses as they would fall from time to time over the bridge of his nose, and then coming down, he'd move them back up, before freeing his hands as they clasped together in a single motion coming down. He'd do so, and then pause briefly before speaking again. These were minimalist gestures as Cuomo let his words wash over his audience. As Robert McElvaine later wrote, Cuomo's success at Notre Dame "was as much the result of what Cuomo was saying as it was his accomplished delivery. The music may have gotten the listener's attention, but the speaker got them to hear his words as well."[100]

About halfway through his remarks, Cuomo chose to once again bundle a number of important social issues together in making his point about abortion—a subject he acknowledged as different with regard to "degree and quality"—compared to the others. Yet Cuomo argued all the same that "my church and my conscience require me to believe certain things about divorce, about birth control, about abortion. My church does not order me—under pain of sin or expulsion—to pursue my salvific mission according to a precisely defined political plan." From here, Cuomo returned to his refrain:

"As a Catholic I accept the church's teaching authority."
"As Catholics, my wife and I were enjoined never to use abortion to destroy the life we created."

The "As a Catholic" refrain was not accidental. Cuomo had used this to begin a little-remembered speech at St. John the Divine Episcopal Church in New York just over a year before his address at Notre Dame. He began that speech with those words. Describing his own religious experience growing up, Cuomo said in that speech, "Ours was a Catholicism closer to the peasant roots of its practitioners than to the high intellectual traditions of Catholic theology."[101] And he spoke of the relationship between politics and faith at the heart of his talk, noting that the answer to the question of "where private morality ends and public policy begins" is reflected "in the one foundation on which all of us as citizens must try to balance our political and religious commitments—the Constitution."[102] Cuomo's speechwriter Peter Quinn is clear that the Notre Dame address grew out of this earlier speech. "If you go back to that St. John's speech, it was the first time a Catholic politician was openly talking about his faith. From that speech on, you can see a sudden change in his tone."[103] Calling the Notre Dame speech "a kind of accident," as Father Richard McBrien had read the text of the St. John the Divine speech in the *New York Times* before inviting Cuomo to campus, Quinn links both addresses to Cuomo's modest upbringing. "Like Reagan, Cuomo could speak to values. His first name was 'Mario.' He was from Queens. He had no contempt for Catholics, no contempt for the middle class. He based his values on Catholic working class social teaching."[104]

Returning to the practicality of matters, each of Cuomo's "As a Catholic" entreaties at Notre Dame was followed by qualifiers.

"But not everyone in our society agrees."
"Our bishops should be teachers, not pollsters."
"There is neither an encyclical nor a catechism that spells out a political strategy for achieving legislative goals."

And then Cuomo chose to invoke the history of the church to make a point about an institution frequently compared to abortion by any number of conservative politicians and religious leaders: slavery. "It has been argued," he reminded his audience, "that the failure to endorse a legal ban on abortions is equivalent to refusing to support the cause of abolition before the Civil War. This analogy has been advanced by the bishops in my own state." Reagan himself had recently compared *Roe v. Wade* to the Dred Scott decision of 1857—a leap many conservatives would make over the years.[105] Cuomo chose the forum provided him now to speak to such ill-conceived "popular illustrations" as he saw them.

> But the truth of the matter is as I'm sure you know, few, if any Catholic bishops spoke for abolition in the years before the Civil War . . . . They weren't hypocrites; they were realists. Remember, at the time, Catholics were a small minority, mostly immigrants, despised by much of the population, often vilified and the object even of sporadic violence. In the face of public controversy that aroused tremendous passions and threatened to break the country apart, the bishops made a pragmatic decision. They believed their opinion would not change people's minds. Moreover, they knew that there were Southern Catholics, even some priests, who owned slaves. They concluded that under the circumstances arguing for a constitutional amendment against slavery would do more harm than good, so they were silent.

As Quinn reflected on the speech over 30 years later, "The central argument of that speech is that we tried this with Prohibition. People were still going to have abortions. He was arguing the practical element."[106] The question for Cuomo wasn't whether abortion was right or wrong. Indeed, he took the extraordinary step to declare publicly that he and Matilda were "enjoined never to use abortion to destroy the life we created—and we never have." But this was a personal decision, rooted in Cuomo's faith—it could not be made to stand for all, certainly not as a matter of constitutional law. For Cuomo, comparing the abortion issue to slavery was engaging history—misapplied at that—on the cheap. And it devalued the real struggle of how to make moral conduct a byproduct of conscious human choice rather than a result of punitive threat from the state. As Cuomo pointed out, "This is in the American-Catholic tradition of political realism. In supporting or opposing specific legislation the church in this country has never retreated into a moral fundamentalism that will settle for nothing less than total acceptance of its views."

Restating his own belief that a constitutional amendment banning abortion "is not the best way" to address the question of abortion ("it would be Prohibition revisited"), Cuomo sought to highlight remedies that went beyond selective enforcement, such as leaving it up to individual states or by reducing Medicaid funding, which would only hurt the poor. In the end, Cuomo saw the issue as a moral one. "The hard truth is that abortion isn't a failure of government. No agency or department of government forces women to have abortions, but abortions go on." Noting that statistically speaking, Catholics show support for and practice abortion at the same rate as those in the general population, Cuomo attempted to redirect focus back onto the church and Catholics themselves. "Are we asking government" he said, "to make criminal what we believe to be sinful because we ourselves can't stop committing the sin? The failure here is not Caesar's. The failure is our failure, the failure of the entire people of God." Later, referencing the Gospel of Luke, Cuomo said Catholics must, like the "physician" spoken of in the Bible, "heal thyself."[107] And finally, to drive home his point, Cuomo put the onus on the community of believers to which he belonged. "Better than any law or rule or threat of punishment would be the moving strength of our own good example, demonstrating our lack of hypocrisy, proving the beauty and worth of our instruction." While St. Francis of Assisi apparently never quite said to "preach the Gospel everywhere and to use words when necessary," Cuomo did speak to one of his teachings: "Let all the brothers, however, teach by their deeds."[108]

In the end, Cuomo sought common ground at Notre Dame. Not one to shy away from erudition (Cuomo once referred a woman at a 92nd Street Y town hall meeting on religion to "pages 53 and 54" of Teilhard's *Divine Milieu*), he stuck for the most part to plain biblical references and familiar authorities such as Pope John II.[109] Cuomo implored his audience to support health care for infant mothers, to expand the Medicaid funding as he had done as governor in New York, to support the furtherance of education for teenage mothers. "If we want to prove our regard for life in the womb, for the helpless," he said, "if we care about women having real choices in their lives and not being driven to abortions by a sense of helplessness and despair about the future of their child, then there is work enough for all of us. Lifetimes of it." And Cuomo reminded his listeners that there were issues beyond abortion that necessitated a believer's reservoir of energies: hunger and homelessness, joblessness, and the scourge of nuclear weapons. These were all part of a tapestry of horrors confronting the world. As he moved to close, he said Catholics had to move beyond advocating the birth of a child "into a world that doesn't care if it is fed properly, housed decently, educated adequately . . . [or] condemned to exist rather than empowered to live." With the silence and attentiveness still present, he finally said, "We can be fully Catholic. . . [a]ppealing to the best in our people, not the worst. Persuading not coercing. Leading people to truth by love. And still, all the while, respecting and enjoying our unique pluralistic democracy. And we can do it even as politicians. Thank you for listening"

Suddenly, the hall packed with about 1,000 students and faculty rose almost as one and burst into spontaneous applause.[110] They had been held for nearly one hour with little room to show their emotions. And then about one minute into the applause, Cuomo began to take his seat, but they were unrelenting, so he rose. And then there was a second, spontaneous burst of applause that lasted another 20 seconds, with Cuomo looking over the auditorium, up into the balcony, a bit of a pleased but weary smile on his face. It seemed to be a decisive moment. Quinn, looking back, said, "It kind of ended the argument. It said so much, nobody wanted to touch it."[111]

Conclusion: "The Things You Should Be Doing."

With his approval rating unchanged and still high among New York Catholics and with an even brighter national spotlight than before— now backed by appearances on *Nightline* and more and more speaking requests from across the country—Cuomo was being asked about 1988.[112] "I'm not a terrific candidate," he told the *New York Times* in late September; "I gave two good speeches." More telling than this typical bit of Cuomo demurring was another statement. "I've done everything just the opposite," Cuomo said about a future route to the White House. "All of the things you should be doing if you wanted to run, I'm not doing—practically all."[113] He was right; 1988 seemed to be of far less concern to him than his reelection in 1986. And 1984 was looking bleaker by the day.

Mondale's running mate was now the one engaged in debate with O'Connor, and Reagan was up by 13 percent in a USA Today poll, looking as strong as ever.[114] All the good news seemed to be being hoarded by Cuomo. The *Times* called his speech "masterly," running an editorial praising him for showing how one "can be devout without imposing religious beliefs on others."[115] The *Daily News* ran large portions of the speech in its next day's edition. The inset was of Cuomo, hands clasped, saint-like and pensive, with an inscription: "We can be fully Catholic . . . . Leading people to truth by love . . . . And we can do it even as politicians."[116] The *New York Post*'s banner headline read "Cuomo vs. The Church" in block letters, suggesting somehow that perhaps the two combatants might be of similar power.[117] The *Post* was sure to note that Cuomo was "booed and hissed" during a question and answer session when he said abortion is "not killing."[118] Cuomo's allusion to murder under ordinary circumstances was not mentioned. For its part, *Newsday*, the last of the hometown papers, said "Cuomo brought to the discussion a voice of reason, thoughtfulness, sensitivity and insight."[119]

The conservative columnist Michael Novak attempted to claim a middle ground, at once criticizing Archbishop O'Connor for letting go unanswered the question of Cuomo's possible excommunication while taking Cuomo to task for not knowing or showing the difference between being "personally opposed to abortion" and "upholding the law permitting abortions."[120] In short, Novak wanted Cuomo to help build a new majority through argument against abortion. The column began with a comparison between slavery and abortion.

What had it all amounted to by Election Day? The convention speech and the lecture at Notre Dame had made Cuomo a star, but they did little to help Mondale. Reagan won with 59 percent of the vote in a colossal defeat that shook up the Democratic Party. Mondale lost the women's vote by 19 points, even having put the first woman on a major party ticket for the vice presidency. Among white ethnics, Mondale captured only the Jewish vote. The only income group Democrats won were the very poor, those making less than $12,500 a year. But they constituted only 15 percent of the electorate. And Reagan captured nearly a quarter of the self-identified Democratic vote, sweeping every state but Mondale's Minnesota and the District of Columbia. But perhaps the most depressing exit poll result for Democrats concerned the future. Reagan won a stunning 61 percent of voters between the ages of 18 and 25, besting Mondale by some 22 points.[121] Where did this leave liberals, let alone Mario Cuomo, who for the time being, still seemed to have deep and strong support in his home state? Other Democrats like Bill Clinton of Arkansas were eschewing the term "liberal" altogether and were ready in 1985 to "take a new tack," forming what would become the conservative Democratic Leadership Council. The group would be committed, in Bill Clinton's words, to "forging a winning message for the Democrats based on fiscal responsibility, creative new ideas on social policy, and a commitment to a strong national defense."[122]

"Well," wrote Reagan in his diary the day after the election, "49 states, 59% of the vote & 525 electoral votes. A short press conf. The press is now trying to prove it wasn't a landslide or should I say a mandate? Then to the ranch on a beautiful day."[123] Since coming to office, Mario Cuomo had delivered several philippics against Reagan, and they seemed to flow over the Great

Communicator, as he was being called, like so many broken arrows. The inaugural address, the keynote in San Francisco, and now the deep dive at Notre Dame—they all were enormous successes for Cuomo. But as they were tied to the central ethos of his party, they may well have suggested ill-portents to the governor—time for a change. But this was not to be the case. Cuomo would deliver other addresses in the coming months, the first major one at Yale University, where he would in today's political parlance "double-down" on liberalism—at least that form of liberalism that echoed down from the New Deal era. But change was in the wind. "He thought [the Democratic Party] was moving away from its roots," Peter Quinn told me in reflecting on this period after the twin successes in the summer of 1984. "What now," Quinn asked, restating the question from that time. "We had just lost the election. Do we change our ideas—or do we still believe in the New Deal philosophy that government can help people?"[124] These never seemed to be more than rhetorical questions for Cuomo. His political philosophy was not up for reconsideration any more than was his faith.

In the weeks leading up to the election, just before it all came apart for Mondale, Cuomo was still forced to grouse with reporters about his future intentions. And reading these intentions became a fascination and perennial pastime for the local and national press. "I know how not to make decisions," Cuomo said at one point about a possible pursuit of the presidency. "I know how to make decisions. Part of the secret of making decisions is to know which decisions not to make."[125] Which decision was Cuomo not making in the fall of 1984? On the most important front, he would have to govern—that was a given. Cuomo had a full two more years to build his record for reelection in 1986. That meant that for all of 1985 and the better part of 1986 he would have to leave the realm of poetry, the one he said was relegated to campaigning. The national spotlight would necessarily die down, and he would have to be about a different kind of business—the one he called "prose."

Part Three

Prose

"*YOU KNOW HOW* he said 'You campaign in poetry and you govern in prose?'" Peter Quinn asked rhetorically. "Well, he did more poetry in government. He was very political—it was not his fault, it was just how it was."[1] Quinn was referring to the political climate in the country in the aftermath of Reagan's electoral victories, the second of which was marked by a Democratic win in but one state—Mondale's Minnesota. As Cuomo's speechwriter, Quinn had been busy helping to craft the language designed to blunt the effects of Reaganism's rise in New York. A dynamic, comprehensive progressive agenda simply wasn't to be had. "It wasn't Cuomo's fault," after all.

Quinn's aside about Cuomo's use of poetry—while governing—suggests an effort on Cuomo's part to portray his governorship as a study in quiet accomplishment rather than the ephemera of oratory. "More than Words," is after all, the title he gave to his collection of speeches. And yet, those speeches seemed to haunt him over time. Given Quinn's reflections, just how much daylight is there between Cuomo's emphasis on prose—which, must be viewed ultimately as his legislative accomplishments while governor—and Quinn's assertion of an Albany record less striking than the words that embellished it? The introduction to Cuomo's public papers from 1985 are heavy on practical accomplishments: the "largest tax cut" in the state's history, the creation of more than 800,000 jobs, $500 million to public schools, Cuomo's vetoing of the death penalty, and a half-billion dollars to help "fund new State prison projects."[2] It was an awkward mix of progressive and conservative values—an acknowledgment that the Sun Belt's pro-business and anti-crime agenda had found a home in liberal New York. In 1985, prison construction was a badge of honor—especially for progressives.

The none-too-subtle shift could be found in Cuomo's Annual Message in January of 1985. "There will always be a strong role for government to play," Cuomo said early in his speech, "but in designing our government we begin by encouraging a strong private sector economy as its foundation."[3] Cuomo was working to keep businesses in New York—particularly upstate, where so many had been leaving in recent decades. His desire not to "impose burdens so heavy that they destroy the productivity and competitiveness we seek to encourage" as a way of strengthening "the whole commonweal" was an example of his evolving "pragmatic progressivism."[4] These were lines not out of any philippic but rather the sober concession to the changing landscape of both national and local politics. Similar language was used to describe Nelson Rockefeller's administration, which ended just over a decade before Cuomo took office. Rockefeller's political biographers James E. Underwood and William J. Daniels referred to his policy disposition as a form of "pragmatic liberalism," perhaps reflecting a time among Democrats and liberal-leaning Republicans when the term "progressivism" was not used as a verbal fig leaf.[5]

But Rockefeller had important advantages over Cuomo, as Dall Forsythe noted in his study of New York's governorship. The "paradox of gubernatorial power in New York" since the fiscal crisis of the 1970s, Forsythe noted, is that the state's governors now hold "an institutionally strong office in a large and important state, yet that institutional leverage seems to confer little advantage in practice."[6]

Rockefeller's 15 years in office were marked by the "transformation of the state university, the downstate mass transit system, the apparatus for urban development," and funding for the arts. But he also left a legacy of punitive and highly racialized drug laws that helped fuel Cuomo's later radical expansion of the state's prison system.[7] When Rockefeller left office to become vice president in 1974, New York was in dire financial straits, a condition that deeply inhibited the legislative and political maneuverability of his immediate successors, Carey and Cuomo. Nevertheless, Rockefeller's liberalism suggests that Cuomo's poetry and prose dance was not all that uncommon in the later stages of New Deal liberalism's influence in New York. A key distinction, however (aside from Rockefeller's being challenged politically from the right) was that Cuomo was still fighting a rhetorical battle against liberalism's dissolution in an era when his political ability to prevent its decline was arguably at its weakest point. Whereas Rockefeller oversaw a period of tremendous government expansion—well over 300 academic buildings constructed on state university campuses, 10,000 new beds in nursing homes, and 90,000 units of new housing are big examples—Cuomo was later derided for having no big policy focus. His was an era of contraction, one of smaller progressive victories.[8]

In his State of the State message delivered in the Assembly Chamber in Albany, that January, Cuomo spoke wistfully about a Hudson progressive era he was hoping to revive:

Look around this room. The future once happened here. In this building, in this very Assembly Chamber, half a century ago, a generation of men and women defined the legislative agenda that eventually changed all of America—and through America, helped change the world. That agenda became the basis of nearly 50 years of prosperity and opportunity. This is now a whole new era. And a whole new opportunity.[9]

Cuomo was hearkening back to a New Deal era which was itself a culmination of progressive politics that made Albany a critical epicenter in liberalism's early 20th-century march, one that had been begun by governors as far back as Samuel J. Tilden and Grover Cleveland. The "future" was now being made by governors from elsewhere it seemed—Georgia, California, and soon enough, Arkansas. Cuomo's august hall was a symbol of a time eclipsed by other, less ambitious visions for government. Years later, as his son guided members of the media on a walking tour of the Assembly and its surrounding environs, its marble columns and ornate chandelier hovering above the legislators' seats, Andrew Cuomo was heard to utter, "This was New York when New York was, in some ways, at its boastful best."[10]

In nearly all those 50 years Cuomo was alluding to before his 1985 State of the State address, Republicans had controlled New York's Senate in every year but one—1965, the year after Lyndon Johnson's massive presidential electoral victory.[11] That political reality meant that Cuomo would be forced to make compromises over the course of his tenure. While the *New York Times* declared in its headline of Cuomo's speech that it was a "plan to revive the New Deal," political realities and the speech's fine print would prove otherwise.[12] Republicans got sizable tax cuts for their troubles, about $1.3 billion proposed over the next three years. It was "these tax cuts" which "exacerbated the cyclical budget problems Cuomo faced several years later."[13] Nevertheless, they were a concession to an increasingly anti-tax electorate. "We've had to drag him, kicking and screaming at first, into the tax relief arena," said Warren Anderson, the Republican majority leader. "Now, just like Hugh Carey, he's pretending that it really was his own idea."[14] Perhaps, but Cuomo received his own pledges that New York Republicans would later claim some success for, as $850 million was proposed to clean up toxic waste sites, and an additional $300 million committed to pay down the state's debt.[15] This was the definition of Cuomo's progressive pragmatism.

The day after Reagan's reelection in 1984, Cuomo reflexively distanced himself from the label of liberalism. "What are you when you reduce public employees by 9,000?" Cuomo asked. "What are you when you say [that] need should be the criterion [for welfare benefits]? What are you when you come out for a tax cut? What are you when you refuse to raise the basic taxes? What are you when you spend more on your defense budget, which we call corrections, than any governor in history?"[16] Over the next five years Cuomo would answer the question, perhaps in ways that would prove unsatisfactory to many liberals. But for many others, he'd do enough to remain a hopeful harbinger of more progressive days. He'd govern with enough from the old system, the old politics, to keep the progressive flame from dying—fewer Democrats were willing to do so, weren't they? And so Cuomo's deflections were all the more forgivable. Over the next five years, he'd have time to build a record, one that wouldn't have to elicit a defensive response as was required in the early days. *What are you?*

The Path to Reelection: 1985–1986

Less than a month after his State of the State address, Cuomo's rising counterpart within the Democratic Party gave the Democratic response to President Reagan's State of the Union address. Bill Clinton served as a moderator that evening as a number of Democratic governors were showcased. Cuomo was among the featured governors, as his record for balancing New York's budget and proposing tax cuts was touted. Reflecting on his own performance in his memoir, Clinton said "Our party took a different tack that year" as he soon got "involved in the Democratic Leadership Council [DLC], a group dedicated to forging a winning message for the Democrats based on fiscal responsibility, creative new ideas on social policy, and a commitment to a strong national defense."[17] However pragmatic Cuomo's progressivism was, it still seemed too liberal for the ascendant politicians within his party. "We want the government off our backs too," Clinton concluded that night, in an early national moment for him, "but we need it by our sides."[18] Just how this balancing act was to be accomplished and fought for by

Clinton and the newly formed DLC remained unknown in early 1985, but it would not remain mysterious for long.

It had been less than a week earlier when Cuomo gave an important address at Yale University. It was, along with his first inaugural speech, his Democratic National Convention address, and his Notre Dame speech, very much in keeping with his philippic presentations against Reaganism. It was an important week in rhetorical contrasts for Democrats, as these two lesser known moments were bookends for the past and future direction of the party. As he began his formal remarks, Cuomo moved not only against Reagan but also against the forces in his own party seeking to alter its commitments. The movement against what would soon be called the politics of "triangulation" was striking:

> The party has an abundance of both candidates and speakers, and if a new philosophy is to be articulated, I'll leave that to others. As a matter of fact, when they describe what that philosophy should be, I'll like to be in the audience, because I can't even think of a new philosophy. The philosophy I believe in— and that I hope was accepted by the people of New York when they elected me in 1982—I described at San Francisco and Notre Dame.[19]

While acknowledging to his audience the need for flexibility in the administration of certain programs and ideas, Cuomo was adamant about his liberal commitments. "Programs and policies change," he said; "our principles *don't*." To put a fine point on it, Cuomo returned to his earlier statements on his political philosophy, delivered the previous summer. "And so," he said, "if I were invited back to give another keynote or to speak at Notre Dame, I wouldn't feel the need to say anything novel."[20]

What was most telling about Cuomo's Yale address is that it explained his political beliefs in nearly spiritual terms. It was a moment that best captured the mixture of both his religious and political sentiments. At the Democratic Convention, Cuomo spoke as a politician. At Notre Dame, he spoke as a Catholic, first and foremost. But at Yale, Cuomo's reasoning was that of a political man speaking absolute truths. Ironically, his model was Galileo, who had argued against church doctrine concerning the nature of the very heavens. "E Pur Si Muove"—"But still it moves"—was the title of his talk, a reference to the Italian astronomer's softly voiced rejection during his trial, in which he countered the idea of a fixed Earth. In a bit of an astounding identification, Cuomo saw in this 17th-century moment a point of similarity. "Despite the events of last November," Cuomo said, "I haven't changed the underlying tenets of my political philosophy. *'E pur si muove.'*"[21]

Fixating on Reagan's masking of his deeply held conservative views, Cuomo said the election of 1984 was not so much a referendum on liberal ideals as on the likability of the president. For Cuomo, Reagan (who had been busy quoting FDR and JFK leading up to the election) became hard to distinguish during the campaign "from a stereotypical 'New Deal liberal.'"[22] Of course, this is the very label Cuomo had been seeking to avoid in New York as he faced an increasingly conservative electorate. After combing through Reagan's less-than-conservative record in deficits and government expansion, Cuomo sought to explain his unease with liberalism as a label. "People expected the programs and policies I spoke of [while running for governor] to conform to their image of liberalism, and when they didn't—when I said things about crime that didn't sound 'liberal' enough or when I talked about the pain we'd have to face in balancing the state budget—some of my supporters got upset."[23] And then, in a bit of sleight of hand, Cuomo returned to a label of his choosing.

> If the liberals asked what progressive pragmatism said about the role of government in our society we'd answer, "It says we should have *all* the government we need." If the conservatives asked, we'd answer, "It says we should have *only* the government we need."[24]

For all this tightrope walking, Peter Quinn was not confused about what was underlying Cuomo's message. "He thought it [the Democratic Party] was moving away from its roots," Quinn recalled about that period. "The speech at Yale really speaks to this. We had just lost the election. What now? Do we change our ideas—or do we still believe in the New Deal philosophy that government can help people?"[25] The answer was obvious to Quinn—and Cuomo said as much at Yale in resting his case on Galileo's authority. And yet, he was still in the business of bracing himself against the political headwinds moving across the country. For Quinn, the Yale speech was a culminating moment. "The thing about that period," he said, "from [Cuomo's] Inaugural to Yale—that defined his whole career. He didn't say much new after that."[26] It seems Cuomo didn't see a need to. At Yale, he reiterated that "from 1932 to 1980, [these principles] worked for a whole nation."[27] Before bowing out of his talk, Cuomo reminded his audience of all the big things the free enterprise system couldn't do of its own accord—"land grant colleges, the GI Bill, the TVA, the Civil Rights Act, the Occupational Safety Act, unemployment insurance, the minimum wage, FHA loans, Medicare, Medicaid, Social Security, Head Start, student loans, the National Highway Act, the Voting Rights Act, Fair Housing."[28] Not one to pretend, he knew they needed reminding.

Having just passed a tax cut in New York that lowered the top tax rate below 10 percent for the first time since the Rockefeller years, Cuomo was seeking to build a record of accomplishment leading in to his reelection campaign in 1986.[29] In what in hindsight registers as a mundane issue, Cuomo's controversial seatbelt law, in effect on the first of the year in 1985, became in time, a powerful, if underappreciated symbol of what government could do. By February, 75 percent of motorists were complying with the law.[30] For Cuomo, the legislation was another example of how "prose" is often overlooked in favor of speech's power to elicit excitement. It was the first seatbelt law of its kind in the United States. It may have saved thousands of lives since its inception. Yet it remains far less impressive in the popular imagination than Rockefeller's "edifice complex" of buildings. As the *New York Times* put it in early 1985, "Mr. Cuomo is in a conservative posture these days, focusing on phraseology that might appeal to a national audience disenchanted with decades of liberal cant."[31] Sometimes that "phraseology" was less in the spoken word than in dry but important legislation. Along these lines, state aid represented 60 percent of the budget passed in April, and motor vehicle fees were cut $100 million—relevant and popular public policies to go along with a $3.1 billion tax cut over the next three years.[32] But these were not collectively, or individually, fodder for presidential speculation. Those conversations were still largely the result of Cuomo's oratorical powers.

By mid-1985 it had become clear that New York had worked its way out of the recession years of 1982 and 1983. There was more to offer voters (Cuomo increased the basic welfare grant by 10 percent on top of his tax cuts)—but it would prove to be a short window, as a second recession would limit Cuomo's actions as governor in the early 1990s.[33] "This is a process I think you do by accretion," Cuomo said at the end of the 1985 legislative session. "[You] pick up a little piece here, a little piece there, and you have to keep working at it."[34] This could not be true for all problems, of course. Many would persist beyond Cuomo's administration, including the growing cauldron of New York's racial inequalities and strife. In a telling line from May 1985, Cuomo pushed for police reform amid a host of racially charged episodes of police brutality. The *New York Times* reported that Cuomo would "appoint a special commission vested with sweeping investigative and subpoena powers to examine the use of force by police departments in the state." For his part, Cuomo said, "Allegations of police brutality have occurred throughout the state and require a statewide response." Going further still, Cuomo said there was "dramatic evidence that the problem has become an insistent and pervasive one [whose] cause is not limited to one city or county. Its solution cannot be discovered by inquiries limited in their scope to a specific incident or jurisdiction."[35]

By the time Cuomo had become governor, New York's prison population had already more than doubled, owing to the passage of the now infamous Rockefeller drug laws that were central to Rockefeller's State of the State address in January 1973.[36]

Cuomo's tough talk on police brutality was part of a balancing act in trying to contain a growing racial conflagration in New York City, as the city's police force became involved in numerous controversial cases involving alleged brutality. While black citizens began to mobilize around the issue, there was also a prevailing mood among whites for stronger "law and order" policies. As Eric Schlosser pointed out, "Cuomo was an old-fashioned liberal who opposed mandatory-minimum drug sentences. But the national mood seemed to be calling for harsher drug laws, not sympathy for drug addicts."[37]

And it wasn't just the white community calling for these measures. "Frederick Douglass Boulevard [in Harlem] looks like Shangri La today compared to what it was in 1972, 1973," the Reverend Calvin Butts III recalls. "But the on the ground sales people peddling [drugs] were in in the community. And many community people were arguing with the Cuomos and others to 'lock 'em up,' 'kill them.' *I was standing right there*. People were saying this to the officials and anyone who would listen."[38] Butts, who is now also president of SUNY-Old Westbury on Long Island (in addition to remaining Abyssinia Baptist Church's Senior Pastor), offered a more complicated view of Cuomo's role in expanding New York's prison system. "Now, the first response should have been to go after the big wigs, the top figures bringing [the drugs] in. But I think it is wrong to saddle some of the political leaders with the issue. No doubt, sentences were draconian to say the least. It was the wrong answer."[39] But Butts would not lay this all on Cuomo or the political leaders of the time—including President Bill Clinton—given the overwhelming sense of desperation felt at the time by members of the black community who had to live with the violent and often deadly consequences of America's drug trafficking. Politically, Cuomo's unwavering opposition to the death penalty also made him somewhat vulnerable on the issue of fighting crime. By the time of his State of the State address in 1987, Cuomo would take credit for having put nearly 10,000 felons behind bars, despite having once in public called the state's prison boom "stupid."[40]

In addition, the police shooting of the African American graffiti artist Michael Stewart in 1984, along with the police killing of an elderly black woman in the Bronx, Eleanor Bumpers, who was late with her rent, were but the beginnings of a near decade-long spectacle of incidents implicating race in New York City. Cuomo would become involved to a greater or lesser extent in nearly all of them. His "outsider" status in relation to the city's black community and the increasingly unpopular Mayor Koch inoculated him somewhat, but he was otherwise part of the mix of powerful state officials who were drawing the ire of a black community increasingly alienated from the administrative arms of the state. A *New York Times* poll from March 1987 revealed that 44 percent of whites and 47 percent of blacks could not identify a single issue in which race relations had improved over the past five years, a period coinciding with the beginning of Cuomo's tenure as governor.[41] This was perhaps the greatest challenge for Cuomo in governing "in prose."

Cuomo would revisit the crucible of race again just after his reelection in 1986 in the aftermath of the Howard Beach killing of a young black man, Michael Griffith, who was chased by a group of bat-wielding whites through the Queens neighborhood and onto a neighboring parkway to his death. The two surviving black men had been beaten with bats and a tree limb.[42] That case would set New York aflame like few others involving race. It was just such conflicts, however, that moved the Democratic Leadership Council and so-called New Democrats to eschew the party's identification with race—and more specifically, the problems of the nation's African American community, as such. As Kenneth S. Baer wrote in his study of the DLC, by 1985, "Stanley Greenberg, a Democratic pollster, presented a report to the Association of State Democratic Party Chairs and to the Democratic National Committee (DNC), arguing that the party was in danger of losing traditional Democratic voters, especially white blue-collar voters, because they viewed the party as too extreme on social issues and too tied to the concerns of blacks and other minorities."[43]

It would turn out that in the 40 years separating the election of Lyndon Johnson in 1964 and the reelection of George W. Bush in 2004, Democrats had elected only southerners to the White House. Bill Clinton's rise to power within the party cannot be divorced from this movement away from the politics of Hudson progressivism—and its close cousin, liberal racial politics. In the spring of 1985, former president Jimmy Carter was weighing in as well, urging Democrats to shift to the right. "In my judgment," said Carter, "the Democrats basically should take the position I took in 1976: a combination of approaches, some of which could be considered quite conservative and some quite liberal."[44] Carter thought Cuomo could fit the bill of such a person heading into the 1988 election.

Cuomo proved to be a poor choice. He was not only preparing for his gubernatorial reelection campaign in 1986, but he was also giving no indication that he was inclined to make a rhetorical shift to the right anytime soon. In June 1985, while speaking at Harvard University's Class Day, Cuomo returned to his assault on the new conservatism that had so enamored members of his own party. "Consider the philosophy that we as a people are being asked to accept," he said. "The only way we can prosper, it's said, is to rape the land, to level the forests, to allow the pollution of the water and the air. The way to help people pull themselves out of poverty, we're told, is to leave them to their own devices. Let those young mothers and their children hack their way through."[45] This was not the language of a centrist or a New Democrat. Cuomo acknowledged the success of Reagan's message while not conceding its intrinsic value. "And, I'm afraid," he said, as he began his conclusion, "it's a philosophy that's succeeding."[46] Invoking Boston's historically black neighborhood, Cuomo once again enlisted the themes of poetry and prose in his defense of liberalism. "It's easier for those of us who've made it to wave the flag and invoke all the symbols and poetry of patriotism than it is to insist our patriotism be translated into the prose of government, into programs that buy some opportunity for a child in Roxbury."[47]

Later that spring, Cuomo would push for New York to divest its financial interests from South Africa, oppose the opening of the Shoreham nuclear power plant on Long Island, and support raising the drinking age in the state to 21. These were progressive, if not signature, public policies; none of them were sufficient to build a national resume for the presidency. Ray Scheppach, who was then executive director of the National Governors Association, was never drawn into the mania surrounding a potential Cuomo bid for the White House. "He didn't have a signature issue or policy like other governors did at the time," Scheppach recalled.[48] And he had an even less appealing disposition toward his fellow state executives. "'I'm a little bit better than the rest of you governors'" was how Scheppach characterized Cuomo's attitude. He was not in the business of making friends with those who might prove crucial to his future nomination. In this regard, he was most unlike Bill Clinton, who was steadily making connections with his fellow governors across the country. "If I looked at Bill Clinton and Mario Cuomo—there were 29–30 [Democratic] governors at the time— Cuomo didn't have a relationship with *anybody*."[49]

When not getting into public spats with Reagan's communications director, Patrick Buchanan, over New York State's tax policy, Cuomo was otherwise locally engaged (Buchanan had called Cuomo's tax plan "neo-socialist").[50] Cuomo's campaign war chest leading into the 1986 race for governor was more than ample. He had amassed over $4 million by the summer and his campaign was debt free.[51] By November, Cuomo's 1982 Republican rival, Lew Lehrman, declared that he would not run against Cuomo in 1986. There were only speculative contenders at year's end as Cuomo was basking in both local and national popularity. Indeed, the Friends of Mario Cuomo raised an additional record $3.4 million in one night. Cuomo characteristically demurred. "This is the biggest fundraiser in history," he said, "but it is regrettable we have to do this kind of thing."[52] Of course, this kind of thing was politics, and Cuomo was not above participating in it. He had pledged that if he were to run for reelection in 1986, it would be an open indication that he would not seek his party's nomination for the presidency in 1988. But he had also been coquettish on the issue. Responding to a question earlier in the year about his pledge not to seek a White House bid, Cuomo said, "I said I didn't want to run for President. I didn't ask you to believe me."[53]

By the end of 1985, Cuomo was feeling his oats. He called the legislature into special session to vote on what would prove to be a series of rather forgettable bills. But with his approval rating at 75 percent, Cuomo didn't want to waste the opportunity to get more done. It smacked of hubris to Republicans in the legislature. The Republican-led Senate voted down five of his six measures.[54] Within a week, Cuomo, perhaps testier than usual, denied the existence of the "Mafia" in rejecting the term as an all-encompassing one to describe organized crime. "Why don't you go to Rikers Island, conclude that 94 percent of them are black, and think up a name that would create that association in people's minds?" Cuomo said.[55] That was but one part of the disaster, small as it was. Cuomo's office would clarify these remarks by day's end, but other public officials, including Rudolph Giuliani, would weigh in. "You can't go so far as to suggest the Mafia doesn't exist," said the then US attorney for the Southern District of New York. Cuomo's denial—"You're telling me that the Mafia is an organization, and I'm telling you that's a lot of baloney"—would be a bit of a thorn in Cuomo's side for the rest of his political career. It was more an indication of his stubbornness than anything else, one that reporters would return to over and over again. In this instance, it was also part of a pattern that suggested his political instincts were least effective when he was out in front politically. As Cuomo entered the next legislative session and his campaign for reelection, there'd be little it seemed on the horizon to chasten him against such carelessness.

Cuomo began the new election year with a State of the State message that emphasized the environment and economic growth. He sought to identify New York with not only economic recovery but also with "resurgence," a difficult task given the still very real challenges of homelessness and poverty facing many of the state's citizens. Like JFK's audacious promise in his inaugural address, Cuomo promised to "do all of this and more."[56] But there were no specific grand plans or sweeping policy prescriptions. Later, in defending his $41 billion budget, Cuomo emphasized his administration's welfare-to-work program and its appeal beyond political labels. It was hard to tell whether he was doing preparatory work toward a possible 1988 White House run, as Ted Kennedy had recently declined to enter the race, leaving the liberal wing of the party open to him, or whether this was simply good policy the governor believed in. "I believe in all [the] government we need," Cuomo told reporters again, "but only government that we need."[57]

Meanwhile, Republicans in early 1986, still without a candidate, were considering a host of long-shot possibilities against Cuomo—including Henry Kissinger, who was "flattered" by the consideration.[58] When Cuomo officially declared his reelection candidacy in May, he finally had a Republican challenger in Westchester County executive Andrew O'Rourke. But the media speculation was still on Cuomo's presidential prospects—all the more so because he declined to promise he'd serve out the full four years if reelected governor. "It's not good for the state. It's not good for me. So why do it?" Cuomo said of such a pledge.[59]

Part of Cuomo's reelection campaign was his tough anti-crime stance. He moved in July to make the possession of crack cocaine an offense that could earn up to life imprisonment. Three vials—or $50 worth of crack—was the amount in possession that could lead to a life sentence. "The answer is not always the stiffest possible punishment," Cuomo said, but given crack's rapid rise and association with violent crime, "I think we need stiffer, sterner punishment— this is not Draconian."[60] Cuomo pondered the measure even as he considered the cost of each new prison cell at $100,000. "A hundred thousand dollars," he said. "Think of it, think of all the good things we could do with that money—a hundred thousand dollars."[61] The concern didn't stop Cuomo from targeting the building of more state prisons as part of his second-term agenda, as the November election drew nearer. In a two-hour interview at the Executive Mansion in Albany in late October, Cuomo pledged to "cut personal income taxes, renew New York City's rent guidelines, and increase aid to local school districts."[62] Cuomo called it a platform of "jobs and justice."[63] This was what was left of the liberal view in New York in the mid-eighties, as Andrew O'Rourke was advocating "shock incarceration" for first-offense drug dealers and people convicted of non-violent offenses.[64]

On Election Day, Cuomo defeated O'Rourke by the largest margin in New York history, winning 65 percent of the vote and 55 of the state's 62 counties.[65] Cuomo had surpassed the long-standing electoral margins of victory held by Grover Cleveland dating back to 1882. Apparently, the *New York Times* didn't think Cuomo's victory was especially noteworthy, given its blowout proportions, as the paper's headline led with "Democrats Gain Control of Senate."[66] The real question was what Cuomo would do about running for president in 1988. Days after the landslide win, he was forced to acknowledge the inevitable. "I'll address it," he told the Associated Press. "It has to be addressed." The next line, simple as it was, made headlines. "I'll take a look and see what's going on," Cuomo said.[67] It all seemed clear sailing on the horizon for Cuomo. His political opposition in the state was mainly relegated to a media growing less enamored with his mercurial nature. Republicans, on the other hand, were seemingly beyond his field of concern. As the January legislative session kicked off in 1987, the usual issues were once again before the governor. A small Westchester delegation of mostly Republicans was making a bit of a fuss over a perennial issue. "'New Yorkers pay major state taxes. This year is a good time to cut them significantly, while the unemployment rate is low," said Assemblyman George E. Pataki of Peekskill, making his first appearance in the *New York Times*.[68]

The First Temptation: 1987–1988

Mario Cuomo began 1987 with the political winds at his back. He announced a five-state travel schedule, reported by the *Times* on the first of the year, that would take him to Iowa—always fodder for presidential candidate speculation—along with California, and three southern states, North Carolina, Florida, and Louisiana. South Carolina's governor, Richard W. Riley, said, "I would suspect that for Mario Cuomo, this is the first stage of something."[69] Riley, mindful of the need for Democrats to win back at least some of the southern states they'd been losing over the years, declared Cuomo's upcoming "look-see" to be a "good thing for him and the Democratic Party. I'd like to see more of it."[70]

Reflecting on his accomplishments from that year in his public papers, Cuomo touted his successful passage of ethics reform in New York along with the "largest personal income tax cut" in the state's history.[71] More money for education was mentioned—the largest increase in education aid in New York history; and Cuomo lauded the Omnibus Prison Overcrowding bill, which created in his words "new prison spaces for 5,800 inmates." He was now also using the language and policy prescriptions of his former Republican adversary, O'Rourke, declaring "a bold and innovative Shock Incarceration Program." There was also careful mention of his balancing the budget, passing environmental protection policies, and new initiatives to address the growing crisis of AIDS. The pattern of mixing preemptive conservative policies, particularly with respect to crime, and more progressive public policies was continued.

There was some irony in Cuomo's "progressive pragmatism," a theme he returned to in describing the New York "miracle" in his second inaugural address. As Cuomo sought to appropriate the rhetoric and selective policy prescriptions of his conservative critics, Reagan was engaged in a similar sleight of hand from the right. As the *New York Times* stated in its editorial review of Cuomo's 1987 inaugural, there was an underlying and intentional confusion to the politics of the time:

Rescuing Roosevelt from the right will be a complex task. Democrats of the Reagan era repeatedly sound like Republicans, complaining prudently about the President's ruinous policy of

borrow and spend, borrow and spend. The President, meanwhile, repeatedly declares himself to be the bearer of Roosevelt's
torch. He claims affinity with New Deal efforts to erase the
fears of poverty and old age. He argues, as did Roosevelt, that
a strong defense is the best shield against war.[72]

What made Cuomo different from the rising conservatives within
his own party, the "New Democrats" that were becoming the voice
of the party? In a word, Cuomo's sojourns to the right were tacti-
cal. They did not emanate from deep-seated personal or politically
held beliefs. And they were used to again inoculate him against
the growing backlash against liberalism—particularly the liberalism identified with the Northeast. As New York's Democratic governor, Cuomo epitomized the caricature of government overreach
Republicans sought to sell an electorate no longer enamored with
liberal programs. At no point however, would Cuomo abandon rhetorically the New Deal ideal he had espoused since his entrance
into politics. This was not to be the case with others, including
Bill Clinton, who would ultimately question the relevance of New
Deal politics for the last decades of the 20th century. Still, not all of
Cuomo's policies—especially those related to crime—were in keeping with the best traditions of liberal governance. And yet, because
his conservatism was at least obliquely tied to questions of black
crime or "preferential treatment" (an issue never far removed from
liberalism's soft racially charged underbelly), it was not out of lock-
step with the types of trade-offs progressives had been making for
decades.[73]

Cuomo took small but important steps to counter the Reagan
administration's efforts to diminish the nation's social welfare
programs and their reach. In early 1987, he proposed a 22 percent increase in the spending allowance for welfare recipients in
the state, many of whom were forced into homelessness, owing to
New York City's skyrocketing rents.[74] He also established a task
force on racial violence in the wake of the Howard Beach attack,
an incident involving the killing of Michael Griffith, a young

Trinidadian-born black man, who was chased from the neighborhood by bat-wielding whites onto Shore Parkway, where he was
fatally struck by an oncoming car. These were not bold policies,
any more than was his call to end "member item" appropriations
in the New York legislature, a move seen as curtailing the sometimes questionable maneuvering of state funds by lawmakers to
their own districts outside of ordinary state procedures.[75] It seemed
that in early 1987, Cuomo was building a clear, if not glittering,
progressive record moving into a campaign year that he would be a
part of. Suddenly, he removed himself peremptorily. On statewide
radio on the evening of February 19, nearly a year before the start
of the presidential primaries, Cuomo ended the growing speculation about his candidacy.

> In my opinion, the Democratic Party offers a number of
> Presidential candidates who can prove themselves capable of
> leading this nation toward a more sane, a more progressive
> and a more humane future. I will not add my name to that
> number. I will not be a candidate, but I will continue to work
> as hard as I can to deal with those problems here in New York
> and to support the selections of our party as vigorously as I can
> in my role as Governor of the State of New York.[76]

New York's elected officials from both sides of the aisle expressed
shock. Denial might be the better word, as both at home and around
the country, Cuomo would continue to be badgered for a different
answer over the next year. His early denial had the effect of being
almost premature in its placement well before campaign season.
"I was so convinced he was going to run and win the nomination,"
said New York Democratic Assembly Speaker Mel Miller, "that
I really didn't hear what he was saying."[77]

It is not clear that Cuomo heard himself at that point. When during a visit to deliver the commencement address at Grinnell College
in Iowa, Cuomo was asked if he was indeed ruling out entering the
primaries, he seemed to do an about face. "No, I'm not," he replied.

And, then when pressed "if he ruled out accepting the nomination if, however unlikely that might be, it was offered by a deadlocked convention, he said: 'Why is it good to foreclose that possibility? What good does it do?"[78] Cuomo's ambiguous response came within a 40-year-long dearth of Democratic presidential candidates from New York's governorship. If Cuomo chose to run, he would be in the tradition of presidential politics that had at one time been defined by Hudson progressives from the Empire State. Such New York stalwarts that earned their party's nomination included Horatio Seymour, Samuel J. Tilden, Grover Cleveland, Theodore Roosevelt, Charles Evans Hughes, Franklin Roosevelt, and Thomas Dewey.[79] Their portraits hung in the state capitol as present reminders of Cuomo's potential legacy. But now, he seemed ambivalent about such history at best. The idea that running for the presidency while governor is difficult cannot be doubted; yet Cuomo returned to that rationale in 1988, and again in 1992, as if there hadn't been a near 100-year history and eight such attempts defying that very notion. Cuomo himself described the conditions for running in 1988 as ideal. "This was the right year," Cuomo told the *Times* after he made his decision. "If you wanted a made-to-order year, this was it."[80]

By the end of the legislative session, one in which Cuomo pushed through a difficult ethics bill, his administration was claiming substantive and symbolic victory. Close aides were now saying the "Hamlet" image of Cuomo as an indecisive leader was gone, that he had taken on a powerful legislature opposed to reform and won. And some still believed that Cuomo had "the potential for a campaign for President should circumstances change and he decide to run after all."[81] In the words of his biographer, Cuomo's "forcing of a confrontation with the legislature, his translation of his personal popularity into meaningful legislation, and his unwavering stand for a tough ethics bill combined to produce the most important victory of Cuomo's years as governor."[82] But with that victory, at perhaps his most opportune moment, he took himself out of the running for the presidency, all but guaranteeing a tumultuous relationship with an increasingly hostile opposition for the next two and half years.

There was considerable speculation at the time—mostly out of desperation—that Cuomo might be willing to be drafted. A long-time Democratic Party insider, New York lawyer Edward Costikyan, penned an op-ed for the *Times* to that effect after Cuomo's announcement.[83] Ed Koch echoed the sentiment, suggesting "lightning might strike" for the governor.[84] After Cuomo's death in early 2015, his biographer Robert McElvaine claimed that Cuomo had in fact, confided in him that he did wish to be drafted—but in 1992, not 1988.

> After the governor decided not to enter the 1992 race, a Draft Cuomo movement was launched and I was asked to make appearances in New Hampshire as a stand-in for the non-candidate. Audiences there were enthusiastic and the movement appeared to be gaining steam. Cuomo had nothing to do with starting the write-in campaign, but my closing argument that he really wanted to be drafted is something that I have never before publicly revealed: Cuomo started talking with me by telephone nearly every day that I was in New Hampshire, asking for details on how the write-in effort was going. It was clear that he wanted it to succeed.[85]

While McElvaine's claim has not been corroborated by anyone associated with the Cuomo campaign of that year to this author's knowledge, it is clear that Cuomo had not ruled out the possibility of a draft in either 1992, or, as was reported by the *Chicago Tribune* and others, in 1988. After going back and forth on the issue with Cuomo's chief spokesperson at the time, Gary Fryer, of the *Tribune* reported that "Cuomo has refused to rule out a draft at a deadlocked convention that went beyond the first ballot, when 2,081 delegate votes will be needed to win."[86] Knowledge of whether he was then or four years later actively encouraging such a scenario seems limited to McElvaine's assertion days after Cuomo's passing.

Fueling further speculation about his presidential ambitions, Cuomo delivered a late summer talk in Chautauqua, New York, on American foreign policy toward the Soviet Union. Calling for a "new realism" in relations with the Soviets, Cuomo, anticipating the end of the Cold War, said, "We can begin by insisting on the common sense of things with a new realism, a new realism that sees the stupidity in the dehumanizing of one another, a new realism that recognizes the obvious—that while we are two strong people with different histories, different ideologies, who will be competitive for many years to come, there is a living world of difference between vigorous competition and violent hostility."[87] The speech was delivered just one month before a scheduled week-long trip to the Soviet Union. While viewed as a successful if not very detailed speech— A. M. Rosenthal of the *Times* called it "a speech full of hope and emotions about the future, soaring above doubt and detail"—it did, backhanded compliments aside, position Cuomo to address his perceived foreign policy weaknesses.[88] Cuomo's presumed political motivations for his visit were also not lost on the press. In his piece for the *Washington Post* titled "Cuomo's Phantom Campaign," Ken Auletta stated the obvious: "From a distance it appears that Mario Cuomo is slyly maneuvering to run for president."[89] Meanwhile, the conservative columnist, William Safire, suggested that "Cuomo's 'new realism' smacked of the old moral relativism."[90]

By the time of his Moscow visit, Cuomo had been brushing up on foreign policy. He had already delivered a commencement address on the subject at Johns Hopkins's School of Advanced International Studies in May. He had spoken at Chautauqua and was reading avidly.[91] Cuomo may have been the most parochial governor of New York in modern times. His cosmopolitanism and genuine acceptance of diversity in all of its forms did not extend to his personal disposition. Weighing his upcoming visit to the Soviet Union, one *Times* columnist questioned, without much irony, "Once in Moscow, will the Governor venture out of his hotel room? His history says maybe not."[92] Cuomo was intellectually curious; he was less interested in seeking out answers that required his physical presence. This was all the more reason to question his political motives for visiting Russia leading up to an election year.

Despite an initial stumble on the first day of his visit, one in which Cuomo seemed to support a Soviet proposal to investigate US human rights violations (which he later backed away from), the trip was viewed by Cuomo and most of the press as a success.[93] Cuomo would not ultimately meet with Soviet leader Mikhail Gorbachev, who was "out of town," a fact that spared both nations a bit of a diplomatic conundrum given Cuomo's stature as a potential presidential candidate.[94] The *Times* did report, not without a bit of cheek, that "Mr. Cuomo has seen more of Moscow and Leningrad than he ever saw of Los Angeles or New Orleans or Detroit or half a dozen other American cities he has visited as Governor."[95] About three weeks later, Cuomo delivered a speech in Washington at the Council on Foreign Relations (CFR), which turned into a bit of a final exam on foreign affairs, as he was questioned about foreign policy for two and a half hours after his talk. The audience was made up of some 250 foreign policy experts including "senators, diplomats, academics and journalists," all of whom were present for his 25-minute address.[96] The now highly controversial Richard Perle—at the time a conservative Democrat—put Cuomo's performance in some perspective. "What he said was unexceptional," said Perle, who had worked at the Pentagon in the Reagan administration. "'But the manner in which he said it was exceptional. He was unusually candid. He's forceful and lively. I agree that was what people were talking about."[97] For his part, Cuomo viewed the reaction to his speech at the CFR as "even better" than the one he received in San Francisco at the Democratic Convention. "That was all emotion," he said. "This was much more intellectual."[98]

Between his visit to the Soviet Union and his speech in Washington, Cuomo saw fit to return to an increasingly discussed topic—that he was not seeking the White House because of personal or familial ties to organized crime. "I keep hearing in-laws," Cuomo told the *Times* in a phone conversation he initiated. "Why would anybody say in-laws?"[99] Cuomo made the call without specifying the nature of the rumors, but what he was alluding to was not lost on anyone who had been following his career in politics. Cuomo "declined to elaborate on the rumors themselves, saying he did not want to give them currency."[100] The impetus for Cuomo's sudden shift to this question appeared to be his interview with *60 Minutes* in which CBS correspondent Lesley Stahl asked him about rumors of "skeletons in his family closet."[101]

The most proximate public issue involving such rumors involved a *New York Times* investigation into the mugging of Cuomo's grandfather Charles Raffa, back in 1984. Raffa was the victim of a violent assault on May 22, 1984, in East New York, Brooklyn. The incident was exceedingly violent—Raffa required plastic surgery to recover, and according to the author, Nicholas Pileggi, who recounted the attack in his lengthy *New York* piece on the mob rumors surrounding Cuomo, Raffa's head had "been sliced open and his scalp was covering his eyes."[102] There were no witnesses to the crime—the incident took place at one of Raffa's rental spaces—and there was no theft reported. Rumors abounded that Raffa's beating was a "mob hit," and that Raffa was "an arsonist" who wanted to burn down his own property for some undisclosed reason. Raffa's account to police did not help—he varyingly described his attacker as "white, Hispanic, and black. Sometimes he said there was one man and sometimes he said there were two."[103] As McElvaine noted in his biography of Cuomo, Sebastian Pipitone, one of Cuomo's personal bodyguards, washed the car Raffa was driven to the hospital in "to remove blood from the exterior before Mrs. Cuomo saw it."[104] This only added further talking points to the whispers surrounding Cuomo's "shadowy" connections. And so it went. Pileggi, who made a living writing works of fiction about "wiseguys" (his book by nearly that same title became the basis for the film "Goodfellas"), went to great lengths to identify all possible associations with Cuomo and the mafia. In the end, his article became the definitive piece for dismissing the rumors. As McElvaine put it, "Pileggi came as close to giving Cuomo a clean bill of health on the subject as any journalist is ever likely to give any politician."[105]

Meanwhile, the *Times* reported the oddities of the case but found no untoward connections to Cuomo.[106] Andrew Cuomo's unofficial biographer, Michael Shnayerson, cited an unnamed staffer who, referencing the Raffa attack, said the Cuomos "were more nervous about that than anything I'd ever seen."[107] Perhaps. But there is no official record from anyone suggesting that the episode was anything more than what it remains, one of any number of mysterious crimes in New York's history. Andrew Cuomo, who visited Raffa in the hospital during his recovery, does not mention the incident in his biography, noting only his fondness for his grandfather.[108] In what seemed like the last word at the time, Cuomo issued a statement after Pileggi's piece in *New York* magazine came out. "If it's a price I pay for being Italian-American, then being Italian-American is well worth the price," he said.[109]

With better news on other fronts, including Democratic gains in New York State in November, Cuomo was nevertheless again lured into weighing in on national politics. There were early indications that Cuomo was somewhat cool toward Massachusetts governor, Michael Dukakis. Illinois senator Paul Simon looked to benefit from Cuomo's support, and perhaps get an endorsement in early November.[110] That proved to be wishful thinking on the part of Simon, with whom Cuomo had become friendly. Even this bit of speculation created national headlines. In an effort to tamp down interest in his own candidacy, Cuomo removed himself from participating in an Iowa debate where he was scheduled to question the Republican candidates. The move didn't do much to quell speculation. Between late December and the early part of 1988, everyone from the gossip columnist Liz Smith ("Don't you owe America a sacrifice?") to the iconoclastic rock star Frank Zappa ("If I can help convince you to accept a draft at the Convention, this note will have been worth writing") were encouraging Cuomo to run.[111] Before long, the administration began responding to constituents with a form letter that Cuomo could personalize; such was the magnitude of incoming requests for his candidacy. Voters weren't the only ones waiting on something more definitive from Cuomo. Much of Democratic Party politics—at least with respect to the presidential race—was frozen in place, with the assumption remaining that Cuomo would still somehow enter the fray. "People can't accept the fact that he's not running," said Representative Nancy Pelosi of San Francisco, a longtime Cuomo supporter.[112]

Somewhat less flattering was the effort by the *Times* to clarify Cuomo's record. The paper ran a lengthy and somewhat critical piece on his governorship in the beginning of the year. The theme was one of a liberal thinker clouded by a record punctuated by more conservative turns at times. "I'm confused by Cuomo," said Donna Shalala, an adviser.[113] Julius Edelstein, who had himself advised FDR and Harry Truman, offered the kind of compliment Cuomo tended to dismiss. "I am reminded of the classification by Max Weber of leadership," he said. "One is charismatic and the other is bureaucratic. Cuomo is clearly of all the governors, except for maybe Rockefeller, the most charismatic governor New York has had going back to Al Smith."[114]

Once again, in his public papers, Cuomo offered a retrospective push-back against his critics and their portrayal of his leadership as one of style over substance. He would list his accomplishments in 1988 as including his Decade of the Child initiative, an increase in the Supplemental Security Income (only the second in the state's history), the creation of an Infrastructure Trust Fund to build new, affordable housing; and on the criminal justice front, Cuomo again touted his anti-crime bona fides—this time with a nod to an increase in "the troop strength of the State Police to an all-time high."[115] In what reads today as the language of an apostate of progressivism, Cuomo also wrote that "we adopted a new law making possession of as few as four vials of crack a felony."[116] There were few, and largely powerless, dissenting voices at the time. With popular tax cuts enacted, unemployment down, a reduction in the state's deficit by $1.2 billion, and a refusal to open the controversial nuclear power plant, Shoreham, on Long Island, there were a number of policy successes Cuomo could point to as indicators that he was more than just an exceptional rhetorician. Perhaps sensing the strength of his support, Cuomo put forth 61 bills for consideration before the legislature at the beginning of its session, an unprecedented number in New York's history. As the *Times* reported, "In the past Mr. Cuomo's proposals, known as program bills, have been submitted one by one as the session progresses. This year, hoping to define an agenda that could be enacted quickly, he decided to release them all during the first full week of the session."[117]

While Cuomo was pushing New York's legislature, something most unusual was afoot in Democratic Party politics. Jesse Jackson, 1984's gadfly candidate, was now doing the unimaginable. He was winning lots of votes—white votes—in the early primaries. And in March he won the state of Michigan outright. This sent shock waves throughout the party and nation. It seemed not beyond reason that Democrats could nominate the first African American to head a major party ticket for the presidency. As late as April, even after three losses took some of the bloom off the rose that had been the Michigan victory, the proudly left magazine, *The Nation*, endorsed Jackson, calling his campaign the "antithesis to Reaganism and reaction."[118] In the wake of Jackson's rise there was increasing pressure on Cuomo to endorse Dukakis. "I reject the suggestion that this presents us with a dilemma if Jesse Jackson wins," Cuomo told the *Times*, arguing that Jackson was good for the party.[119] Some analysts saw Cuomo's praise of Jackson as self-serving; that if Jackson somehow entered the convention with the most delegates, a draft Cuomo movement would be triggered. The thought of a black man heading the Democratic Party ticket was beyond the thinking of the vast majority of the party's leadership and rank and file. When asked if he thought Jackson could in fact win, Cuomo responded with a simple "yes."[120] In an analysis that would carry future implications for another, perhaps less unlikely, but equally remarkable bid for the White House by an African American candidate, the *Times* reported in June, that Jackson had tripled his votes among whites since 1984.[121]

The thought of Cuomo entering the 1988 race to rescue Democrats from the possibility of nominating a black candidate contained a great many holes—some theoretical and others practical. For starters, Cuomo was by late spring dealing with a $300 million shortfall in the state's budget. A newly explosive episode of racial unrest was unfolding—this one involving a young girl named Tawana Brawley, who had claimed she was abducted and sexually assaulted by a group of white men in Dutchess County, New York. And then there was the finale of the popular but nonetheless controversial closing of the Shoreham nuclear power plant on Long Island. Shoreham was perhaps a small matter when weighed against the possibility of Cuomo's entering presidential politics, but it was not difficult to see how the issue could fuel voter discontent given the possibility of increasing utility rates.[122] All told, by the time Michael Dukakis had become the Democratic Party nominee, there were enough distractions at home to justify Cuomo's reticence to enter the race. Longtime Cuomo friend Nicholas D'Arienzo's presumption that Cuomo would run if the "duty was imposed upon him"—an allusion to the draft Cuomo idea—may have been more real in the minds of his then-supporters then it ever was truly viable in his own.[123] By early fall, the *Times* was reporting insinuations from Cuomo's camp that the next race the governor was thinking about was his own—a shot at a historic third term as governor of New York.[124]

Cuomo's help for Dukakis was perfunctory and passionless. He penned an op-ed for the *Times* just before the election and gave all the right verbal cues of support. But Cuomo's efforts were hardly critical to the outcome. George H. W. Bush was elected to succeed Reagan by a 53 to 46 percent margin, one quite similar to Barack Obama's 2008 electoral victory over John McCain. The difference was in the Electoral College where Bush won 426 electoral votes to 111 for Dukakis.[125] Democrats won only 10 states and the District of Columbia. It was an only slightly less devastating rebuke than the legendary thumping of Mondale in 1984. But it lent credence to the idea that old-style liberalism was dying, and that candidates like Cuomo—progressive, northeastern, ethnic—had seen far better days. The fact that Bush carried every southern state by at least

10 points also fueled speculation, already growing since the convention in 1984, that Democrats were going to have to shift gears and become a different kind of party. "New Democrats" did not seem to be seeking someone like New York's exciting but otherwise geopolitically handicapped governor.

Three-Term Governor: 1989–1990

Michael K. Osborn of Colorado wrote a two-word letter to Mario Cuomo in February of 1988. Someone—perhaps Cuomo—jotted a note to the governor's press secretary Gary Fryer to "Prepare reply." Osborn's plea read:

> Dear Governor Cuomo:
> Run, goddamnit.
> Sincerely,
> Michael K. Osborn

A little over two weeks later, Cuomo did in fact return Osborn's pithy note, with an equally pointed rejoinder.

> Dear Michael:
> I did. In 1986. I won. My next chance is in 1990. Thanks.
> Sincerely,
> Mario Cuomo[126]

Cuomo's reply to the Denver resident was perhaps more than an effort at levity and repartee with a potential voter. It somehow also smacked of how Cuomo was engaged politically; one legislative session, one political season at a time. With 1988 behind him, Cuomo seemed to indeed be looking to 1990 rather than the next presidential election in 1992.

And then there was simple clear-eyed reality. "This is not going to be a year of many new programs," Cuomo said ahead of the 1989 legislative session. "We don't have the money for them."[127] He was alluding to a new $2 billion shortfall in the state's budget. Cuomo would spend the next three years and presidential cycle weighing those budgetary realities against his ambitions. The truth was, the tax cuts he had initiated, and thought he needed politically, were now coming home to roost. But Cuomo was unwilling to abandon them. In his State of the State message, he couched New York's woes in national terms:

> This time a sudden shrinkage of expected revenues has shaken states from coast to coast, from California to Massachusetts, ours included. It is now already clear that at least for a while our revenues will simply not support the generous rate of growth and expenditures that we've seen the last several years, unless we raise corporate, sales or income tax rates. And that I oppose, because it could badly damage our competitive position.[128]

Cuomo did tout an increase in state aid to elementary and secondary education in his state papers of that year. And, for the first time, there was a true emphasis on rehabilitation in fighting the so-called drug war. But Cuomo also praised what he called the "successful, innovative Shock Incarceration Program," designed to provide a six-month "boot-camp" type experience along with treatment to non-violent offenders under 30.[129] By 1990 there were some 1,209 prisoners in the program. "I have to give him good marks in our business," said the executive director of the New York State Chiefs of Police Association, Joseph Dominelli, at the time.[130] As the *Times* reported after Cuomo's State of the State address, "Mr. Cuomo's call for an intensified war on drugs drew bipartisan support in the Legislature."[131] Cuomo described the drug problem as the nation's "single most ominous phenomenon of our time."[132] In his State of the State address he was unequivocal. "I was asked recently what were New York's three most serious problems," Cuomo said. "I answered, 'Drugs, drugs and drugs.'"[133] Few seemed to disagree. In New York City, the prison population in March 1989 reached the size of a small American city—18,630—the largest ever in its history.[134]

The focus on the drug war was beginning to present an unwelcome possibility for Cuomo—namely, that the legislature would be able to garner enough votes to override his veto of the death penalty. In March, Democrats were just one vote shy of having the 100 needed to effectuate an override. It had been just over 25 years since someone had been executed in New York by the state. Democrats had been switching their votes to support of the death penalty, and statewide polls were showing 70 percent support for it across the state. Cuomo's fierce and unprecedented construction of new prisons in New York is best understood in the context of this political climate. As the *Times* reported, the State's Senate majority leader, Ralph J. Marino, a Republican from Oyster Bay, "criticized [Cuomo's latest] veto, saying Mr. Cuomo was turning his 'back on the people of New York, who overwhelmingly support the restoration of capital punishment in our state.'"[135] While Cuomo's position on capital punishment had long been tied to his faith, his position on incarceration seemed more tied to politics. Cuomo was hardly unconcerned with political labels. He had displayed a tendency in off-year elections to present himself in more liberal colors. Indeed, as the former US attorney in Manhattan, Rudolph Giuliani, sought the Liberal Party endorsement for mayor, Cuomo was vocal in his ideological opposition. "He's a Republican true to the Reagan commitment, and the Reagan commitment was not good for the City of New York," Cuomo said.[136]

There were other impasses with the legislature beyond capital punishment. Cuomo's budget was a major point of contention, and for the fifth year in a row, the budget was passed after the legal deadline.[137] Cuomo also vetoed an increase in tuition to state and city universities. Along with the abortion issue, Cuomo was also compelled to weigh in on an effort to ban abortions in state hospitals (he opposed the prospective ban) and the controversy over flag burning brought up by a recent Supreme Court case (the Court supported the right as an expression of free speech). After a relatively quiet summer, Cuomo was faced with yet another budget shortfall, this one appearing to be close to $1 billion. This was nearly twice as large as had been expected. "Our situation has gotten a good deal worse," said State Budget Director Dall W. Forsythe.[138] This was news that had serious implications for Cuomo's third-term bid the following November, let alone any presidential ambitions three years later. The budgetary crisis in New York would elicit a promise from Cuomo just over a year after he and the state's voters learned of the enormity of the deficit. "'There's no way you could say, 'No, that's not really important, I'll solve the problems from Washington,' and then take off and campaign from coast to coast," Cuomo would say. "I couldn't do it and I wouldn't do it."[139]

Among the other things Cuomo couldn't do was pass the $400 million tax cut he wanted to give voters in 1990. The new budget was going to create some $1.4 billion in taxes instead. The political consultants were not waiting to assess Cuomo's prospects for 1992. "It lays down a tremendous amount of negatives," said Charlie Black, the Republican consultant who worked on President Bush's 1988 campaign.[140] "And you don't have to be a genius to present the record and compare it to how he would do as President. He would be reduced to running on his personality and his charisma rather than on his record."[141] Even the usually effusive Introduction to his State Papers was muted by the difficult realities facing Cuomo and the state. "One of New York's greatest assets in responding to the fiscal challenge facing the State and nation is the solid economic foundation we have built." The statement was supported by a list of International Trade Acts, "additional efforts in strategic industries," and "new laws and programs to help protect the value of New York's transportation infrastructure." There didn't seem to be much to brag about.[142]

The growing sense of Cuomo's vulnerability led some to believe that Giuliani, who had lost to David N. Dinkins in New York's mayoral race, could best Cuomo in 1990's gubernatorial election. The sentiment would prove overly hopeful—but there were ominous signs for Cuomo's political future, ones that had not been there since his first run for the governorship, in what was seeming like a long time ago. By January, 1990, Cuomo had been governor seven years, won two elections, and become a liberal icon and the national face of the Democratic Party. He had delivered the convention speech of many voters' lifetime and had been the darling would-be aspirant to the White House in 1988. But now, at the beginning of his eighth year in office, he seemed vulnerable and perhaps beyond his moment. And there was reason to believe he might not even be given the chance to seek the presidency given New York's woes. He may have been looking to 1990 rather than 1992, as he had been suggesting all along. The difference was that now, few insiders were doubting him. "I'd like to see him challenge Mario Cuomo," said Diane McGrath-McKechnie, New York City's Republican mayoral candidate in 1985, referring to Giuliani. "He would give Mario one heck of a race."[143]

Conclusion

Despite Cuomo's woes entering the 1990 race for governor, there was still no heir apparent or obvious challengers from the Republicans in New York State. Cuomo still had a formidable war chest and tremendous name recognition. The depth of his support may have been diminishing but it was still wide. Pierre Rinfret, a former economist in the Nixon administration and owner of a consulting firm, would ultimately become the Republican Party's sacrificial lamb in what was deemed an unwinnable race. As the *Times* reported in May at the time of Rinfret's announcement to seek the governorship, "[Republican] Party leaders were repeatedly rebuffed by potential candidates in awe of the $8 million Cuomo campaign treasury and the Democratic Governor's high standing in polls, at least earlier this year."[144] With President George Bush at a 72 percent approval rating owing to Saddam Hussein's invasion of Kuwait and a war-time setting for the nation, Cuomo was hardly the only Democrat focusing on his or her own backyard. There were few early candidate visits to Iowa in the late summer of 1990. "It's pretty dead," said David Yepsen, political correspondent for the *Des Moines Register*, in August.[145]

Despite governors from Connecticut, Vermont, and Massachusetts choosing to forgo reelection campaigns amid declining popularity, Cuomo remained a very strong, if no longer invulnerable candidate. There were nevertheless, unfavorable trends. Notwithstanding Cuomo's anti-crime stance and all the new prisons, crime was up 20 percent in New York. The percentage of taxes that state residents were paying had gone up—despite the large tax cuts. It had become clear that Cuomo was defying the odds in a region that was experiencing its own backlash against liberal policies over the years.[146] As the campaign season moved past Labor Day, Cuomo pledged 5,000 more police officers for New York City. Perhaps such gestures were working. In a Marist poll conducted in September, Cuomo led Rinfret by a margin of 60 to 15 percent, this despite the fact that those surveyed indicated a growing concern with crime and the economy.[147]

In hindsight, the poll did not quite reflect Cuomo's vulnerability. The third party candidacy of Herbert London hurt Rinfret tremendously; the two conservative candidates would garner about 45 percent of the vote, a sign that Republicans could have made a serious challenge had they had a candidate to rally around.[148] Cuomo understood his weaknesses it seems, and at Harvard's Kennedy School of Government, he tried to put them in some perspective that September. "Today, we have a 'fend-for-yourself' federalism, which forces the states to try to go it alone," he said.[149] Assailing the New Federalism promoted by Reagan and Bush, Cuomo said that instead "we should return to the recognition of *national* responsibility for *national* problems, *local* responsibility for *local* problems, and *shared* responsibility for *shared* problems."[150] He dubbed this "progressive federalism." The argument had its novelty, but it was, unlike previous philippics, a case made from a defensive posture rather than one of confidence. The *Times* put it plainly after the Harvard address: "By using his speeches to denounce the Federal Government, Mr. Cuomo seeks to shift blame for those crises from Albany to Washington."[151]

The strategy may have worked but it hardly did wonders. In the general election, Cuomo defeated Rinfret with 53 percent of the vote, down some 10 points from his 1986 victory. Democrats also lost the state Senate, and Cuomo's $1.9 billion environmental bond issue was defeated. "I think some of the luster is taken out of Cuomo's Presidential candidacy," said Roger Stone, a Republican political consultant, after the election. "It was a sort of hollow victory for him."[152] The conservative columnist William Safire, sensing perhaps the end of Cuomo's national appeal, was more colorful. "The dismal Cuomo showing has forced the Governor's national boosters to eat humble pie with melancholy Danish," Safire wrote in the *Times*.[153] One could hardly begrudge Safire and other conservatives their moment. Cuomo had been on a near-decade-long run of positive state and national media coverage, going back to his elevation to lieutenant governor under Carey in 1978 and his rise to the governorship in 1982. But now, with Republicans on the rise nationally, and with a wartime president at the height of his popularity, a 53 percent majority for Cuomo somehow transmitted an aura of defeat.

"I ain't worried about Mario Cuomo," Lee Atwater, the Republican strategist is purported to have said after George Bush's defeat of Michael Dukakis in 1988. "Bill Clinton does worry me."[154] By 1990, that perspective seemed at least half-right. Mario Cuomo had the look of a politician whose star was falling. And George Bush seemed all but invulnerable. The world of prose, of difficult governance had produced some victories for Cuomo, but it had also bloodied him. As 1990 faded into the New Year, however, such premonitions would prove to be immature, if not incorrect. Mario Cuomo was returning—however improbably—to the world of campaigning, to the favorable terrain of prose.

Part Four

Party

MARIO CUOMO WAS sworn in for his third term as governor without much fanfare, the *New York Times* reported in January 1991. Noting that his administration faced a budget gap of perhaps upwards of "$4 billion," the *Times* also noted that the year was one in which Cuomo "is expected to decide whether he will seek the presidency."[1] New York's budgetary concerns and Cuomo's presidential ambitions were on parallel tracks it seemed, and those paths were likely to cross at some point in the year. In his budgetary address to the legislature on January 31, Cuomo recognized what everyone involved in the state's politics knew—the direction forward was foreboding. "Nothing in my eight years as governor," Cuomo told the legislators that day, "not even the potentially deadly prison uprising that initiated my first term, has been more difficult or challenging."[2] The same recession that was undermining George Bush's once formidable reelection chances were now bedeviling Cuomo's ability to govern, let alone contend for the presidency. After being sworn in, Cuomo told a pool of reporters, "The months immediately ahead of us are going to be perhaps more difficult than any since the Great Depression."[3]

At least a portion of Cuomo's woes were national. Some were structural and historic, owing to New York's increasingly post-industrial economy. But Cuomo also earned tough marks from those who worked within his administration. "I thought Cuomo was a great owner or manager of a five and ten cent store who became owner of Bloomingdales," one official told me on condition of anonymity. "I can't think of anyone I was closer to than Cuomo—what he believed, what I believed. But Carey was the far superior governor."[4] The official, familiar with the administrations of Carey and Cuomo, argued that Cuomo's small inner circle, one less "impressive" than Carey's, prevented him from getting the type of counsel from a wide array of people necessary to run a state as large and diverse as New York. "Cuomo thought he was the smartest person in the room. Carey did not."[5]

How much of New York's fiscal crisis, among its other challenges, were owed to Cuomo's management shortcomings as governor is difficult to say. But he was scored somewhat harshly by voters in his less than striking electoral margin of victory in 1990, and he would enter the "decision" year for satisfying whatever presidential ambitions he had knowing that New Yorkers and the rest of the country were watching him. When asked whether he was, in fact, in a decisive year for seeking the White House, Cuomo was characteristically coy. "If I were going to make plans, or plan to make plans, I would have to start with that question," he said.[6] Unsurprisingly, Cuomo did not accept the budgetary crisis as a self-inflicted wound. "The cumulative weight of this decade-long shift of the burden combined with shrinking revenues as a result of the national recession, is crushing many states, including New York," he said in his State of the State address.[7] Washington was to blame.

Meanwhile, the Democratic Leadership Council was not so quietly building a national organization of moderate Democratic leaders and grassroots chapters.[8] Speaking at its annual meeting held in Cleveland in May 1991, Clinton argued, "Too many of the people who used to vote for us, the very burdened middle class we're talking about, have not trusted us in national elections to defend our national interest abroad, to put their values in our social policy at home or to take their tax money and spend it with discipline. We've got to turn these perceptions around, or we can't continue as a national party."[9] And with a nod to his own state's welfare-to-work policy, Clinton said to great applause, "Work is the greatest social welfare program this country has ever devised."[10] It was the kind of language rooted in a personal, if not a civic, sense of responsibility that became the ideological way station from which Democrats would seek to win back disaffected voters, now part of the Reagan coalition. Clinton's speech was said to have given him "an inexorable movement to a presidential run."[11] While premature, Clinton's Cleveland DLC speech did show that centrist Democrats were on the assault. Conversely, progressives were largely facing the brunt of anti-liberal Washington sentiments—from within their own party. Jesse Jackson's lack of an invitation to the DLC meeting was not the only divisive issue facing those at the annual gathering. There were debates over free trade, civil rights, and the use of racial quotas as a "form of discrimination."[12] Covering the event for the *New York Times*, Gwen Ifill took particular notice of the corporate backing and feel of the surroundings:

> The meeting hall here was decorated with signs and flags that lent the room the look, but little of the energy, of a major political convention. Many voting delegates were corporate lobbyists who paid $35 to join the organization and $50 to attend the convention. The leadership's executive director, Al From, said the corporate backers, which included A.T. &T., RJR Nabisco and Philip Morris Companies, contributed from $3,000 to $25,000 to underwrite the three-day event.[13]

A little over a week later, by way of contrast, Cuomo was dealing with a budget deficit crisis that had ballooned by some reports from the already startling $4 billion to a whopping $6.5 billion within a matter of months.[14] While the final number was in dispute, Cuomo was hardly able to engage in national Democratic politics, even if he were inclined to do so. With New York City some $3 billion short of state aid entering the last days of budget negotiations, and with the state short of funds even to build five new promised prisons, Cuomo was enmeshed in his greatest political crisis, one gaining increased visibility nationally day by day.[15] Still, the politics of the moment was predictably far removed from the electoral climate of 1992. In March 1991, with the budget crisis looming in New York and with President Bush still relatively popular, Bush led Cuomo in an NBC/Wall Street Journal presidential trial heat poll 78 percent to 17 percent. By way of comparison, Carter had led Reagan the March before the election by 14 points.[16] Indeed, by November, one year out from the 1992 election, a Los Angeles Times/Mirror Poll showed Bush losing to an unnamed Democrat for the first time, with Cuomo leading the pack of prospective Democratic candidates by 12 points (while still falling to Bush).[17] Cuomo's problems were not insurmountable, trying as they were; but their resolution required the type of political timing necessary to vault him, if he so wished, back into the center of discussions of presidential possibilities. By mid-1991, that timing was in some question.

New York's budget passed nine weeks after the deadline, on June 4. By allowing the legislature to lead in presenting its budget rather than hammering out an agreement over details of his own, Cuomo was dependent on his limited veto powers over portions of the budget he could strike down. Describing the budget talks as "venomous," the *Times* reported the "grim" facts that "local governments, for example, are facing a $360 million cut in unrestricted state aid, to $600 million. State school aid, too, is to be cut by $400 million, to roughly $8.3 billion, and state agencies' budgets are being sliced by 2 percent to roughly $13 billion."[18] Decrying some of the legislature's cuts, Cuomo spoke candidly, if not tactfully. "They have done some truly stupid things with some of these cuts," Cuomo said. "No, not stupid—stupid means they made a judgment. Mindless is a better word because they did not know what they were doing."[19]

The battle proved costly. Cuomo had spent tremendous capital in the state's most trying economic times, getting a budget passed that he was ultimately unhappy with. True, there was little to work with given the deficits, but the increased rancor in Albany was not without considerable contributions from the governor. Nor would the issue go away in the next session. Cuomo had effectively bought himself a summer, and perhaps a fall, to right his political winds— and more important, the economic winds of the state; this would allow confidence in his leadership and in New York's economic future to be at least marginally better. And somehow, over the next half year, circumstances sometimes working at cross-purposes, provided him with ample room to once again be positioned at the top of considerations for his party's nomination to become president of the United States. Cuomo was 58 and in the middle year of his first as a newly elected three-term governor; despite his wounds, his political future was still the envy of perhaps all but one of his peers.

Maneuvering: The Summer and Fall of 1991

A combined survey over the summer months of 1991 showed Cuomo at 21 percent to be the first choice of Democrats to be their nominee in 1992. Al Gore and Lloyd Bentsen followed at 14 and 13 percent, respectively. Bill Clinton, still very much an unknown nationally, was at 2 percent.[20] Cuomo's secure national profile among Democrats did not lead him to neglect showing his strong hand in New York politics. Cuomo went on to veto some 384 items in the state budget proposed by the legislature. The cost to the state in total expenditures he vetoed totaled nearly $1 billion. Was Cuomo trying to burnish his image as a more centrist figure than the wild-eyed liberal he was likely to be depicted in a national race? He certainly tried to dispel such talk, even as it grew. "I heard the people talking about treachery and disloyalty and complicated political motivations, running for President, moving to the right, all the schemes," Cuomo said. "I heard it all, and it's not pleasant to hear."[21]

As Cuomo was making deals to restore some of the slashed funds to the state from his vetoes, Bill Clinton was one of a few

Democrats eager to form a presidential exploratory committee.[22] With Bush's popularity still high from the Persian Gulf War victory and with a new coup attempt in the Soviet Union in late August, few of the Democratic Party standard-bearers were anxious to take on a sitting president. Cuomo was also in late summer likely to be drawn into another racial conflagration in New York City, as the death of a black boy, Gavin Cato, struck by a Hasidic motorist in Crown Heights, Brooklyn, touched off days of unrest when the motorist was not indicted.[23] It was the very picture of northeastern, urban, racial volatility that Republicans had been running against since the mid-1960s. Cuomo's troubles at home, such as they were, seemed to have at least momentarily dampened expectations of his getting in the presidential race. "I don't see any signs that he actually is going to run," Nancy Pelosi said during a San Francisco fundraiser headlined by Cuomo in September. "I say that with discouragement, frankly, but this is a subject that he just won't talk about when you try to bring it up."[24] There had once been an idea that Cuomo's flirtation was political strategy. "He runs by not running," said Tom Hayden, a California legislator, during a 1987 Cuomo swing through Los Angeles. "He creates demand by reducing supply."[25] By the fall of 1991, that seemed like so much wishful thinking.

As Cuomo's former budget director Dall Forsythe would note years later, Cuomo's budget vetoes were part of his willingness to take unilateral action as governor. As examples, Forsythe includes Cuomo's vetoes against the death penalty and his refusal to approve the emergency evacuation plan for the nuclear plant in Shoreham.[26] His decision to run for the White House may have been a similarly honed, unilateral decision. It appears that up until the eleventh hour, even Andrew Cuomo was unaware of his father's decision regarding a presidential run—and Andrew was not only his closest adviser, but his son.[27] Cuomo's lack of clarity about a presidential decision over the summer had the effect of renewing talk about a possible candidacy given the perceptions of a weak Democratic field. The Democratic National Committee chairman, Ron Brown, saw Cuomo's non-commitment as costly. "The threat of a Cuomo candidacy was freezing Democratic activists and contributors who by this point might have been choosing another candidate to support," Brown said.[28]

If Cuomo could freeze the field, couldn't he win the nomination as well? The *Times* speculated about whether Cuomo had any interest in the obligations of the presidency, never mind its allures. "Of the 3,187 days that Mr. Cuomo has been Governor, he has, by his staff's count, spent only 36 nights away from the Executive Mansion," the *Times* reported in September of 1991.[29] Cuomo might be interested in the job of president, but perhaps not in its performative requirements. The state's issues also continually drew him in. In September he was busy presenting plans to revitalize New York City—the type of large-scale government plan that had made the Rockefeller and Carey legacies. "Rockefeller left the road system, the mall in Albany, all the universities," Assembly Speaker Mel Miller said as the plan was unveiled. "Hugh Carey's monument is that he saved the city from bankruptcy. Maybe it sunk in that what you're remembered for as a Governor are the institutions you create and the temples you leave."[30] Cuomo's plan included large new public works in the city, including a light rail system; a state takeover of Medicaid, long desired by Mayor David Dinkins; a new Westside development plan; and, a large new science library, among other items. The plan was hailed by the editorial board of the *Times* as one of "leadership and hope."[31] Cuomo also said that month that he would not "release" his supporters to back other Democratic candidates. "Who am I, Charlton Heston?" he mused.[32] He likewise played down his forthcoming trip to Japan as a way to build his foreign policy chops. Once again, Cuomo had the look of a presidential candidate—and he was doing things to raise that possibility with one hand while batting it down with the other.

By making his broad proposal for New York in the midst of the state's budgetary crisis and aftermath, Cuomo went on the offensive, and it seemed to largely buoy him in New York. It directed press and media attention toward large-scale and future-oriented problems. Cuomo even found the time to pen a lengthy response to *New York* magazine's Joe Klein, who raised questions about the feasibility of his plans.

> We are not doing anything as dramatic as building airports. We are simply rebuilding the economy and the spirit of the city. We are rolling up our sleeves and doing the hard, sweaty, non-glitzy work of speeding the flow of goods and services and people, of unclogging the arteries of the city's aging network of roads, rails, ports, and waterways that support our economy.[33]

It was the type of argument on progressive terms Cuomo wanted to have. But there were early signs of skepticism, and not just from Klein. The *Times* captured the skepticism well, reporting that "Mr. Cuomo also revealed that his plan is based on assumptions that local tax collections would grow by an average of 5 percent a year and that Medicaid costs would grow by 12 to 13 percent a year through the end of the century. That led the Senate majority leader, Ralph J. Marino, Republican of Oyster Bay, L.I., to call the plan 'a house of cards built on overly optimistic forecasts.'"[34]

The timing of the plan to revitalize New York was perhaps not accidental. Days after Ralph Marino's "house of cards" comment, Cuomo shifted the political terrain even further. At a private breakfast meeting for supporters on October 11, Cuomo acknowledged that he was thinking of running for the presidency. "They said, 'Will you think about it?'" Cuomo said. "I said, 'Sure, I'll think about it. I'm always thinking about it.' I said I'd have to be mindless not to think about it. I don't talk about it, but I think about it. Of course I do."[35] This latest flirtation did not go over well with some declared candidates. "You can't be the reluctant maiden for year after year and then expect to jump into the process in midstream," said Bill Clinton on getting word of Cuomo's renewed interest in joining the contest. "The time is really past when candidates should be thinking about whether to get in. The time is at hand to either do it or not do it."[36] Over the next 10 weeks the seriousness with which Cuomo was speaking would become evident, despite his initial efforts to tamp down expectations of a run. He was not a declared candidate, but he was in fact, weighing seriously the possibility of a presidential run. Just how seriously would unfold over that time span. "This is not just dithering," one adviser told reporters. "He's really torn."[37] New York Democratic chairman and close Cuomo adviser, John Marino, added that in actuality, Cuomo had until November to get into the race. There was still time. And so began a clock that would begin to tick down from that first November deadline until the last day of the fall in 1991. Clinton's frustration was shared by Ron Brown and others within the Democratic Party. Some of it was because of the disruption to the field of declared candidates, and some because Cuomo could, in fact, be clearly positioned well enough to get the nomination if he fought for it. But did he want it?

Hamlet, No More

Try as he might to maintain his noncommittal posture concerning a run for the White House, it was clear that Cuomo had opened the door. His advisers were preparing for that possibility—what some in Washington began to think of as an inevitability. Would he in fact decide, once and for all, to run? The question was again posed in October by an audience member at the 92nd Street Y, where Cuomo was part of a panel on perhaps the only more vexing topic of "Who is God?" What if God asked Cuomo to run, someone in the crowd had the good humor to ask. "Only if he guarantees that someone will balance the state budget while I'm schlepping in Iowa," was his response.[38] The remark underscored the ever-present concern about the state of New York's economy, where on the same day the *Times* covered Cuomo's talk at the Y, it reported that the state had lost 300,000 jobs since May, nearly twice as many as had been predicted. And it also noted that there was likely to be a "budget gap" of $155 million.[39] Meanwhile, calls were coming into the Democratic chairman of Colorado's office inquiring "What the hell is he going to do?"[40] The fact that insiders were raising questions again meant Cuomo had reclaimed the spotlight. But to what end? William Safire took to writing an entire column from "inside the mind" of Cuomo. Safire had Cuomo's brain choosing to run.[41] Cuomo wasn't quite there, but he once again, this time more forcefully, acknowledged that he was "looking at running." "There's still time left until sometime in November," he told reporters after a speaking engagement in Chicago on October 20. "By then you have to either be in or not be in. There's only a few weeks to go and we'll see," he said.[42]

As Cuomo weighed entering the race, a Draft Cuomo for President Committee was established in Congress (without Cuomo's objection) as he arranged a meeting with Democratic National Committee chairman Ron Brown to discuss the future. These machinations belie the idea that Cuomo elected not to enter the 1992 presidential race because it was, as one political scientist put it several years later, "a suicidal endeavor." This hardly seemed the case, particularly in late 1991, given the national economic decline and Bush's increasing vulnerability.[43] Indeed, before Cuomo tipped his hand at his October 10 breakfast gathering with reporters, he had only days earlier sought out Democratic strategist Bob Shrum about his chances. Cuomo had met with Shrum before, in 1987, and whether it was for seven hours as Cuomo remembered, or two, as described in Shrum's account, Cuomo had more going for him in 1992 than he or Dukakis did in 1988.[44] In any case, Cuomo's languid movement toward a decision is probably poorly read as disbelief in his chances. "What does my heart tell me?" Cuomo told News 12 Long Island, at the time. "Go out and tell them, Mario. Take your best shot, whether you win, lose or draw. But don't finish this game until you've taken your best shot."[45]

Yet by the end of October, Cuomo was calling the legislature back into session. The state's budget deficit was now nearing $700 million.[46] As Republican consultant Roger Stone put it, if Dukakis ran on the Massachusetts miracle, Cuomo would have to run on "the New York nightmare."[47] New York's fiscal woes would be piled on Cuomo's anti-death penalty stance, along with his perceived Northeast, liberal (and ethnic) insularity. In hindsight, it seems inevitable that Democrats would naturally move away from the technocratic Greek governor of liberal Massachusetts to a more moderate and highly emotive Arkansan. But in the fall of 1991 there were no such inevitabilities, and while Cuomo's weaknesses were evident, his was also a different personality from that of Dukakis. Cuomo had a real ability to connect with working-class voters, and while he was hardly a southerner, it is not hard to imagine him connecting with religious-minded voters on issues of faith and conscience. In a few decades of brawling in New York politics against the likes of Edward Koch, it is hard also to imagine Cuomo playing "soft" against the array of attacks he'd undoubtedly face in a primary or general election. Perhaps, in the end, his troubles in New York would have proven insurmountable, but as Bill Clinton would go on to show, all sorts of heretofore impediments to winning a national election went out the window in 1992. The biggest difference tactically is that while Cuomo had been thinking of running in recent weeks—perhaps months—Clinton had been making connections across the country, first with Democratic governors, but also with local officials through the infrastructure of an organization he had helped build. Clinton had been wanting it all along.

And yet Cuomo was still very much present, ready to shake up the race. The *New Yorker* may have been glib but not entirely inaccurate in repeating the political class's mantra about the Democratic field for 1992: "Eeny, Meeny, Miney, and Mario."[48] To underscore interest in Cuomo's entry into the race, the *Washington Post* and New York *Daily News* began running "Cuomo Watch" and "Waiting for Mario" columns, respectively.[49] It is hard to know from the closed circle of Cuomo advisers what was going on in the governor's mansion on the subject of a prospective run in the days leading up to Cuomo's decision. Andrew Cuomo's 2014 biography is curiously silent on the subject, covering perhaps his family's most significant political season by mentioning only Andrew's September 1991 work heading up Mayor David Dinkins's Cuomo Commission on homelessness, and then, abruptly four pages later, completing his coverage of the electoral season with a most curious non sequitur of a sentence: "Shortly after the 1992 election, I got a call from Congressman Tom Downey."[50] Suffice it to say, it has not been a well-covered moment, as the chief players have either passed on or have next to nothing to say about it. Mario Cuomo told Craig Horowitz of *New York Magazine* years later that "Matilda and I have never talked about it. The family and I have never talked about it."[51] Perhaps we should believe him.

The Socratic striptease, as Maureen Dowd described it, was coming to an end.[52] One way or another, Cuomo was going to turn his eyes toward, or away from Washington—most likely for good. After 1988, this was his second bite at the apple; anticipating a third would be more than unrealistic. Who in the Democratic Party would believe him (or want him) again? Some began to think after the national elections on November 6 that Cuomo might read the tea leaves as favoring his entrance into the race. Democrats scored a surprise upset in the Senate election in Pennsylvania, as Harris Wofford defeated the state's attorney general Dick Thornburgh. Perhaps Wofford's message of economic discontent and the need for health care might carry beyond Pennsylvania. Was Cuomo warming to the idea? It seemed so. He directly attacked his most likely chief rival, Bill Clinton, for the first time, in *New York* magazine, calling Clinton's college loan plan "a bunch of baloney."[53] He also jabbed at Clinton's welfare plan. "He says they shouldn't be on welfare forever. Maybe in his state they are. In mine they are on for an average of two years."[54] Joe Klein, who authored the article, picked up on something between the two men, something brewing within the Democratic Party for years—and it seemed personally embodied in the two governors. "Cuomo has this thing about Clinton, a moderate who may emerge as his most credible challenger," he wrote.[55] Meanwhile, Clinton adviser Frank Greer offered a more cautious jab, telling Klein, "I think Mario may be worried that someone has developed a message that addresses the concerns of the middle class in creative ways."[56] It was enough of a pushback without entreating Cuomo to enter the race outright.

The "thing" Cuomo had about Clinton was likely both personal and political. Clinton was a political and social climber, a man of deep ambition. And he was working at it, openly and artfully politicking and making his case for leadership within the party. Clinton was also an inveterate talker, a schmoozer—someone who didn't mind the type of *"cerimonia"* Cuomo's father had raised him to disdain. It is hard not to imagine Cuomo comparing himself to Clinton—and Clinton was now earning his stripes as an effective if not yet great orator. "In my state," Cuomo had reassured Klein. "Maybe in his state," he also averred.

The political component to this had to do with the term "moderate" that Klein used to describe Clinton. Philosophically, the two men were different Democrats. Cuomo was unapologetically New Deal–oriented, a man born in the year of FDR's election. Conversely, Clinton's searing political experience was 1968—graduation from Georgetown, Oxford, and the draft, the Vietnam War, the Chicago Convention. Liberalism under great fire. And he too, was passionate about his position—though for Clinton, politics seemed more about position than deeply held beliefs. And perhaps this too rankled Cuomo, a man driven by first principles—perhaps less than he imagined, but no doubt motivated by them. It was late in the game when Cuomo's first salvo was fired—the *New York* magazine was out on November 18. Late as it was, Cuomo was not holding his powder. He seemed to be a man bent on making an attack. Today, many are inclined to forget that this assault had perhaps only slightly less to do with Reaganism than it did with what pundits would one day soon be describing as the politics of the "Middle Way." Cuomo may have governed in the shaded areas, but he was at heart a black and white Manichean.

Hedging his bets some, Klein nevertheless came away from his interview with Cuomo more convinced than not that he would run. "Over the past few weeks, Cuomo seems to have made progress— glacial perhaps; reversible, undoubtedly, toward a yes."[57] There even appeared to be an opening over the budget impasse in Albany. On November 12, the *New York Times* reported that Cuomo and legislators were weighing the possibility of drawing up a multi-year budget, one that would include selective cuts in programs along with a spending freeze.[58] The deal would potentially eliminate the $689 million state deficit. It would also offer a political boon to Cuomo—and the state's legislators—because it would take the budget off the table as a campaign issue, both nationally for Cuomo, and locally, for the state's pols. The deal would carry over into March or June of 1993, when Mario Cuomo might well be serving as the nation's 42nd president.

But the stars were not so neatly aligned. The very next day, New York's Republican comptroller and the State Senate majority leader, Ralph Marino, were throwing cold water on the plan. "It's just not acceptable," Marino said. "We cannot have deficit spending continuing until the start of the fiscal year."[59] More tellingly, the Bush White House took notice, as White House spokesman Marlin Fitzwater told reporters at a Bush fundraiser in New York City that "no amount of fancy footwork will relieve [Cuomo] of the responsibility of his own state's fiscal affairs."[60] To make matters worse, just one week after the *Times* reported the possibility of a multi-year budget plan, Cuomo's aides acknowledged that the budget deficit might actually double in the coming fiscal year.[61] The new budget gap was now forecast at $3.6 billion.[62] The window was closing, if it ever was truly open. Recognizing the futility of his fight with Marino and the state's Republicans, Cuomo said simply, "There is no more time."[63]

Cuomo didn't give up entirely—either on the budget or on pushing back against the Bush White House. He took time out to express umbrage with Vice President Dan Quayle's repeated use of Cuomo's first name "Mario" on a Sunday talk show. Marlin Fitzwater said Cuomo "better get used to it. Mario, Mario, Mario, Mario, Mario, Mario."[64] Cuomo was being *Dukakised* and he hadn't even entered the race. Anna Quindlen of the *Times* remarked, "The fact that the Vice President called the Governor Mario means that the 1992

Presidential race has officially begun."[65] While Cuomo viewed the first-name-calling as a not so thinly veiled reference to his ethnicity, it was far from his biggest challenge. Meanwhile, the New Hampshire primary filing deadline of December 20 was now looming. Cuomo acknowledged as much on *Good Day New York*. "If you want to run in the primary in New Hampshire, which I would want to, then that's a date,"[66] Cuomo said on December 3. He was a little over two weeks away from that reality. The day after reporting Cuomo's comments about New Hampshire, Cuomo advisers John Marino and Brad Johnson were busy meeting in the Manhattan office of Michael Del Giudice, Cuomo's former chief of staff, putting together a list of "prospective campaign managers, media consultants, press secretaries, election lawyers, pollsters and issues advisers."[67] In 1987, Cuomo spoke of such maneuvers as the "things I should be doing if I were running." He was starting to do them now, however late in the game.

Just as things seemed to be settling a bit—Cuomo had reached a deal with Democratic Assembly Speaker Mel Miller about spending cuts that would potentially eliminate the deficit in 15 months—things became surreal. Shortly after Cuomo had told reporters that "the only piece missing now is the [Republican] Senate," Miller was convicted in a Brooklyn court on federal fraud charges.[68] The Democratic Speaker lost not only his Speakership but also his 44th Assembly District seat. To make matters worse, at least as far as Cuomo's presidential prospects were concerned (never mind passing a budget), Democrat James R. Tallon of Binghamton, who immediately succeeded Miller, was to be challenged by Saul Weprin, a Queens Democrat, who headed the Ways and Means Committee. This meant there would have to be an election for the Speaker's seat, and there was no date set.[69] Fortunately for Cuomo, Tallon conceded the next day, recognizing he'd have little power to hold off a downstate contender with Weprin's power and experience.

This wasn't how Cuomo wanted to set the table for a presidential run. The Democrats had held their first debate; the Florida straw poll was won by Bill Clinton; New York's budget was a mess—and its Democratic Assembly leader had now been convicted. These were not favorable conditions by any means. Yet, on December 16, Joseph Grandmaison, former chairman of the New Hampshire Democratic Party, "picked up a primary form for Mario M. Cuomo" and was set to mail it to John Marino, New York's Democratic Party chairman. Grandmaison had wanted to keep this document—but at the time, he perhaps imagined far more important ones ahead involving New York's governor. Cuomo was to sign that document and then send it in with a certified check for $1,000. Why hadn't Grandmaison sent the form to Cuomo directly? Cuomo had not asked for it, Marino said.[70]

On a chilly Tuesday, before the Friday filing deadline in New Hampshire, Mario Cuomo appeared in a dark overcoat and tan fedora-style hat leaving Syracuse for Albany. He was crushed by reporters, with the *New York Post* among others, wanting to know, "Will he toss that hat into the ring?"[71] Few probably recognized that line about another prospective progressive candidate—Teddy Roosevelt—from a more ebullient time for reform governors from the Northeast. What people did seem to be more confident about was Cuomo's candidacy. "More calls are being made. This thing is getting serious."[72] This is what anonymous sources were telling reporters. John Marino, still noting the governor's uncertainty, was openly pushing Cuomo to get in. "Let's join the race now. The time is now—that's my attitude."[73] Another aide was reported saying, "It looks and smells like a 'go.'"[74] Was Cuomo tipping his hand as well? Had he made what appeared to be a Freudian slip when he told reporters days before the filing deadline, "[Republicans] have [held up the budget] before, *when I wasn't running for president.*"[75] Cuomo insisted he hadn't just made an announcement, but it was hard to resist the signs. Arthur Browne of New York's *Daily News* began his December 19 column with unabashed confidence in upcoming events:

There won't be a state budget agreement tomorrow, but there will be a Cuomo-for-President campaign. As there has been for several weeks, if not longer. The governor will file to enter the New Hampshire Democratic primary, completing a lap of the race in which he demonstrated that he could run well by standing still. Then, in all likelihood, he'll return to Albany for as long as possible, the national press corps at his heels. Cuomo has never said any of this, nor have his aides, but to believe otherwise you have to accept the idea that after all this attention, he's prepared to tell the nation he's not up to running because he couldn't make a deal by an arbitrary date with Ralph Marino, the state Senate majority leader from Muttontown. Pulleeeze.[76]

Cuomo had until 5:00 pm on Friday to decide. To be Hamlet, no more.

"A Call to Arms"

With a few pages of notes in his hands, Mario Cuomo took to the podium in Room 250 of the state capitol, just after 3:30 pm on Friday, December 20, 1991. It is uncertain how many individuals, other than perhaps Andrew Cuomo, Joe Grandmaison, and John Marino, knew what he'd say at that moment. Cuomo had been with his advisers much of day, conferring about the budget. According to Andrew Cuomo biographer Michael Shnayerson, Andrew had been lobbying his father to enter the race. When asked by supporters throughout the day if his father was finally getting into the race, Andrew had answered, "I don't know." Cuomo had not finished writing his statement until 2:00 pm. There is good reason to believe that down to the wire, Andrew did not, in fact, know.[77] In short order, Cuomo would say as much when asked if he had consulted with members of his "inner staff about his decision." Cuomo's reply was terse but revelatory. "I don't do it that way. We do a lot of it by osmosis. We do a lot of it by shrugs."[78]

After a quick sip of water, Cuomo began reading from his statement, in a calm, and deliberate manner. "Republicans," he said, "have responded to every reasonable offer of compromise by the Assembly and the Governor with new and predictably, unacceptable demands."[79] He went on to talk about the damage to the state and its credit should the problem go on unresolved. "It is my responsibility as Governor to deal with this extraordinarily severe problem. Were it not, I would travel to New Hampshire today and file my name as a candidate in its presidential primary. That was my hope and I prepared for it." *He was saying no.* The planes were ready; his supporters, fundraisers, and political opening, they were all there; and he was at the podium, increasingly grave, now sounding exasperated, and saying no. He wanted to be a good Democrat, he said, accepting "the judgment of the national chairman of our party that it would be in the best interest of the Democratic Party that I abandon any such effort now so as to avoid whatever inconvenience and disruption to the process is created by the uncertain possibility of another candidacy." *He was abandoning the race.* He had said it.

"Governor, Is This One of the Greatest Disappointments of Your Career?"And then came a familiar refrain, to those who had been paying attention to Cuomo since 1977. When the short four-minute statement was over and he was taking questions, one came in that gave him some pause: "Governor, is this one of the greatest disappointments of your career?"

"It would be enormously ungrateful," Cuomo began, first shaking his head and wincing even as the reporter delivered the question, "to talk about disappointments. I have said over and over just being governor was more of a privilege than I ever expected to receive and probably more of a privilege than I ever felt I deserved. It would have been nice to run for President, but it's difficult for me to complain in any form at all." Cuomo was back to gratitude, the man from the "little grocery store in Queens," the humble family roots in southern Italy. Cuomo wanted to run, but bringing himself to do so—and to do so at the possible economic expense of his state—cut against every moral sensibility he had had since St. John's Prep. Was this not the answer? I asked Peter Quinn, whom Cuomo had invited back into the inner circle in the run-up to the 1992 campaign. Why bother to bring Quinn back, if not for a run? Quinn had left speech-writing for Cuomo after the Notre Dame speech in 1984 for a new career at Time, Inc. So, I asked Quinn: *What happened in 1992? Do you have an opinion about why he didn't run?* "I called him the next morning, after he announced at the press conference he wasn't going to run," Quinn told me. "I said 'What the fuck was that all about?' He had put a campaign together. Brad Washington who had set up the Washington campaign had a nervous breakdown over it. I mean, he had set things up to run."[80] This was still not quite an answer, so I pressed.

AUTHOR: *Why didn't he?*

QUINN: Only he knows. It was something he took with him to the grave. He said it was the Republican Leader, Ralph Marino.

AUTHOR: *And the budget, right? That his hands were tied.*

QUINN: And that's total bullshit.

AUTHOR: *And people have their own speculations.*

QUINN: And that's something I don't want to do.

Seeing where Quinn was going—or rather not going—I decided not to press.

New York's tabloids were predictably colorful the next morning. *Newsday's* "No Show" headline was accompanied by a large photograph of "The empty podium in Concord, New Hampshire."[81] Reporters, flanking the podium and its half dozen or so microphones, were reduced to taking pictures of the empty space, the space Cuomo was supposed to fill. The *Daily News* front page placed a photo of Cuomo framed inside a stop sign, the headline reading, "Mario No Go."[82] The *Post's* front page offered a punchy "Cuo-no!" while the *Times's* just-the-facts headline ("Cuomo Says He Will Not Run for President in '92") was flanked by the photo of the empty podium from Concord.[83] Many of the nation's newspapers, notably the *Washington Post* and *Chicago Tribune* among them, mentioned the two planes on the tarmac in Albany, waiting for Cuomo to board for New Hampshire.[84] The planes were instant symbols of the high drama of the moment but also of something important somehow inexplicably aborted. As one aide to a rival Democrat told the *Post*, "There are many people in this party who've been waiting for Mario Cuomo to run since before he made that speech in '84. It must hit some people in our party hard."[85] The biggest of the rival Democrats, Bill Clinton was magnanimous. "Had Gov. Cuomo chosen to run, he clearly would have been the favorite to win the nomination, and a formidable opponent," Clinton said.[86] The not-so-quiet battle between the two most impressive Democratic governors of their generation had come to an end.

In his press conference, Cuomo noted that he wasn't "particularly eager to see the story all over the world," even as he was mindful of trying to meet reporters' deadlines for the evening news.[87] But the story did travel around the world, and Cuomo likely knew that it would. Italy's *La Repubblica*, which had covered Cuomo's rise in American politics over the better part of two decades, offered an intriguing analysis. The article noted the challenges faced by Italian Americans in US politics; it also mentioned the suspicions of mob ties to Cuomo, including a short account of Charles Raffa's mysterious beating in Brooklyn. There was also an emphasis on having to prove one's "innocence" as an Italian in American politics—and it included Geraldine Ferraro in this history. The article concluded with Cuomo refusing to accept a reporter's notion that he was somehow abandoning his dream of becoming president. "Non sono ancora arrivato a quel grado di presunzione e di egoismo" ha ribattuto Cuomo "ma ci sto provando." "I will work toward that level of egoism," Cuomo said, "but I haven't arrived at it yet."[88]

Mario Cuomo, "L'Hamlet de l'Hudson," *Le Monde* of France reported, would not in fact run in the upcoming presidential election. More interestingly, the paper focused on the divide in the Democratic Party and the new, more moderate direction Bill Clinton of Arkansas wanted to take it ("Alors que Mario Cuomo représentait le parti traditionnel, porte-parole des Noirs, des femmes et des syndicats, Bill Clinton, lui, cherche à regagner une classe moyenne qui s'estime opprimée par le fisc et menacée par la montée en force des minorités ethniques"). Yes, the traditional party of blacks, women, and unions was moving to recover those middle-class voters who had begun to feel threatened by "ethnic minorities."[89] It was spot-on coverage.

Meanwhile, the *Times* of London reported on Cuomo's "refusal to run" even as "hotels were booked and planes chartered" to enable his filing for the New Hampshire primary.[90] The *Times* also noted, "The announcement was welcomed privately last night by White House aides who have become increasingly concerned about the Cuomo threat in a depressed US economy."[91] The paper likewise had the "more conservative" Bill Clinton as the candidate who benefited the most. It was clear that Cuomo's decision not to run had implications well beyond his own personal political career. It was rightly seen, not only in the United States but also abroad, as likely heralding a shift in Democratic Party and liberal politics into the future. And indeed, it was just that. But understanding Cuomo's motives was still the subject of intense speculation. As Elizabeth Kolbert of the *New York Times* wrote, "Those who saw the Governor's equivocations as elements of a master plan, and said so on national television, are now faced with an extravagant mystery."[92] Her answer? "Those who always doubted that a man who hates to sleep in strange beds could run for President now seem strangely credible."[93]

With Cuomo now officially out of the race, it was time to reassess. He still had the budget crisis in front of him. He also had three years left in his third term as governor. What did he wish to do in that time? Was he really serious about his plan to rebuild, or at least, make over, much of New York City? On December 22, Cuomo would wake up for the first time in more than seven years without being one of his party's biggest stars and figures of the future. Unlike his mayoral loss in 1977, there would be no chants among supporters for future races. There was no campaign looming on the horizon—at least not for him. What would Mario Cuomo do in prose when there was no poetry beckoning him? Harold Holzer, a Cuomo aide and confidante, recalled at the time, listening to Cuomo read to him over the telephone the morning of December 20, before he decided what course to take, the version of his statement having him running for the presidency. "It was," Holzer remembered, "a call to arms."[94]

Two More Novembers

Back in October, when Cuomo's candidacy was still very much up in the air, Bill Clinton had already announced his own candidacy and given his first major policy speech at his alma mater, Georgetown University. At Georgetown, Clinton spoke of the "New Covenant," one aimed at tackling the "greed" that had overcome much of the nation—not only the private sector but also our own "government, which should have been setting an example."[95] He spoke about crime, and the rise of gangs, and the scourge of drugs. This new covenant was to be forged by a new Democratic Party, he said, one that would put people on welfare to work because "we can no longer afford to have you on welfare forever." It was a call for responsibility and good citizenship. He also promised to "put an end to welfare as we know it." And he pushed against the "scandal of absentee parents who run off and leave their children no financial support"—the "deadbeats" as he called them. The speech contained a number of long-standing Democratic truisms of the past, but it was notable mainly for its moderate, even conservative tone. Ending welfare, getting the deadbeats to pay—locking up the gangbangers; getting those who won't work, back to work. It was a powerful speech. And it was one Cuomo had been largely arguing against, even up until his days before opting out of the race. Yet within little over seven months, Cuomo would stand in front of a podium in his home state—in "the greatest state in the greatest nation, in the only world we know"—and he would be the person putting forth Bill Clinton's name as the nominee of the Democratic Party for president of the United States.

Between that time and his exit from a race he never truly entered, Cuomo went back to work. He once again tried to get

Republicans in the State Senate to reconsider his 15-month budget plan to eliminate the deficit. "If they don't do it, they're dead politically," he said on Christmas Eve. "If they don't do the 15 months, they're going down."[96] But Cuomo was now in some respects, a lame duck—the prestige he had wielded just days before was now greatly diminished. Cuomo would call the Senate back to Albany for a special session over the usual Christmas holiday break, but to no avail, as they rejected his proposal out of hand. The mystique around Cuomo was also clearly gone, as he was heckled by a Queens assemblyman during his State of the State address.[97] To make matters worse, New York's credit rating was downgraded in January by Moody's and would not remain "out of the woods" even when a budget deal was finally agreed to in April 1992. The deal came at the cost of programs at the heart of the liberal state—nearly $1 billion worth of cuts to Medicaid and welfare.[98] Back in January, Cuomo vowed not to cut welfare "simply to pander."[99] But he made the cuts all the same. And in another sign of the political winds shifting about him, a number of prominent New York Democrats declared their support for Bill Clinton before the end of January.[100]

Cuomo's only moment back in the national spotlight at the time was the result of the release of a tape of Bill Clinton and his purported mistress, Gennifer Flowers, whose recording of Clinton had the Arkansas governor responding to her suggestion that Cuomo might have "some mafioso connections," as "he acts like one." Cuomo was livid—and unforgiving, as Clinton's apology went unaccepted, leaving Clinton hung out to dry. The *Times* captured the deeper political significance of the rift, noting that "Mr. Cuomo regularly assailed the moderate agenda set by the Democratic Leadership Council, which was led by Mr. Clinton, while Mr. Clinton once referred to Mr. Cuomo as 'a powerful spokesman for the Northeast liberal base of the party.'"[101] While Clinton was racked by the Flowers revelation and other troubles, including the release of an anti–Vietnam War letter from his days in Oxford, he managed to turn a second-place finish behind Paul Tsongas in New Hampshire into a political victory of sorts. Meanwhile, a not-so-underground write-in campaign for Cuomo in New Hampshire proved to be all smoke and no fire, as Cuomo got scant support—a meager 4 percent of the vote.[102]

Back in Albany, the budget crisis provided an unexpected reprieve of sorts for one of the state's biggest challenges—a prison population that was 118 percent over capacity. New, less draconian laws were at last being looked at in an effort to reduce the number of incarcerated. The plan would save some $65 million per prison needed to house the overpopulation. A staggering 750 new prisons were projected to be built to meet the current crisis.[103] Ironically, the prison uprising at Sing Sing that occurred in Cuomo's earliest days in office was now a symbol, in a sense, of the failure of the state and its governor to resolve a root cause of the uprising in the first place. It proved to be a trenchant example of liberalism's failure to address a challenge head-on whose remedy serves to disproportionately benefit the lives of men and women of color.

As Cuomo sought out solutions to the budget crisis, politics went on. Cuomo stayed out of the primary season, choosing not to endorse a candidate. Talk of a brokered convention and other wild scenarios for bringing Cuomo back into the mix as a candidate were no longer taken seriously after Clinton's April 7 win in the New York primary. As James Carville put it, "The party is full of people who want the glory of being President but not the agony of having run."[104] Few had to think long about whom Carville had in mind. Cuomo's agonies were already plenty. Another racially charged case—this time in Brooklyn—was raging, as the stabbing death of a 29-year-old Hasidic scholar the summer before in Crown Heights by an unconfirmed number of African Americans, seemed unlikely to produce a prosecution from the Brooklyn District Attorney's Office. The DA, Charles Hynes, had been appointed by Cuomo in 1986, as a special prosecutor in the Howard Beach case. Now, Hynes was facing pressure from both the black community—who wanted a prosecution in the death of Gavin Cato, who was struck by a motorist in Crown Heights (the event that precipitated the stabbing death of Yankel

Rosenbaum)—and members of New York's Jewish community, who viewed Rosenbaum's death as a modern pogrom. Hynes was beside himself with what to do. "There's nothing you can do with this kind of office that will get the assent of the majority," Hynes said. "Brooklyn is sui generis. It's wildly eclectic. There are 96 different ethnic or religious groups and at any given time they all hate each other."[105] This was not the version of the "wonderful mosaic" that Cuomo had so often spoken of in his speeches over the years. And it could only be imagined how Republicans would have used such incidents against him had he decided to run. As it was, it was but another example of liberalism's struggles in its northeastern core.

As the spring session in Albany closed and with the Democratic National Convention arriving in New York soon, Cuomo was still winding his way through the more mundane morass of issues affecting New York State—redistricting controversies, attempts to fend off accusations that the new budget deal struck in April was based on faulty accounting (such as selling off the state prison at Attica to a state agency), a West Side revival plan for Manhattan that looked like it might actually work. Amid these issues, Cuomo seemed nonplussed that it seemed unlikely that he would be invited to speak at the convention. "So I had a once-in-a-lifetime opportunity—why should they give you a second opportunity?" he said.[106]

Meanwhile, the presidential race was becoming harder to assess as billionaire Ross Perot was running as a populist and third party candidate. With Bush vulnerable and Clinton with his own difficulties, almost anything seemed possible. What was clear was that Republicans were zeroing in on what Bill Clinton had previously called the "risk" of having the Democratic Convention in New York City. Calling Cuomo "liberalism's sensitive philosopher king," Vice President Dan Quayle assailed New York as the epicenter of liberalism's failures. "In so many ways the liberal Democrats chose the perfect site for their convention—almost as if they feel a strange compulsion to return to the scene of the crime," Quayle said. "And as we watch this spectacle on our televisions, I suspect many Americans from around the country will be left with this conviction: We must not let them do to the rest of America what they have done to the people of New York City."[107] The lines, rehearsed as they were, were not altogether dissimilar from the sentiments expressed by the Democratic Leadership Council in its early history. And it was the basis for Clinton's fears of having the party too closely identified with New York City.

In the end, Clinton made the New York backdrop work to his advantage—and with the help of Ron Brown, Cuomo's old law student at St. John's University—got Cuomo to agree to give the nominating speech, just one week before the convention was under way.[108] Cuomo also appeared to be on Clinton's short list for vice president, but Cuomo, having foresworn leaving New York for a shot at the presidency, was hardly willing to make that move for a position reminiscent of his hound dog days as lieutenant governor under Hugh Carey. Still, with Cuomo now giving the nominating speech, the *Times* saw the moment as one of rapprochement, marking an "improvement in relations between two men who are considered leading spokesmen for the Northern liberal and Southern moderate wings of their party."[109] Cuomo's late addition elevated the level of star power for both Clinton and the party. CBS decided to add an hour of coverage given Cuomo's speaking role. All in all, it was one of those occasions when the politics of the moment worked to the advantage of the two rivals. "We think the speech by Gov. Mario Cuomo may be the most compelling television event of this convention," said Lane Venardos, director of CBS News's special-events unit.[110] Given 1984, it was a good bet.

After a short and inspiring biographical video, Cuomo took to the stage just a little past 9:00 pm on July 15 to nominate Bill Clinton as the Democratic Party's candidate for the presidency. Cuomo immediately went back to his moment in 1984, one that was on the minds of anyone old enough to remember.

Eight years ago, in San Francisco, some of us tried to convince America that while President Reagan was telling us we were all one "Shining city on a hill," there was another city, were people were struggling, many of them living in pain. And we tried to tell America that unless we changed policies, unless we expanded opportunity, the deterioration of the other city would spread. Well, we Democrats failed to reach enough Americans with that message, and now the nation has paid an awful price. We cannot afford to fail again.[111]

He then spoke of the weaknesses of supply side and "trickle down" economics which "has failed us again." And Cuomo did his best before a rapt crowd to hold onto Democratic Party first principles even as he acknowledged Clinton's recognition that "a great political party must apply the best of its accumulated wisdom to the new configurations of a changing reality." He argued that "Bill Clinton believes, as we all here do, in the first principle of our Democratic commitment; the politics of inclusion, the solemn obligation to create opportunity for all our people. Not just the fit and the fortunate. For the aging factory worker in Pittsburgh; the school child in Atlanta; for the family farmer in Des Moines; the eager immigrants, sweating to take their place alongside of us here in New York City, and in San Francisco."

And he derided Republicans whose hands were callused from "polo mallets" rather than hard work. He spoke of giving people "back their dignity" and the Governor of Arkansas's plans to produce real jobs. He hit hard on the savings and loan scandal, raising his voice to great applause: "And then Americans discovered that wealthy bankers, educated in the most exquisite forms of conservative Republican banking, through their incompetence and thievery, and the government's neglect, had stolen or squandered everything in sight! The world's greatest bank robbery!" Like a good party soldier, he repeated the refrain, "We need Bill Clinton," throughout his speech, emphasizing the need for change, for a movement away from desperate times. Cuomo was playing off the familiar notes he had struck in 1984—and he and his crowd became almost one in anticipating the attacks on Republican "values" that "through the courts . . . tell us what god to believe in, and how to apply that god's judgment to our school-rooms, our bedrooms and our bodies."

These were lines delivered with great conviction. It would have been hard to believe they would be the last ones delivered from a stage of this magnitude in the political career of Mario Cuomo. He was 60 now, but he still had tremendous fight and an uncanny abil-ity to connect with an audience. But Clinton, at 45, was the future. Cuomo had declined a chance to run; he had declined another chance to serve as Clinton's vice president. He would later not accept a posi-tion on the Supreme Court. He had much he would not do—but it was evident, that in these moments, he was very much acting in his will, and in his calling. Finally, came his conclusion—the crescendo, one that sought to turn the success of the Persian Gulf War against Bush:

Ladies and gentlemen, a year ago in this great city . . . we had a great parade . . . to celebrate the return of our armed forces from the Persian Gulf. I am sure you had one, too. But as joyous as those parades were, I'd like to march with you in a different kind of celebration—one, regrettably, that we can-not hold yet. I'd like to march with you behind President Bill Clinton through cities and rural villages where all the people have safe streets, affordable housing, and health care when they need it. I want to clap my hands and throw my fists in the air, cheering neighborhoods where children can be child-ren, where they can grow up and get the chance to go to col-lege, and one day own their own home.

I want to sing proud songs, happy songs, arm in arm with workers who have a real stake in their company's success . . . . I want to march behind President Bill Clinton in a victory parade that sends up fireworks, celebrating the triumph of our technology centers and factories, out-producing and out-selling our overseas competitors. I want to march with you knowing that we are selecting justices to the Supreme Court who are really qualified to be there . . . . I want to shout out our thanks because President Bill Clinton has helped us make the greatest nation in the world better than it's ever been.

So step aside, Mr. Bush!

The Madison Square Garden crowd was euphoric. Clinton's campaign manager, James Carville, would say afterward, "There are two things I don't do—criticize Michelangelo's paintings and Mario Cuomo's speeches." The major networks were more than pleased— ABC opted to rebroadcast the speech "almost in its entirety."[112] News anchors from all the networks were glowing. ABC's David Brinkley said simply, "He's still the best," while CBS's Charles Kuralt mused, "I'm still in glow of that speech."[113] Nevertheless, after that moment, it was Bill Clinton's party, and in many ways it remained so, at least until 2008. Clinton won a plurality of votes in the November election, becoming the nation's 42nd president and first Democrat in 12 years. He won with only 43 percent of the vote, but as political scientists Paul J. Quirk and Jon K. Dalager pointed out, when excluding Perot, who won 19 percent of the vote as a third party candidate, Clinton's victory "was roughly comparable to Bush's victory over Dukakis in 1988," when Bush gained 53.9 percent of the two-party vote; in 1992 Clinton won 53.5 percent.[114]

However the numbers were dissected, there was clearly a shift in the political winds of the nation, most assuredly defined, at least in part, by those blowing within the Democratic Party. Mario Cuomo was now down to one November before him, and it was two years away. He would be seeking a historic fourth term as New York's governor. It was that or nothing else—no cabinet position or administrative role of any kind was remotely desired on his part—though Bill Clinton would try to bring Cuomo's gifts to the Supreme Court. No, Cuomo was again looking away from Washington, most likely for good now. He had his challenges, ones he could have turned away from, had he wished to. But the work in Albany beckoned and he had decided. The 1992 presidential election would spawn many "alternative histories" and "what ifs" among political aficionados over the next several decades. It remains a mystery to many, and for good reason. There hadn't been a comparable political moment in American history, one where a party's favored candidate spurned the chance to run in such dramatic fashion and at the last minute. But it was what was to come in Washington that signaled its significance more than anything. America would not be turning away from Reaganism. There would be none of those "parades" that Cuomo spoke of from the Madison Square Garden floor in July. Clinton's years in Washington might represent a break, or a "preemption" from conservatism, historically, but it cannot be said they were a restoration of liberalism, certainly not of the stripe Cuomo had been arguing for in his adult life. Perhaps that was never possible. The alternative histories are never marshalled from reason. The questions are unanswerable, and as Peter Quinn said, Mario Cuomo took those answers "with him to the grave."

Conclusion: "With the People I Was Born and Raised Up With"

After a somber State of the State address in 1993, and with the now routine haggling over New York's budget at the beginning of a new year in Albany, Mario Cuomo was presented with the possibility of serving as a justice on the Supreme Court of the United States. It was a compelling possibility, as now President Bill Clinton, recently inaugurated, was looking to replace Justice Byron White, who was retiring at the term's end. The *Times* could not resist speculating about "the spectacle of a Justice Cuomo in verbal bash-ups with another loquacious lawyer from Queens, the right wing's Justice Antonin Scalia."[115] By all accounts, Cuomo's family favored the move—one that would have been "natural" for him. Years later, Cuomo would tell *New York* magazine, "I learned so much [as governor] that I thought it would be a waste to just bury that under a black robe and limit myself to the very important work of a justice of the Supreme Court."[116]

The process, if not the finality of Cuomo's decision, was far more tortured. By George Stephanopoulos's account, Cuomo had declined the offer, then later told Andrew, who was working as his intermediary with the Clinton White House, he'd accept it, before declining again. Cuomo then put himself back into contention by saying he'd accept a seat on the Court if Clinton offered it to him and "really put it to him."[117] Finally, 15 minutes before Clinton was to call Cuomo with the offer at 6:00 pm on June 12, Andrew called Stephanopoulos, who recalled his "stomach sinking to his knees." Cuomo was once again backing out, with Stephanopoulos's hopes dashed as his desire to get his hero on the Court had left egg on his face. "Most liberals . . . understood that Clinton wasn't really one of us," he said in his memoir. And now, the one who had transcended "McGovern, Carter, Mondale, and Dukakis"—the "only Democrat [who could] still stir the party faithful" in a manner on a par with the Kennedy brothers—was leaving the field of battle.[118] While Cuomo disputed Stephanopoulos's account later, he told the *Times*, "If George says I called him, I'm sure I called him."[119] And then he offered a final note on the matter: "To be a justice of the Supreme Court, to sit there and listen, to study, to conclude and write and not have to worry about the polls, nothing would have been more perfect," Cuomo told the *Times*. "But on the other side, I think I have probably been in a better position to speak out on the issues."[120] With Cuomo, there was always *the other side*.

For the rest of 1993, Cuomo dealt with deeply serious and at times banal issues as governor. The World Trade Center had been bombed, but remained standing. He was in a fierce legal fight with Donald J. Trump over the building of Indian casinos in New York (Trump didn't want them, saying they discriminated against him).[121] Cuomo was also busy trying to keep the Yankees from leaving New York while working to pass an anti-discrimination bill against gays—the first of its kind in the state, something he had been working on since 1991.[122] And, in an odd twist of fate, former Assembly Speaker Mel Miller's conviction for fraud was overturned.[123] Would Cuomo have run had Miller been able to stay on in late 1992? Probably not, but Miller's removal from office all but killed any realistic chance that Cuomo would have joined the race. And while Cuomo could not point to any mammoth structures he had built as governor, with the revamped West Side Highway complex still in the works, there was new ground being broken in New York City to revitalize and transform Times Square. It was an effort, Cuomo said, "to rebuild the most famous crossroads in the world."[124]

More than a year away from his reelection bid, and with Senator Al D'Amato having finished his own flirtations with challenging Cuomo for governor in 1994, there were indications that there would be another little-known Republican to take on Cuomo. It wasn't until November 9 that a Peekskill "lawyer and farmer" named George E. Pataki declared his candidacy against Cuomo.[125] Pataki's credentials, sparse as they were, included eight years in the state legislature. There seemed to be little notice or fear in the Cuomo camp. Nevertheless, half of those surveyed by Marist opposed a fourth term for Cuomo, despite his large lead over Pataki (48–24 percent) in a late 1993 poll.[126] More revealing, however, Cuomo's approval rating was at its lowest point in 11 years as governor. New Yorkers were uneasy about both Cuomo and the idea of a governor staying on for 16 years. At the year's end, Cuomo was proposing another round of tax cuts to boost his chances heading into 1994. It was a season of change—Rudolph Giuliani was now New York's Republican mayor, after having ousted David Dinkins in November. Cuomo positioned himself accordingly, with the *Times* noting that "by calling for tax cuts, a crackdown on crime and a welfare program that emphasizes work," Cuomo was trying to "outflank" Republicans determined to end his tenure as governor.[127] In Washington, the Republicans' second most powerful House member, Newt Gingrich, was making taxes and crime national issues. Clinton was thus engaged in his own flanking maneuvers as president, recognizing the national mood was dead set against the status quo. By the summer of 1994, Pataki's fundraising was outpacing Cuomo's.[128]

Back on January 7, Cuomo had said "I don't need polls to tell me that at this moment the people are concerned and angry, and they are registering their strong disapproval with those of us in command. I know that makes us underdogs as we enter this race."[129]

Cuomo was counting on heavy turnout in the African American community to reverse his fortunes. But many prominent black officials were ambivalent at best about Cuomo by 1994. "He's very condescending, very arrogant," Calvin Butts III was quoted as telling the *New York Times* weeks before the election.[130] Twenty-two years later, Butts was pained to recall events. "Well, the critical piece was we begged of him to pay more attention to the African American community in 1994 in his last campaign. We said, 'Come to Abyssinia, come to see us.' But it was sort of like, 'Where are you going to go? You gotta stick with us.' The Democratic Party, not so much him, took the black vote for granted. And we invited Pataki and he came to Abyssinia and made an appeal. And I remember it was a turning point at that time in his campaign."[131] In the end, Cuomo increased his support among black voters in 1994 over his 1990 election—but that had been a poor showing for Cuomo. In the end, he was unable to match David Dinkins's turnout among black voters—something thought to have been a necessity at the time.[132]

Try as he might, it was hard to depict a three-term governor and former party star as an underdog to the farmer from Peekskill. In the end, Cuomo was defeated by Pataki, as "an icon of liberalism" was ushered out of office in a historic wave election that led to Republicans taking control of the House and Senate for the first time in 40 years.[133] It was also the first time since 1970 that Republicans controlled a majority of the nation's statehouses.[134] Pataki gained 48.8 percent of the vote to Cuomo's 45.4 percent, becoming the first Republican governor in New York in 20 years. Even with Giuliani's backing, Cuomo made little headway with New York City's population, whose voter turnout was near a paltry 50 percent. In an election marked by the issue of crime, Cuomo lost voters who favored the death penalty—some 60 percent of those voting—by 2 to 1.[135] Cuomo, who said he did not pray for victory, was gracious to Pataki in defeat, while allowing that above all, voters were perhaps punishing him for being aloof. The *Times* saw him as philosophical rather than embittered. "Wistful? I'm from Queens. We don't get wistful. We don't get wan."[136]

Four days after the defeat, Cuomo sat down with *Times* reporter Kevin Sack for an interview in the executive mansion in Albany. He reached back to his faith after discussing the politics of it all. Campaigns are like life he said. "They start with conjecture and hope, they are filled with unexpected gifts, undeserved rejections, inexplicable pain, incredible joy, confusion, vindication, everything," Cuomo said. "How do they end? I come from a religion where the whole symbol of the religion ended in condemnation and crucifixion. But that wasn't the measure of the experience. That's just the way it ended."[137] Cuomo's last political defeat was in 1977, when he lost to Ed Koch in New York's mayoral race. He said then, "I am where most people thought I ought to have been in the beginning, and that is with the people I was born and raised up with, the people I helped protect against the blunders of politicians, with the neighborhoods, with the little people."[138]

The political history of Hudson progressivism came to an end with Mario Cuomo's defeat. George Pataki would go on to serve three of his own terms as governor, dousing, as best as he could, the embers of liberalism in the state while making his own concessions to its underlying appeal. Pataki would be succeeded by Democrat Eliot Spitzer, who had all the trappings of progressive leadership, but his tenure was marred and cut short by scandal. He did not make it to the mid-point of his first term. Likewise, David Patterson, New York's first African American governor, who succeeded Spitzer, was unable to govern effectively, as he too was damaged by personal scandal. Between Spitzer and Patterson, there were but four years of Democratic rule to Cuomo's 12. And then, finally, in 2010, Cuomo's son, Andrew, became New York's 56th governor. He was elected to a second term in 2014. It is too early to assess his tenure—there have been progressive achievements, but this Cuomo appears less comfortable governing from the ideological position of liberalism than his father. His is a decidedly results-oriented administration. But the language and attention to first principles is missing. And Andrew Cuomo views that as altogether welcome. The two Cuomos thus have had different purposes and objectives, and by all accounts, they are two very different men politically, if not temperamentally. As one Cuomo family friend put it, "Andrew is operating in the family business in the shadow of a father" who would be called "the great philosopher statesman of the American nation."[139] By any measure, no New York governor—or Democratic political figure since Mario Cuomo—has captured the national spotlight as progressive political spokesman for as long as Cuomo held it; nor has anyone matched his conviction and ranging intellect. While Andrew Cuomo's legacy is still unfolding, by design, it will unquestionably be his own, not his father's.

On January 2, 2015, Mario Cuomo died at age 82, just six hours after his son had been sworn in to begin his second term as governor. At the funeral, Andrew Cuomo said his father "wasn't really a politician at all. At his core, at his best," he said, "he was a philosopher and he was a poet. And he was an advocate and a crusader. Mario Cuomo was the keynote speaker for our better angels."[140] They were elegant and well-chosen words. They capture the essence of Cuomo, if not his totality. For the more complete picture must acknowledge that Mario Cuomo *did* govern, that he was a leader, as he had suggested, of "more than words." But he was also limited as a man governing out of his time, against a tide of politics that was washing out the old ways. His rule therefore had to be as devoted to speech as to the world as it was. George Stephanopoulos had upon reflection, called him *"Our Reagan."*[141] But in truth, that figure has not come, as Cuomo's time reflected the wilderness years of his party. While he was not ultimately, the titanic national leader hoped for by so many liberals, Cuomo's was undoubtedly that *John* voice that predates political resurrection. Cuomo was not Reagan. But like no other, he held up a banner on the rampart for that longed-for appearance. He held it high, where it remains.

Epilogue: Tramonti

THERE IS NO easy route to Tramonti, Italy. One embarks on the Autostrade, the main highway from Naples, but is soon thrown into a small world of hills, more like little mountains, and winding roads that undulate without end. When my research assistant Àngels Miralda and I reached the Municipio—the local town hall, set amid so many red tiled roofs surrounded by green cliffs, we encountered a sole policeman, quietly at his desk filing papers. "Where can we find records about Mario Cuomo?" I asked, and then waited, as the translation from Àngels came back to me. "If you want to know about Mario Cuomo, you should see Giordano Maddalena. She is up the hill near the church, and she will tell you all you want to know," he said.

After a short drive we rang the bell to what from outside looked to be a rather large apartment complex. It soon revealed itself to be a small home—a kind of petit villa. "We are here from America— an American professor wishes to talk to you about Mario Cuomo," Àngels pleaded in Italian. "Well, who sent you?" came the reply, before we explained it was the policeman at the Municipio who had sent us. "What can *I* tell you?" replied the voice.[1] But we were soon buzzed in.

Before long, an older, strongly built woman appeared, hair streaked with blonde highlights, wearing red Max Mara glasses and a yellow housedress. She was Maddalena Cuomo, cousin of the former governor of New York. "How can I help you?" Before long we were invited into her home, where in the kitchen hung an autographed photo of Mario Cuomo. After small talk and some time overlooking the grounds where the young mother of Mario Cuomo, Immacolatta, was raised, she told us of the old times, how Cuomo's parents had been married in the quaint church just down the road. Over freshly brewed Italian coffee, I summoned the courage to ask a question I feared might end the conversation altogether: "Why didn't Mario Cuomo ever run for the presidency?"

"I will tell you," Maddalena said, firmly. "He was told by the Mafia—in both America and Italy—that he would end up like John Kennedy if he did. He was for the blacks *("per i neri)*, and for the poor *("per i poveri")*. He was going to be bad for business. And they threatened his life."

Why was she talking about this so casually now, to strangers no less? "The world has changed. That was thirty years ago. You have Obama now. Things are different. People didn't talk about it then, but now, it is talked about here all the time," she insisted.

"Ask her, Àngels, 'What about Andrew Cuomo, would such a threat be placed against him today if he decided to run?'" "No," came the reply. "Things are different now." Àngels, speaking slowly in Italian, recounted our conversation a few nights earlier with some university experts on southern Italy while in Rome—Vanda Wilcox from John Cabot University and Nick Dines of Middlesex University in London; we were told that the Mafia, centered in Naples, "had no reach," in fact, in the small town of Tramonti. We relayed this to Maddalena, anxious for her response. She absorbed the observation for a moment and then, looking away, gave a short, chilling laugh.

I did not visit the birthplace of Cuomo's parents with the express purpose of unearthing some heretofore undisclosed ties to organized crime. I was interested in Cuomo's family as economic and perhaps political migrants—people leaving southern Italy during the fascist era out of fear or some longing. I wanted to learn about the experience of Rosario Cuomo (Mario's father's cousin) in the Italian Army, whether the Cuomos, like many other Italian families, had brought a more conservative political orientation with them to the United States in the 1920s and 1930s, and how this might have contributed to their slower movement to New Deal politics than other immigrant groups of that time. I was also hoping to glean more of how a young Mario Cuomo might have experienced liberal politics through a familial worldview perhaps less inclined to see the role of the state in the lives of its citizens favorably. But the question of La Camorra—the Neapolitan mob—was thankfully raised by someone other than me. And I was admittedly curious.

In our conversation, Maddalena spoke of Cuomo's mother, Immacolatta, receiving death threats from La Camorra over the phone. She said Immacolatta feared for her son's life and reminded him of "what happened to the last Catholic president." According to Maddalena, Cuomo's mother advised him not to run. She held to this story the following summer of 2013, when I visited Tramonti again. I went back hoping to learn more of whatever I could. For starters, Maddalena had told me during my first visit that Cuomo was not born in the United States but was rather born in Italy—an astounding claim. Could Cuomo have been "birthered" before Obama? Was this an explanation for his not running? It was an intriguing and extraordinary remark, one repeated to us later by another Tramonti local. I thought with Ángels's assistance, I could track down the relevant birth records while perhaps getting other local accounts of Maddalena's theory about La Camorra and Cuomo.

We started out on July 23, 2013, for Nocera Superiore, where Andrea Cuomo was raised. If in fact Mario Cuomo had been born in Italy, his father's hometown was the place to check.[2] In meeting with Gigi Mauro, Nocera's municipal registrar, it became apparent that there was no record of an Italian birth for Mario Cuomo, at least as far as official records went. And Mauro provided his own recollection of Cuomo's Brooklyn birth. Later that day, Maddalena brought us to meet her cousin Anna, whose memory was impeccable. She too confirmed that Mario's older brother Frank was born in Italy to Andrea and Immacolatta, and that Mario was born in Brooklyn, giving the correct birth years for both off the top of her head. Maddalena deferred to Anna's authority and that was that.

Sort of.

Gigi Mauro had also mentioned Cuomo's wife Matilda's concern with the ubiquity of the Cuomo name in southern Italy, and how many Cuomos were, in his words, "not with the law."[3] Many "Cuomos"hoped to use their surname to ingratiate themselves with the governor during her visit to Nocera in the 1980s. Another Cuomo cousin, Rosy, would confirm as much during our visit to her business in Nocera on July 26, 2013. There were lots of Cuomos running around it seemed, but not *the* Cuomos related to Mario, Rosy noted.[4] This was not hard to see as there was at least one street in Tramonti—via Cuomo—that I had mistakenly thought was named in honor of Mario Cuomo, only to learn it bore no relation to him whatsoever. The number of Cuomos in the archives in Nocera and the businesses in and around Naples and even down to Salerno proved how common the name was. In effect, it would mean nothing to suggest or even substantiate that there were Cuomos connected somehow to organized crime in southern Italy. It's akin to noting that the Smiths and Fitzgeralds have Wall Street connections. They'd be there if you bothered to look. The *New York Times* reported on this in 1983, noting how in Nocera, after Cuomo became New York's first Italian American governor, "all of a sudden, everyone [became] a relative," at least by one local's account.[5]

Would Cuomo not have run for the presidency to spare his family even this tangential and unrelated (yet journalistically simple) connection that might well have been made? It's ultimately unknowable, but I find it unconvincing to say the least—any more than Cuomo would have halted a run for the White House over one or more threatening phone calls (giving Maddalena's memory on this front the benefit of the doubt). Public officials, even at Cuomo's level, live with that sort of thing. Would the media's closer scrutiny and intrusion upon his family have been seen by him as simply not worth it? Perhaps, but again, this is a great stretch, one that can be bested with other, and I think more proximate, explanations. And yet, just several months before I finished this book, reports began circulating from a *Guardian* article whose headline read "Mafia planned to kill Mario Cuomo during trip as New York governor."[6] The article claimed Cuomo was "targeted for assassination by the Sicilian mafia."[7] The report was based on the "confession" of Maurizio Avola, who is serving a life sentence for his role in 43 murders. This was to have been a hit directed at the Italian state rather than the Cuomos per se, the *Guardian* reported, as Cosa Nostra (the Sicilian mob) wanted to send a message that those who testify against the organization and seek refuge in the United States would not go unpunished. Avola told the *Guardian* that the assassination was to take place during a Cuomo visit to Messina, but it was called off as "the American politician arrived with extremely tight surveillance, lots of bodyguards and a bullet-proof car. It made the assassination impossible."[8]

What can be made of such claims? For starters, Cuomo's visit occurred well after he declared that he was no longer a presidential candidate. In fact, Cuomo arrived in Rome weeks after the election, on November 19, 1992. If Avola is to be believed, the attempt on Cuomo's life was not dependent upon his becoming president; he was an equally good target and political "symbol" (the term Avola used) as governor. Beyond this is the question of whether Cuomo would have balked at a run knowing of these types of threats. He'd certainly want Matilda's support. Didn't Alma Powell, at least by a number of accounts, dissuade her husband Colin Powell, from seeking the presidency in 1996 because of her fear of a possible assassination against the nation's prospective first black president?[9] For the record, Cuomo had always said any presumed ties to the mob would be a reason he *would* run, rather than not. The thought of disproving such an association, one Cuomo was subtly tagged with his whole political life, would have fueled his fire, he had suggested. Again, the answer is unknowable, but there are likelier, and perhaps less remarkable, reasons that Cuomo elected not to enter the 1992 race—at least until proven otherwise. Nevertheless, I did during the course of my research make an official request to the Federal Bureau of Investigation to release its file on Mario M. Cuomo through a Freedom of Information Act (FOIA) request. The FBI's response proved unsatisfactory, if not a touch ominous:

> For your information the records . . . which may be respon-sive to your Freedom of Information Acts (FOIA) request, were destroyed on 2/11/1989 and 11/20/2005. Since this material could not be reviewed, it is not known if it was responsive to your request.[10]

I have not to date appealed the denial, as I was notified I could at the letter's end. I may yet, but it's hard to argue for destroyed documents.

The search for some Rosetta stone to unlock the mystery of Mario Cuomo has proven facile. He had told us all along about his deep-est motivations and interests. He made allusions to Andrea in his speeches—almost always in some self-deprecating way: he didn't need or covet the *cerimonia*, that elegant Italian word Cuomo used, channeling his father, to convey the pomp of politics. The big house in Albany was big enough—better than he could have imagined. Being governor was as great a blessing as any—to ask or want for more would be almost profane. *He was the governor of the greatest state in the greatest country in the only world we know.* All these things were more than enough.

In *Federalist* 72, Alexander Hamilton makes an intriguing argument for rejecting term limits in the American presidency. "Even the love of fame, the ruling passion of the noblest minds," Hamilton wrote, would deter a leader from launching into an office knowing "that he must quit the scene before he could accomplish the work."[11] But Cuomo's love of fame, a love he surely knew he had, and part of his own self-effacement, was attached to another, smaller scene, one he did not wish to quit. It was a level of fame commensurate with his best self-image, one cultivated at least since prep school, where the Vincentians instructed him against vainglory and the temptations of this world. In this sense, Cuomo was least like the statesman Madison had in mind in *Federalist* 51. Cuomo countered his own ambition. He had been taught to do so, first by Andrea, and then the Vincentians. It was, ironically enough, not his desire to want more. "You have to really put it to him," Andrew had told George Stephanopoulos about the Supreme Court offer. *He was going to have to be made to take it.* To be told he was needed, convinced, that his own desires were somehow not in play.

I met Mario Cuomo only once, sometime after his defeat to George Pataki, back in the mid-1990s. He had returned to practicing law in New York, and it was there, on the streets of Manhattan, somewhere on the East Side between 3rd and Lexington Avenues, where I ran into him. I was with my cousin, who was also practicing law at the time, and we both knew immediately who was walking in front of us. We stopped him to say hello, and to thank him for his time as governor. He asked about the schools we attended. David had recently graduated from New York University's School of Law, and that drew a smile from Cuomo. We made a bit more small talk, and now others started to approach. Other New Yorkers were hovering a bit and giving their thanks, some calling out from a distance. Cuomo, pressed for time, came back to me. "And what about *you?*" I told him I had recently finished my undergraduate degree at Georgetown. Perhaps sensing his opportunity, he smiled, and with a wave of the hand and feigned disappointment, exclaimed, "Jesuits!"

He then turned, and was gone.

Notes

PROLOGUE

1. "Cuomo Rejects Bid for President in '92," *Washington Post*, December 21, 1991.
2. Bruce Miroff, *The Liberals' Moment: The McGovern Insurgency and the Identity Crisis of the Democratic Party*, Lawrence: University Press of Kansas, 2007, 45. Author's telephone interview with Joseph (Joe) Grandmaison, Tuesday, September 30, 2014.
3. Author's telephone interview with Joseph (Joe) Grandmaison, Tuesday, September 30, 2014.
4. Author's telephone interview with Joseph (Joe) Grandmaison, Tuesday, September 30, 2014.
5. "Cuomo Won't Run for the Presidency," *Newsday*, December 21, 1991.
6. "In Concord, It's Ready, Set, but No Go," *Newsday*, December 21, 1991.
7. Author's telephone interview with Joseph (Joe) Grandmaison, Tuesday, September 30, 2014.
8. "Cuomo Says He Will Not Run for President in '92," *New York Times*, December 21, 1991.
9. "The Mario Effect: Last Time a Group of Presidential Challengers Was This Unimpressive, There Was a Reason," *Capital Playbook*, Steve Kornacki, April 10, 2011, http://www.capitalnewyork.com/article/politics/2011/04/1812706/mario-effect-last-time-group-presidential-challengers-was-unimpress?page=all.
10. "Cuomo Says He Will Not Run for President in '92," *New York Times*, December 21, 1991.
11. This was Robert S. McElvaine's 1988 book *Mario Cuomo: A Biography*. Cuomo did not run for the presidency in 1988.

12. Saladin Ambar, "The Rise of the Sunbelt Governors: Conservative Outsiders in the White House," *Presidential Studies Quarterly*, March 2014.
13. David Marannis, *First in His Class: A Biography of Bill Clinton*, New York: Simon and Schuster, 1995, 417.
14. "Cuomo Says a Bid for Presidency Would Rule Out a 2d Term in '86," *New York Times*, September 30, 1984.
15. New York State Archives, Albany, New York, Series 13682, Campaign Finance/Presidency, Boxes 113, 114.
16. Author's telephone interview with Joseph (Joe) Grandmaison, Tuesday, September 30, 2014.

Part One

1. "Giovane, entusiasta, fiducioso il congressman Florio deciso a diventare governatore del NJ," *Il Progresso Italo-Americano*, May 1, 1977.
2. "Cuomo ufficialmente candidato a sindaco," *Il Progresso Italo-Americano*, May 11, 1977.
3. See Bruce Miroff on the Democratic Party and identity politics in the McGovern campaign in *The Liberals' Moment: The McGovern Insurgency and the Identity Crisis of the Democratic Party*, Lawrence: University Press of Kansas, 2007, 300–301.
4. Daniel Patrick Moynihan, *Daniel Patrick Moynihan: A Portrait in Letters of an American Visionary*, edited by Steven R. Weisman, New York: Public Affairs, 2010, 463.
5. John Dickie, *Darkest Italy: The Nation and Stereotypes of the Mezzogiorno, 1860–1900*, New York: St. Martin's Press, 1999, 1.
6. Matthew Frye Jacobson, *Whiteness of a Different Color: European Immigrants and the Alchemy of Race*, Cambridge, MA: Harvard University Press, 1998, 62.
7. Eagleton Institute of Politics, Center on the Governor, Rutgers University fireside chat with NJ Governor Thomas Kean, December 14, 2010. https://www.youtube.com/watch?v=YvEVRf5Mt70. The full quote is "I was regarded as a liberal Democrat and that made me laugh," Cuomo said, "because I had been rejected in my first campaign because I was Italian American, Catholic, President of the Italian American Lawyers Guild, had five children and had big hands."
8. Robert S. McElvaine, *Mario Cuomo: A Biography*, New York: Charles Scribner's Sons, 1988, 409.
9. Daniel J. Tichenor, *Dividing Lines: The Politics of Immigration Control in America*, Princeton, NJ: Princeton University Press, 2002, 130.
10. See Adrian Lyttelton, *Liberal and Fascist Italy*, Oxford: Oxford University Press, 2002, 108.
11. Nathan Glazer and Daniel Patrick Moynihan, *Beyond the Melting Pot: The Negroes, Puerto Ricans, Jews, Italians, and Irish of New York City*, Cambridge, MA: MIT Press, 1976, 184.

12. Donna Gabaccia, "When the Migrants Are Men," in Donna Gabaccia and Vicki Ruiz, eds., *American Dreaming, Global Realities: Rethinking US Immigration History*, Chicago: University of Illinois Press, 2006, 193.

13. It was precisely this image that at least for a moment, fused what Ira Katznelson has described as the "boundaries between ethnicity, race, and territoriality" with regard to urban politics, and that of class. Ira Katznelson, *City Trenches: Urban Politics and the Patterning of Class in the United States*, Chicago: University of Chicago Press, 1981, 6.

14. "Profiles: Governor-1," *New Yorker*, April 9, 1984.

15. H. Paul Jeffers, *The Napoleon of New York: Mayor Fiorello LaGuardia*, New York: John Wiley, 2002, 284.

16. Frank Freidel, *Roosevelt: A Rendezvous with Destiny*, Boston: Little, Brown, 1990, 270.

17. Conrad Black suggests Roosevelt's support among Italian Americans— based in part on his "cautious policy during the Spanish American War"—helped keep a number of important states (including New York) in his win column in the 1940 election. Conrad Black, *Franklin Delano Roosevelt: Champion of Freedom*, New York: Public Affairs, 2003, 599.

18. Mason B. Williams, *City of Ambition: FDR, La Guardia, and the Making of Modern New York*, New York: W.W. Norton, 2014, xi.

19. Ibid., 77.

20. Andrew E. Busch, *Reagan's Victory: The Presidential Election of 1980 and the Rise of the Right*, Lawrence: University Press of Kansas, 2005, 127.

21. In this vein, Stuart Hall wrote, "We would get much further along the road to understanding how the regime of capital can function *through* differentiation and difference, rather than through similarity and identity, if we took more seriously this question of the cultural, social, national, ethnic, and gendered composition of historically different and specific forms of labour." Stuart Hall, "Gramsci's Relevance to the Analysis of Racism and Ethnicity," UNESCO, August 1, 1985.

22. McElvaine, 72.

23. *Vincentian*, {1952}

24. Ibid., 79.

25. Ibid., 80.

26. All quotes from Dr. Nicholas D'Arienzo are from the author's interview with him on February 23, 2015.

27. Author's interview with Joseph Mattone in his Queens office, February 6, 2015. Glenn's *A Class Manual in Formal Logic* was published in 1947.

28. McElvaine, 82.

29. From Woodward's forthcoming book *Getting Religion*. Woodward is a former religion editor at *Newsweek*, http://www.firstthings.com/article/2015/03/a-joust-with-mario-cuomo.

30. Pierre Teilhard de Chardin, *The Divine Milieu*, New York: Harper Perennial, 1960, 22.
31. McElvaine, 84.
32. "The Prose (and Poetry) of Mario M. Cuomo," *Atlantic*, December 1990, http://www.theatlantic.com/past/docs/issues/90dec/cuomo.htm.
33. Ibid.
34. Ibid.
35. Author's interview with Joseph Mattone, February 6, 2015.
36. McElvaine, 164.
37. Ibid, 164.
38. Robert A. Caro, *The Power Broker: Robert Moses and the Fall of New York*, New York: Vintage, 1974.
39. "Willets Point, This Era's Cuomo?" *Crain's New York Business*, September 23, 2007, http://www.crainsnewyork.com/article/20070923/SUB/70922025/willets-point-this-eras-cuomo.
40. "City Acts to Foil Queens Park Foes," *New York Times*, August 14, 1964.
41. Roberta Brandes Gratz, *The Battle for Gotham: New York in the Shadow of Robert Moses and Jane Jacobs*, New York: Nation Books, 2010, 292.
42. McElvaine, 169.
43. Ibid., 169.
44. "City Acts to Foil Queens Park Foes," *New York Times*, August 14, 1964.
45. "Willets Point: A Development Waterloo?" *New York Observer*, February 19, 2008, http://observer.com/2008/02/willets-point-a-development-waterloo/.
46. "The Prose (and Poetry) of Mario M. Cuomo," *Atlantic*, December 1990.
47. McElvaine, 172.
48. Ibid., 172.
49. Mario Cuomo, *Forest Hills Diary: The Crisis of Low-Income Housing*, New York: Random House, 1974, 6.
50. McElvaine, 172.
51. Richard Sennett, *The Fall of Public Man*, New York: W.W. Norton, 1976, 301.
52. Douglas S. Massey and Nancy Denton, *American Apartheid: Segregation and the Making of the Underclass*, Cambridge, MA: Harvard University Press, 1993, 56.
53. McElvaine, 173.
54. The author cannot account for the "missing" 10 homes in this *Newsday* account. "Beat City Hall": Corona Does It," *Newsday*, December 2, 1970.
55. Ibid.
56. "Out of the Melting Pot, into the Race," *Newsday*, April 21, 1974.
57. *New Yorker*, July 18, 1977
58. "A Curious Politician," *New York Review of Books*, September 19, 1974.
59. McElvaine, 179.

60. Cuomo, *Forest Hills Diary*, 8.
61. McElvaine, 181.
62. Ibid.
63. Ibid., 180.
64. "The Queens Theme: Niggers Get Out!" *Amsterdam News*, October 28, 1972.
65. Joseph P. Viteritti, ed., *Summer in the City: John Lindsay, New York, and the American Dream*, Baltimore: Johns Hopkins University Press, 2014, 67–68.
66. McElvaine, 183.
67. "Forest Hills: No Compromise," *Amsterdam News*, July 22, 1972.
68. "Forest Hills 'Solution' Pleases No One," *Newsday*, July 27, 1972.
69. "Lindsay Backs Forest Hills Cutback," *Newsday*, July 27, 1972.
70. Cuomo, *Forest Hills Diary*, 138.
71. Mario Cuomo, *Report of Investigation Concerning Forest Hills Low-Income Housing Project*, July 25, 1972, 5, http://chpcny.org/assets/MarioCuomo-Forest-Hills-Report.pdf.
72. Ibid.,14.
73. "To Run, or Not to Run," *New York Magazine*, March 21, 1977. Cuomo biographer McElvaine writes that the position offered by Carey was for City Council president. McElvaine, 196.
74. St. John's would go on to have three graduates serving simultaneously as governor: Cuomo in New York, George Deukmejian in California, and Alex Farrelly, in the US Virgin Islands.
75. Cuomo, *Forest Hills Diary*, xii.
76. "To Run, or Not to Run," *New York Magazine*, March 21, 1977.
77. Author's interview with Joseph Mattone, February 6, 2015.
78. Troy, who was later to betray Cuomo's trust, was the Queens County Democratic Chairman. McElvaine, 199.
79. "Cuomo Rising," *Village Voice*, April 18, 1977.
80. Ibid.
81. "Around City Hall," *New Yorker*, June 27, 1977.
82. Interestingly, William Safire attributed President Ronald Reagan's use of "Forgive me," which often prefaced controversial remarks in his speeches to a form of parrhesia. Safire likewise linked an early modern appearance of the rhetorical device to Cicero. See William Safire, "On Language: Forgive Me, But," *New York Times*, October 21, 1984.
83. McElvaine, 200.
84. Ibid., 203.
85. Eagleton Institute of Politics, Center on the Governor, Rutgers University fireside chat with NJ Governor Thomas Kean, December 14, 2010, https://www.youtube.com/watch?v=YvEVRf5Mt70.
86. Jonathan Soffer, *Ed Koch and the Rebuilding of New York City*, New York: Columbia University Press, 2010, 111.
87. "How Not to Be a Candidate," *Newsday*, June 14, 1974.
88. "Out of the Melting Pot, into the Race," *Newsday*, April 21, 1974.

89. McElvaine, 211.
90. "Around City Hall," *New Yorker*, September 30, 1974.
91. Ibid.
92. Ibid.
93. Ibid.
94. "Cuomo May Be NY Ombudsman," *Newsday*, December 11, 1974.
95. McElvaine, 212.
96. "Cuomo May Be NY Ombudsman," *Newsday*, December 11, 1974.
97. "Democrats Flounder in Search of a Leader," *Newsday*, December 4, 1976.
98. "Democrats Weigh Cuomo for Nassau," *Newsday*, June 18, 1976.
99. "Trying Hard to Be Only Number 2," *Newsday*, September 7, 1974.
100. "Carey's Appeal Gets Italian Dressing," *Newsday*, October 24, 1974.
101. "'Freebies' Are a Way of Life in Albany," *Newsday*, May 12, 1975.
102. "Cuomo Finds Lobbyist within Law," *Newsday*, March 4, 1975.
103. McElvaine, 215.
104. Dall Forsythe, "The Governor of New York," in Gerald Benjamin, ed., *The Oxford Handbook of New York State Government and Politics*, New York: Oxford University Press, 2012, 268.
105. McElvaine, 216.
106. Ibid., 217.
107. Soffer, 119.
108. "Carey Urges Less Localities' Aid, Budget Cut, 10c Gasoline Tax Rise," *New York Times*, January 9, 1975.
109. McElvaine, 227.
110. "Battle of the Brains: Lehrman vs. Cuomo," *New York Magazine*, November 1, 1982.
111. "Around City Hall," *New Yorker*, July 18, 1977.
112. Ibid.
113. Ibid.
114. Ibid.
115. Ibid.
116. "Around City Hall," *New Yorker*, May 30, 1977.
117. Ibid.
118. "Around City Hall," *New Yorker*, September 5, 1977.
119. Ibid.
120. Ibid.
121. "Koch, Cuomo Debate," *Newsday*, September 15, 1977.
122. Ibid.
123. McElvaine, 250.
124. "Carey: Decision on Cuomo Inevitable," *Newsday*, October 2, 1977.
125. "Koch Decries 'Scurrilous Tactic,'" *Newsday*, October 1977.
126. Ibid.
127. Mario Cuomo, *Diaries of Mario M. Cuomo: The Campaign for Governor*, New York, Random House, 1984, 251.
128. Soffer, 139.

129. Michael Snayerson, *The Contender: Andrew Cuomo*, New York: Twelve, 2015, 37–38.
130. McElvaine, 254,
131. Ibid., 251.
132. "Poll: Koch Far Ahead," *Newsday*, November 4, 1977.
133. "Koch, Bellamy Sweep in City," *Newsday*, November 9, 1977.
134. "Democrat Is Mayor," *New York Times*, November 9, 1977.
135. "Statistics Spoil Cuomo's Dream," *Newsday*, November 9, 1977.
136. "Around City Hall," *New Yorker*, November 21, 1977. The line was quoted by Pete Hamill of the *Daily News* on October 28, 1977.
137. Krupsak had "felt shut out of Carey's inner circle." "Around City Hall," *New Yorker*, August 7, 1978.
138. McElvaine, 264.
139. "Around City Hall," *New Yorker*, August 7, 1978.
140. "News You Probably Missed," *New York Magazine*, August 28, 1978.
141. McElvaine, 267.
142. Peter W. Colby, ed., *New York State Today: Politics, Government, Public Policy*, Albany: State University of New York Press, 1985, 86.
143. McElvaine, 269.
144. Cuomo, *Diaries of Mario M. Cuomo*, 25–26.
145. Ibid., 30, 45.
146. McElvaine, 273.
147. Ibid., 280.
148. Cuomo, *Diaries of Mario M. Cuomo*, diary entry, September 22, 1981.
149. "Profiles: Governor—I," *New Yorker*, April 9, 1984.
150. Cuomo, *Diaries of Mario M. Cuomo*, diary entry, January 15, 1982.
151. "Profiles: Governor—I," *New Yorker*, April 9, 1984.
152. "Cuomo Enters Gubernatorial Race against Koch," *New York Times*, March 17, 1982.
153. Around City Hall, *New Yorker*, March 22, 1982.
154. McElvaine, 289
155. Soffer, 232.
156. Ibid., 233.
157. "Cuomo's War Chest No Match for Koch's," *New York Times*, July 17, 1982.
158. "Mayor Delivers a Strong Attack against Reagan," *New York Times*, September 1, 1982.
159. Cuomo, *Diaries of Mario Cuomo*, 149.
160. "Excerpts from the Remarks by Cuomo, Koch, and Leherman (sp.)," *New York Times*, September 24, 1982.
161. Author's interview with Ray Scheppach, November 21, 2014.
162. "Excerpts from the Remarks by Cuomo, Koch, and Leherman (sp.)," *New York Times*, September 24, 1982.
163. Cuomo, *Diaries of Mario M. Cuomo*, 319.
164. Cuomo, *Diaries of Mario M. Cuomo*, diary entry, October 28, 1982.
165. McElvaine, 299.

166. "Aide Says Reagan Visit for Lehrman Is Unlikely," *New York Times*, September 28, 1982.

167. "The New York Primary; Cuomo Sticking with Familiar Style," *New York Times*, September 25, 1982.

168. "Cuomo, a Politician Who Hates Politics, Is Running Hard to Be the Governor," *New York Times*, October 22, 1982. The quote is attributed to union leader, Norman Adler.

169. "Mario Cuomo for New York," *New York Times*, October 28, 1982.

170. "Male-Female Split on Politics Found a Key Factor in Polls," *New York Times*, October 27, 1982.

171. "The New York Gubernatorial Campaign: A Referendum with National Overtones," *New York Times*, October 31, 1982.

172. "Around City Hall," *New Yorker*, November 22, 1982.

173. Ibid.

174. McElvaine, 303.

175. Cuomo, *Diaries of Mario M. Cuomo*, diary entry, November 3, 1982.

176. Soffer, 234.

177. "Profiles: Governor—I," *New Yorker*, April 9, 1984.

178. Mario Cuomo, *More Than Words: The Speeches of Mario Cuomo*, New York: St. Martin's Press, 1993, 7.

179. Cicero was consul of Rome in 63 bc and increased his fame tremendously by defeating the conspiracy of Catiline. Cicero was ultimately displeased to draw the governorship of Cilicia, at Pompey's behest. His tenure was a short-lived one month. Author conversation with Peter Dennis Bathory.

180. Ibid. My transcription of Cuomo's 1983 Inaugural is taken from both his written text and television coverage of the live speech, which included a number of ad lib additions, https://www.youtube.com/watch?v=5SvwQ_7mB5k.

181. Ibid.

182. Ibid., 9.

183. Ibid.

184. Ibid.

185. Ibid., 10.

186. Ibid.

187. Ibid., 11.

188. Ibid., 12.

189. These were not part of Cuomo's formal remarks, https://www.youtube.com/watch?v=5SvwQ_7mB5k.

190. McElvaine, 306.

191. "Elected Blacks Hail Cuomo's Inaugural," *Amsterdam News*, January 8, 1983.

192. "NAACP Sees Closer Ties with Governor," *Amsterdam News*, January 15, 1983.

193. Cuomo, *Diaries of Mario M. Cuomo*, diary entry, January 1, 1983.

194. Ibid.

195. Mario Cuomo, *More Than Words*, 11.

PART TWO

1. "Around City Hall," *New Yorker*, June 13, 1983
2. "Cuomo's First Year: Pride and Disillusion," *Newsday*, January 1, 1984.
3. Ibid.
4. "Profiles: Governor—I," *New Yorker*, April 9, 1984.
5. "Cuomo's First Year: Pride and Disillusion," *Newsday*, January 1, 1984.
6. Ibid.
7. "Cuomo's Minority Appointments," *Amsterdam News*, January 7, 1984.
8. "Cuomo's 1st Year: Style Is Hands On," *Newsday*, January 17, 1984.
9. "Cuomo's First Year: Pride and Disillusion," *Newsday*, January 1, 1984.
10. "Cuomo Urged to Pare Objectives," *Newsday*, January 8, 1984.
11. "For Cuomo, Revolt in Ranks," *Newsday*, January 17, 1984.
12. Robert S. McElvaine, *Mario Cuomo: A Biography*, New York: Charles Scribner's Sons, 1988, 313.
13. Ibid., 310.
14. Ibid., 311
15. "The Prison Industrial Complex," *Atlantic*, December 1998, http://www.theatlantic.com/magazine/archive/1998/12/the-prison-industrial-complex/304669/.
16. "Setting the State's Course for a Political Year," *Newsday*, January 5, 1984.
17. Ibid.
18. Author telephone interview with the Reverend Dr. Calvin Butts, III, June 9, 2016.
19. "Cuomo's First Year: Pride and Disillusion," *Newsday*, January 1, 1984.
20. McElvaine, 339.
21. "In Hart's Words, An Echo of Cuomo," *Newsday*, March 30, 1984.
22. Ibid.
23. "Cuomo's Liberalism Remains Faithful to Traditional Values," *Newsday*, June 4, 1984.
24. "Reagan Theme Recast," *Newsday*, January 5, 1984.
25. "Around City Hall," *New Yorker*, September 26, 1983.
26. "Result of the Primary '82; Cuomo and Koch Are Out of the Race for the Vice-Presidential Nomination," *New York Times*, June 19, 1984.
27. Ibid.
28. "Reagan's Recession," Pew Research Center, December 14, 2010, http://www.pewresearch.org/2010/12/14/reagans-recession/.
29. "Around City Hall," *New Yorker*, December 26, 1983.
30. "Reagan's Recession, Pew Research Center, December 14, 2010, http://www.pewresearch.org/2010/12/14/reagans-recession/.
31. "Cuomo Named Keynote Speaker," *New York Times*, June 22, 1984.
32. "Around City Hall," *New Yorker*, June 18, 1984.
33. "Cuomo Named Keynote Speaker," *New York Times*, June 22, 1984.
34. Reagan ridiculed the Ferraro pick as tokenism. Referring to Great Britain's Margaret Thatcher, Reagan said that unlike Ferraro, Thatcher was chosen "not because she was a woman but because she was the best person for the job." "Ron: I pick by merit," *New York Daily News*, July 14, 1984.

35. Quoted in Michael Nelson, ed., *The Elections of 1984*, Washington, DC: Congressional Quarterly, 260.

36. "The Governor Has Faded, but He Still Has Promise," *Newsday*, February 12, 1984.

37. "Glad It Wasn't Mario," *New York Daily News*, July 15, 1984.

38. "Cuomo, un Uomo," *National Review*, July 13, 1984.

39. "A Political Journal," *New Yorker*, August 13, 1984.

40. Ibid.

41. Ibid.

42. Ibid.

43. "Just Call Him Foxhole Fritz," *New York Daily News*, July 1, 1984.

44. "Cuomo Is Tuning Up for Keynote," *Newsday*, July 9, 1984.

45. Andrew M. Cuomo, *All Things Possible: Setbacks and Success in Politics and Life*, New York: HarperCollins, 2014, 81–82.

46. My two sources for recounting the address are from Cuomo's published version of the speech found in his book *More than Words: The Speeches of Mario Cuomo,* and C-Span's coverage of the address as delivered. Cuomo delivered a number of ad-libbed lines. The full text of the speech can be found in the Appendix to More than Words. http://www.c-span.org/video/?3443-1/mario-cuomo-19322015.

47. All subsequent quotes from this address are taken from the remarks delivered on C-Span cited above, again, not to be confused with the printed text.

48. The concept seems to originate (at least in more recent decades) with Winston Churchill's physician Lord Moran. See Thurston Clarke's discussion in *Ask Not: The Inauguration of John F. Kennedy and the Speech that Changed America*, New York: Penguin, 2004, 75–76.

49. Author's email exchange with Elizabeth Drew, August 18, 2015.

50. "A Political Journal," *New Yorker*, August 13, 1984.

51. David Axelrod, *Believer: My Forty Years in Politics*, New York: Penguin Press, 2015, 160.

52. Douglas Brinkley, ed., *The Reagan Diaries*, New York: Harper Collins, 2007, 255.

53. David Maraniss, *First in His Class: A Biography of Bill Clinton*, New York: Simon and Schuster, 1995, 417.

54. "A Political Journal," *New Yorker*, August 13, 1984.

55. Wilson Carey McWilliams, *Redeeming Democracy in America*, edited by Patrick J. Deneen and Susan J. McWilliams, Lawrence: University Press of Kansas, 2011, 179.

56. "Around City Hall," *New Yorker*, August 20, 1984.

57. "Essay: The Unhappy Family," *New York Times*, July 20, 1984.

58. Kenneth S. Baer, *Reinventing Democrats: The Politics of Liberalism from Reagan to Clinton*, Lawrence: University Press of Kansas, 2000, 58–62

59. Official Proceedings of the 1984 Democratic National Convention, Democratic National Committee: Washington, DC, 1984, 217.

60. Lou Cannon, *Governor Reagan: His Rise to Power*, New York: Public Affairs, 2003, 177.
61. I've updated Winthrop's old English spelling here. See his speech in Isaac Kramnick and Theodore Lowi's edited volume, *American Political Thought*, New York: W.W. Norton, 2009, 16.
62. McElvaine, 349.
63. "The Chord Cuomo Struck Still Hasn't Stopped Resonating," *Newsday*, July 18, 1984.
64. "A Political Journal," *New Yorker*, August 13, 1984.
65. "A Revival Meeting," *New York Times*, July 22, 1984.
66. "Mario Cuomo: A Lawyer's Brief for America," *Amsterdam News*, July 21, 1984.
67. Author telephone interview with the Reverend Dr. Calvin Butts, III, June 9, 2016.
68. "The Morning After," *New York Daily News*, July 19, 1984.
69. "Bravo Mario!" *New York Daily News*, July 18, 1984.
70. "Essay; The Unhappy Family," *New York Times*, July 20, 1984.
71. "Around City Hall," *New Yorker*, August 20, 1984.
72. "Liberalism Old and Eloquent," *Newsday*, July 19, 1984.
73. "Grading Cuomo: C for Substance, A for Delivery," *Newsday*, July 19, 1984.
74. "A Buoyant Cuomo Plans Administrative Shakeup," *Newsday*, July 18, 1984.
75. "A Political Journal," *New Yorker*, August 13, 1984.
76. Ibid.
77. McElvaine, 351–352.
78. "Cuomo to Challenge Archbishop over Criticism of Abortion Stand," *New York Times*, August 3, 1984.
79. McElvaine, 92.
80. "Cuomo to Challenge Archbishop over Criticism of Abortion Stand," *New York Times*, August 3, 1984.
81. "Cuomo Plans Church-State Lectures," *Newsday*, June 28, 1984.
82. Ibid.
83. Ibid.
84. Soffer, 242.
85. Michael Nelson, ed., *The Elections of 1984*, Washington, DC: CQ Press, 1985, 279.
86. "Press Off the Wall, Says Ron," *New York Daily News*, July 8, 1984.
87. "Archbishop Asserts that Cuomo Misinterpreted Stand on Abortion," *New York Times*, August 4, 1984.
88. Ibid.
89. "Cuomo Praises Archbishop's Statement," *New York Times*, August 4, 1984.
90. "Essay; Christian Republican Party?" *New York Times*, August 27, 1984.

91. "Mondale—God Isn't Republican," *New York Post*, September 6, 1984.

92. McElvaine, 352.

93. Garry Wills, *Under God: The Classic Work on Religion and Politics*, New York: Simon and Schuster, 1990, 310.

94. My citations of the address at the University of Notre Dame are based on Cuomo's remarks captured on C-Span, as opposed to the printed remarks as included in his book, *More than Words*, http://www.c-span.org/video/?c4520678/cuomo-notre-dame.

95. Cuomo's vagueness was approaching insincerity in his passive language here, as he noted, "In early summer, an impression was created in some quarters that official church spokespeople would ask Catholics to vote for or against specific candidates on the basis of their political position on the abortion issue. I was one of those given that impression."

96. John Locke, *A Letter Concerning Toleration: Latin and English Texts*, edited by Mario Montuori, The Hague: M. Nijhoff, 1963, 21.

97. "Reagan, at Prayer Breakfast, Calls Politics and Religion Inseparable," *New York Times*, August 24, 1984.

98. Ibid.

99. Ibid.

100. McElvaine, 353.

101. *Diaries of Mario M. Cuomo: The Campaign for Governor*, New York: Random House, 1984, 463.

102. Ibid., 465.

103. Author's telephone interview with Peter Quinn, Monday, September 14, 2015.

104. Ibid.

105. Reagan's analogy was made in his article for the *Human Life Review* in the spring of 1983. See Timothy Noah's article for Slate, October 11, 2004, http://www.slate.com/articles/news_and_politics/chatterbox/2004/10/why_bush_opposes_dred_scott.2.html.

106. Author's telephone interview with Peter Quinn, Monday, September 14, 2015.

107. The scripture is Luke 4:23.

108. Greg and Jennifer Willits, *The Catholics Next Door: Adventures in Imperfect Living*, Cincinnati, OH: Servant Books, 2012.

109. "Ruminating on God, Cuomo Talks of Politics (and Cuomo)," *New York Times*, October 16, 1991.

110. Audience estimate in "Gov: Separate God, Politics," *New York Daily News*, September 14, 1984.

111. Author's telephone interview with Peter Quinn, Monday, September 14, 2015.

112. McElvaine, 353–354.

113. "Cuomo Says a Bid for Presidency Would Rule Out a 2nd Term in '86," *New York Times*, September 30, 1984.

114. "Reagan Up by 13% in State: New Poll," *New York Post*, September 12, 1984.

115. "A Faith to Trust," *New York Times*, September 15, 1984.
116. "Church and State: Catholicism and Consensus," *New York Daily News*, September 14, 1984.
117. "Cuomo vs. the Church," *New York Post*, September 14, 1984.
118. Ibid.
119. "Cuomo's Insight on Religion and Politics," *Newsday*, September 17, 1984.
120. "Archbishop, Governor, and Veep," *National Review*, September 21, 1984.
121. Exit poll numbers are from the Roper Center: http://www. ropercenter.uconn.edu/polls/us-elections/how-groups-voted/how-groups-voted-1984/.
122. Bill Clinton, *My Life*, New York: Alfred A. Knopf, 2004, 319.
123. Reagan, 227.
124. Author's telephone interview with Peter Quinn, Monday, September 14, 2015.
125. "Cuomo Says a Bid for Presidency Would Rule Out a 2nd Term in '86," *New York Times*, September 30, 1984.

Part Three

1. Author's interview with Peter Quinn, Monday, September 14, 2015.
2. State of New York, *Public Papers of Mario M. Cuomo, 1985*, Albany: State of New York, 1989, xix–xxi.
3. Ibid., 6.
4. Ibid.
5. See James E. Underwood and William J. Daniels, *Governor Rockefeller in New York*, Westport, CT: Greenwood Press, 1982.
6. See Dall Forsythe, "The Governor of New York," in Gerald Benjamin, ed., *The Oxford Handbook of New York State Government and Politics*, Oxford: Oxford University Press, 2012, 263.
7. Ibid., 265, 267.
8. Underwood and Daniels, 215.
9. State of New York, *Public Papers of Mario M. Cuomo, 1985*. Albany: State of New York, 1989, 95, 96.
10. "Capitol Redux," *New York Times*, March 10, 2013, http://www. nytimes.com/interactive/2013/03/10/nyregion/a-tour-of-the-new-york-state-capitol.html?_r=0.
11. "GOP Senators from New York City and LI Get New Power," *New York Times*, January 10, 1985. The run of nearly uninterrupted Republican control of the Senate dated from 1939.
12. "Cuomo Plan Seeks Revival of Spirit of the New Deal," *New York Times*, January 10, 1985.
13. Forsythe, 269.
14. "Cuomo Plan Seeks Revival of Spirit of the New Deal," *New York Times*, January 10, 1985.
15. Ibid.

16. John Kenneth White, "Political Conflict in New York State," in Jeffrey M. Stonecash, John Kenneth White, and Peter W. Colby, eds., *Governing New York State*, Albany: State University of New York Press, 1994, 15.
17. Bill Clinton, *My Life*, New York: Alfred A. Knopf, 2004, 319.
18. https://www.youtube.com/watch?v=pNQD0v0SLbs.
19. Mario Cuomo, *More Than Words: The Speeches of Mario Cuomo*, New York: St. Martin's Press, 1993, 55.
20. Ibid., 56.
21. Ibid.
22. Ibid., 57.
23. Ibid., 60.
24. Ibid., 61.
25. Author's Interview with Peter Quinn, Monday, September 14, 2015.
26. Ibid.
27. Ibid., 63.
28. Ibid., 64.
29. Hy Rosen, *From Rocky to Pataki: Character and Caricatures in New York Politics*, Syracuse, NY: Syracuse University Press, 1998, 118.
30. "A Reporter's Notebook: Governors and Seatbelts," *New York Times*, February 1, 1985.
31. "Reporter's Notebook: Cuomo's Care over Words," *New York Times*, February 12, 1985.
32. "Abundant Budget," *New York Times*, April 6, 1985.
33. "Cuomo Approves Rise in Basic Welfare Grants," *New York Times*, April 21, 1985.
34. Robert S. McElvaine, *Mario Cuomo: A Biography*, New York: Charles Scribner's Sons, 1988, 341.
35. "Cuomo to Order Review of Police across the State," *New York Times*, May 21, 1985.
36. "The Prison-Industrial Complex," *Atlantic*, December 1998, Issue 1.
37. Ibid.
38. Author's telephone interview with the Reverend Dr. Calvin Butts, III, June 9, 2016.
39. Ibid.
40. Ibid.
41. "New York Race Tension Is Rising Despite Gains," *New York Times*, March 29, 1987.
42. "Attack Victim Too Ill to Help, Lawyer Says," *New York Times*, December 26, 1986.
43. Kenneth S. Baer, *Reinventing Democrats: The Politics of Liberalism from Reagan to Clinton*, Lawrence: University Press of Kansas, 2000, 68.
44. "Carter Urges Party to Offer a Policy Mix," *New York Times*, April 3, 1985.
45. Cuomo, *More Than Words*, 81–82.

46. Ibid., 83.
47. Ibid.
48. Author's telephone interview with Ray Scheppach, November 21, 2014.
49. Ibid.
50. "Cuomo Angered by Reagan Aide," *New York Times*, June 9, 1985.
51. "Cuomo Political Fund Has Gifts of $240,000," *New York Times*, July 28, 1985.
52. "Fete for Cuomo Sets Fund Mark of $3.4 million," *New York Times*, November 20, 1985.
53. "Reporter's Notebook: Cuomo's Care over Words," *New York Times*, February 12, 1985.
54. "At Special Albany Session, Senate Votes Down 5 of 6 Cuomo Plans," *New York Times*, December 11, 1985.
55. "Cuomo Condemns Use of 'Mafia' for Describing Organized Crime," *New York Times*, December 18, 1985.
56. "Cuomo, in State of State Message, Offers Environment and Job Plans," *New York Times*, January 9, 1986.
57. "In Budget, Cuomo Tries a Conservative Theme," *New York Times*, January 18, 1986.
58. "Kissinger Says He May Oppose Cuomo in Fall," *New York Times*, January 31, 1986.
59. "Cuomo Seeks 2nd Term; Presidential Bid Left Open," *New York Times*, May 20, 1986.
60. "Cuomo Asking for Sentences of up to Life for Crack Sellers," *New York Times*, August 16, 1986.
61. Ibid.
62. "Cuomo and O'Rourke: What Each Pledges to Do if Elected," *New York Times*, October 27, 1986.
63. Ibid.
64. Ibid.
65. "Democrats Gain Control of Senate," *New York Times*, November 5, 1986.
66. Ibid.
67. "Cuomo to 'Take a Look' at 1988 Presidency Bid," *New York Times*, November 11, 1986.
68. "Delegation in Albany Outlines Priorities," *New York Times*, January 25, 1987.
69. "Cuomo Plans Trips to Five States in Early '87 and More Later," *New York Times*, January 1, 1987.
70. Ibid.
71. State of New York, *Public Papers of Mario M. Cuomo, 1985*. Albany: State of New York, 1988, xix–xx1.
72. "Franklin Delano Cuomo," *New York Times*, January 4, 1987.
73. See, for example, Ira Katznelson's *When Affirmative Action Was White: An Untold History of Racial Inequality in Twentieth Century America*, New York: W.W. Norton, 2006.

74. "Nightmarish Search for Housing Haunts New York's Welfare Recipients," *New York Times*, February 1, 1987.

75. "Cuomo Assails Grants to Lawmakers' Projects," *New York Times*, February 19, 1987.

76. "Cuomo Remarks Barring Race for the Presidency," *New York Times*, February 20, 1987.

77. Ibid.

78. "Cuomo Sends Out Conflicting Signals on '88 Race," *New York Times*, May 19, 1987.

79. Jeffrey M. Stonecash, John Kenneth White, and Peter W. Colby, eds., *Governing New York State*, Albany: State University of New York Press, 1994, 133.

80. "Cuomo Remarks on Decision Not to Run in '88," *New York Times*, February 20, 1987.

81. "Cuomo Finally Puts His 'Hamlet' Image to Rest," *New York Times*, July 12, 1987.

82. McElvaine, 376.

83. "Don't Count Cuomo Out," *New York Times*, March 8, 1987.

84. "Will Cuomo and Baker Enter Presidential Race?" *Lakeland Ledger*, March 13, 1987.

85. "Why Mario Cuomo Played Hamlet so Well," *New York Daily News*, January 4, 2015.

86. "Cuomo Stays Cagey on any Endorsement," *Chicago Tribune*, March 9, 1988.

87. "Cuomo Calls for a 'New Realism' by US in Relations with Soviet," *New York Times*, August 24, 1987.

88. "On My Mind; The Minds of Mario Cuomo," *New York Times*, August 28, 1987.

89. "Cuomo's Phantom Campaign," *Washington Post*, September 20, 1987.

90. "Essay; the Weightless Wordsman," *New York Times*, August 30, 1987.

91. McElvaine, 381.

92. "Cuomo's Travels: Seclusion Gauges a Political Style," *New York Times*, September 7, 1988.

93. "Cuomo Supports Stand by Moscow on Rights Proposal, then Recants," *New York Times*, September 22, 1987.

94. Ibid.

95. "A Tourist's Coming of Age," *New York Times*, September 26, 1987.

96. "Experts Grill Cuomo, and He Passes, Sort Of," *New York Times*, October 15, 1987.

97. Ibid.

98. McElvaine, 387–388.

99. "Cuomo Assails Rumors of Past Family Misdeeds," *New York Times*, October 4, 1987.

100. Ibid.

101. "Mario Cuomo and Those Mob Rumors," *New York Magazine*, November 2, 1987.

102. Ibid.
103. Ibid.
104. McElvaine, 411.
105. Ibid., 412.
106. "Unorthodox Steps in Inquiry on a Cuomo Relative," *New York Times*, October 28, 1987.
107. Michael Snayerson, *The Contender: Andrew Cuomo*, New York: Twelve, 2015, 75.
108. Andrew Cuomo, 243–244. xxxx
109. "Cuomo Faults Rumors on Organized Crime," *New York Times*, October 27, 1987.
110. "Senator Simon Looks Strong, Says an Uncommitted Cuomo," *New York Times*, November 6, 1987.
111. "Won't You Toss Your Hat into the Ring, Mario Cuomo?" *Sarasota Herald Tribune*, December 24, 1987. Frank Zappa letter to Mario Cuomo (undated), New York State Library, Public Papers of Mario M. Cuomo. Note: The original handwritten letter from Frank Zappa to Cuomo is undated. However, it is accompanied by a typewritten letter from Mr. Zappa's representative Kathryn Thyne, dated March 9, 1988. Cuomo responded on March 17, 1988.
112. "Waiting for Cuomo," *Golden State Report*, January 1988.
113. "Cuomo Years: The Words vs. the Deeds," *New York Times*, January 6, 1988.
114. Ibid.
115. State of New York, *Public Papers of Mario M. Cuomo, 1985*. Albany: State of New York, 1988, xix–xx.
116. Ibid.
117. "Cuomo Seeks Quick Legislative Action," *New York Times*, January 12, 1988.
118. "For Jesse Jackson and His Campaign," *Nation*, April 16, 1988.
119. "Cuomo Remains Unflustered at Jackson Gains," *New York Times*, March 30, 1988.
120. Ibid.
121. "Jackson Share of Votes by Whites Triples in '88," *New York Times*, June 13, 1988.
122. "Cuomo vs. Legislators: Hand-to-hand Combat over Shoreham," *New York Times*, August 1, 1988.
123. McElvaine, 415.
124. "Candidate Cuomo," *New York Times*, September 30, 1988.
125. Michael Nelson, ed., *The Elections of 1988*, Washington, DC: CQ Press, 1989, 78.
126. Letters from the Politics and Presidency file (1988), New York State Library Mario M. Cuomo Collection, dated February 16, 1988, and March 4, 1988, respectively.
127. "Budget Plight in the Wings in Albany," *New York Times*, January 3, 1989.

128. "Excerpts from Cuomo Address: Challenge of Difficult Times," *New York Times*, January 5, 1989.
129. State of New York, *Public Papers of Mario M. Cuomo, 1989*, Albany: State of New York, 1989, xx–xxi.
130. "Criminal Justice: Hard Goal for Cuomo," *New York Times*, October 2, 1990.
131. "Praise and Skepticism Greet the Drug Plan," *New York Times*, January 5, 1989.
132. Ibid.
133. State of New York, *Public Papers of Mario M. Cuomo, 1989*, Albany: State of New York, 1989, 11.
134. "Officials Offer Sing Sing Prison in an Exchange," *New York Times*, April 10, 1989.
135. "Cuomo Vetoes Death Penalty Seventh Time," *New York Times*, March 21, 1989.
136. "Cuomo Warns Liberal Party on Giuliani," *New York Times*, March 27, 1989.
137. "New York Missing Legal Deadline Again," *New York Times*, April 1, 1989.
138. "Bigger Shortfall Now Faced by Cuomo for Next Budget," *New York Times*, October 27, 1989.
139. "The 1990 Elections: New York—Cuomo's Re-Election Unchallenged Victor," *New York Times*, November 7, 1990.
140. "Fiscal Woes Have Hurt Cuomo, but How Much?" *New York Times*, June 4, 1990.
141. Ibid.
142. State of New York, *Public Papers of Mario M. Cuomo, 1990*, Albany: State of New York, 1989, xix–xx.
143. "The 1989 Elections: Giuliani, Shouting for Quiet, Fights to Concede Graciously," *New York Times*, November 8, 1989.
144. "Pierre Rinfret, Economist, Chosen by G.O.P. to Run against Cuomo," *New York Times*, May 24, 1990.
145. "Few Approach Starting Gates for 1992 Presidential Stakes," *New York Times*, August 13, 1990.
146. "Cuomo's Campaign: Crime? Taxes? Look Elsewhere," *New York Times*, September 5, 1990.
147. "Cuomo Not Being Blamed for State Ills Poll Finds," *New York Times*, September 18, 1990.
148. James G. Gimpel, *National Elections and the Autonomy of American State Party Systems*, Pittsburgh: University of Pittsburgh Press, 1996, 49.
149. Mario Cuomo, *More than Words*, 212–3.
150. Ibid, 213.
151. "For Cuomo, Albany Road Runs Past Washington," *New York Times*, September 22, 1990.

152. "Cuomo Omnipotence Blunted, Gets Back to Budget," *New York Times*, November 8, 1990.
153. "The Bush Victory," *New York Times*, November 8, 1990.
154. Steven M. Gillon, *The Pact: Bill Clinton, Newt Gingrich, and the Rivalry that Defined a Generation*, Oxford: Oxford University Press, 2008, 86.

PART FOUR

1. "Cuomo Is Sworn in for Third Term without Festivities," *New York Times*, January 1, 1991.
2. State of New York, *Public Papers of Mario M. Cuomo, 1985*, Albany: State of New York, 1991, 223.
3. "Cuomo Is Sworn in for Third Term without Festivities," *New York Times*, January 1, 1991.
4. Cuomo official, (anonymous) telephone interview, February 5, 2016.
5. Ibid.
6. "Cuomo Is Sworn in for Third Term without Festivities," *New York Times*, January 1, 1991.
7. "Cuomo Prescribes Austerity, Not Activism," *New York Times*, January 10, 1991.
8. Kenneth S. Baer, *Reinventing Democrats: The Politics of Liberalism from Reagan to Clinton*, Lawrence: University Press of Kansas, 2000, 176.
9. "Democrat Session Previews '92 Race," *New York Times*, May 8, 1991.
10. The speech can be viewed online at C-Span, http://www.c-span.org/video/?17869-1/democratic-leadership-council-keynote-address.
11. Baer, 178.
12. "Democratic Group Argues over Goals," *New York Times*, May 7, 1991.
13. Ibid.
14. "Playing Numbers Game in Albany Budget Battle," *New York Times*, May 15, 1991.
15. "Budget in Turmoil as Cuomo Rejects Lawmakers' Plans," *New York Times*, May 20, 1991.
16. See "How Reliable Are the Early Presidential Polls?" Pew Research Center, February 14, 2007.
17. "Poll Finds Bush in Dead Heat if Vote Were Held Today," *Los Angeles Times*, November 12, 1991.
18. "New York State Budget Approved Nine Weeks after the Deadline," *New York Times*, June 4, 1991.
19. "Battle of Budget: Park as Political Football?" *New York Times*, June 6, 1991.
20. The survey was done by Louis Harris and Associates, https://ropercenter.cornell.edu/public-perspective/ppscan/26/26013.pdf.
21. "Cuomo Lobs 384 Balls Back to the Legislature," *New York Times*, June 16, 1991.

22. "Arkansas Governor Forms Presidential Panel," *New York Times*, August 16, 1991.

23. "Black Marches in Protest at Hynes's Summer Home," *New York Times*, September 8, 1991.

24. "California's Democrats Take Cuomo at Word," *New York Times*, September 14, 1991.

25. Ibid.

26. See Forsythe in Gerald Benjamin, ed., *Oxford Handbook of New York State Government and Politics*, Oxford: Oxford University Press, 2012, 269.

27. Michael Shnayerson, *The Contender: Andrew Cuomo, a Biography*, New York: Twelve, 2015, 123.

28. Marty Cohen, David Karol, Hans Noel, and John Zaller, *The Party Decides: Presidential Nominations before and after Reform*, Chicago: University of Chicago Press, 2008, 212.

29. "For Mario Cuomo, All Roads Lead to Home," *New York Times*, September 22, 1991.

30. "Cuomo's Blueprint: Building a Legacy," *New York Times*, September 26, 1991.

31. "The Governor's Gift: Energy," *New York Times*, September 25, 1991.

32. "Cuomo Says Bush Can Be 'Handled,'" *New York Times*, September 26, 1991.

33. Letters: "Quid Pro Cuomo," *New York Magazine*, October 28, 1991.

34. "Cuomo Details His Medicaid Plan, and Reviews Are Less than Raves," *New York Times*, October 10, 1991.

35. "Cuomo Utters a 'Maybe,' but Hastens to Add, 'Not,'" *New York Times*, October 12, 1991.

36. Ibid.

37. Ibid.

38. "Ruminating on God, Cuomo Talks of Politics (and Cuomo)," *New York Times*, October 16, 1991.

39. "New York Seen Facing New Budget Gap," *New York Times*, October 16, 1991.

40. "In 'Waiting for Mario,' Only the Plot Goes On," *New York Times*, October 16, 1991.

41. "Reading Mario's Mind," *New York Times*, October 21, 1991.

42. "Cuomo Says He's 'Looking at' 1992 Race," *New York Times*, October 21, 1991.

43. The term was applied to Cuomo, Bill Bradley, and Jay Rockefeller, by Betty Glad in Stanley A. Renshon, ed., *The Clinton Presidency: Campaigning, Governing, and the Psychology of Leadership*, Boulder, CO: Westview Press, 1995, 11.

44. See Steve Kornacki, "The Mario Effect," in *Politico*, April 10, 2011, http://www.capitalnewyork.com/article/politics/2011/04/1812706/mario-effect-last-time-group-presidential-challengers-was-unimpress?page=all. Shrum's account can be found in his *No Excuses: Confessions of a Serial*

Campaigner, New York: Simon and Schuster, 2007, 174–175. Cuomo recalled Shrum's meeting in Albany in his December 20, 1991, press conference announcing his decision not to run, http://www.c-span.org/video/?23494-1/cuomo-declines-presidential-campaign.

45. "Opinions Vary on '92 Bid by Cuomo (Including His)," *New York Times*, October 29, 1991.

46. "Cuomo to Call Back Legislature to Cope with Budget Deficit," *New York Times*, October 31, 1991.

47. "Assessing Flaws and Strengths of Cuomo, the Perpetual Potential Candidate," *New York Times*, November 1, 1991.

48. "Around City Hall: Waiting," *New Yorker*, December 30, 1991.

49. Ibid.

50. Andrew M. Cuomo, *All Things Possible: Setbacks and Success in Politics and Life*, New York: HarperCollins, 2014, 128–132.

51. "Mario Cuomo: Keeping the Faith," *New York*, http://nymag.com/nymetro/news/people/features/2426/.

52. "Cuomo, Through His Own Looking Glass," *New York Times*, November 4, 1991.

53. "Mario's Messianic Humility," *New York*, November 18, 1991.

54. Ibid.

55. Ibid.

56. Ibid.

57. Ibid.

58. "Leaders in Albany Drafting New Plan on Budget Deficits," *New York Times*, November 12, 1991.

59. "Cuomo Comes to Defense of Fiscal Plan," *New York Times*, November 13, 1991.

60. Ibid.

61. The state did find emergency resources—$40 million—to install 3,000 more prison beds. "New York to Install 3,000 More Prison Beds," *New York Times*, December 8, 1991.

62. "Cuomo Aides See Doubling of Gap in Albany Budget," *New York Times*, November 20, 1991.

63. "Talks Stall on Cuomo Budget Proposal," *New York Times*, November 21, 1991.

64. "Public and Private; Don't Call Me Ishmael," *New York Times*, November 23, 1991.

65. Ibid.

66. "Cuomo Seems Closer to Decision on Running for President," *New York Times*, December 4, 1991.

67. "Cuomo Advisers Discuss Possible Campaign Aides," *New York Times*, December 5, 1991.

68. "Governor Reports Progress on Multiyear Budget Plan," *New York Times*, December 13, 1991.

69. "Conviction Adds New Troubles for Cuomo and the Budget," *New York Times*, December 14, 1991.

70. "Getting Cuomo's Entry Form, Just in Case," *New York Times*, December 17, 1991.
71. "Gov's Mum—but Insiders Say He's about to Join Race," *New York Post*, December 18, 1991.
72. Ibid.
73. Ibid.
74. "Finally! Looks like Mario's Ready to Run," *New York Post*, December 19, 1991.
75. "Cuomo's Slip Is Showing . . . that He's Gonna Run," *New York Post*, December 18, 1991. The italics are mine, for emphasis.
76. "Gov Runs Best in Place," *Daily News*, December 19, 1991.
77. Shnayerson, 123.
78. The full statement and press conference can be viewed on C-Span, http://www.c-span.org/video/?23494-1/cuomo-declines-presidential-campaign. All quotations from the address are taken from the text and video coverage from this C-Span link.
79. Ibid.
80. Author's telephone interview with Peter Quinn, September 14, 2015.
81. "No Show: Cuomo Says He'll Forgo Run for Presidency," *Newsday*, December 21, 1991.
82. "Mario No Go," *Daily News*, December 21, 1991.
83. "Cuo-No!" *New York Post*, December 21, 1991; "Cuomo Says He Will Not Run for President in '92," *New York Times*, December 21, 1991.
84. "Cuomo Rejects Bid for President in '92," *Washington Post*, December 21, 1991; "Cuomo Says N.Y. Woes Snuffed Out Bid," *Chicago Tribune*, December 22, 1991.
85. "Cuomo Says N.Y. Woes Snuffed Out Bid," *Chicago Tribune*, December 22, 1991.
86. Ibid.
87. Text, press conference, December 20, 1991, C-Span.
88. "La Renuncia di Cuomo Spiana la Strada a Bush," *La Repubblica*, December 22, 1991, http://ricerca.repubblica.it/repubblica/archivio/repubblica/1991/12/22/la-rinuncia-di-cuomo-spiana-la-strada.html.
89. "M. Cuomo Forfait Pour la Maison Blanche," *Le Monde*, December 22, 1991.
90. "Cuomo Refuses to Run," *Times*, December 21, 1991.
91. Ibid.
92. "A Cage of Equivocation," *New York Times*, December 21, 1991.
93. Ibid.
94. "No Show: Cuomo Says He'll Forgo Run for Presidency," *Newsday*, December 21, 1991.
95. Bill Clinton, New Covenant Address, Georgetown University, October 21, 1991. All quotations related to this speech are taken from the C-Span recording and text, http://www.c-span.org/video/?23518-1/clinton-campaign-speech.

96. "Without Presidency to Shoot for, Cuomo Takes Aim at Republicans," *New York Times*, December 25, 1991.

97. Robert F. Pecoralla and Jeffrey M. Cash, eds., *Governing New York State*, Albany: State University of New York Press, 2012, 132.

98. "Wall Street Says New York State's Credit Rating Not Out of the Woods," *United Press International*, April 3, 1992.

99. "Mr. Cuomo's Sobering Speech," *New York Times*, January 9, 1992.

100. "Pragmatism Is a Big Winner as Clinton Gains in New York," *New York Times*, January 21, 1992.

101. "Clinton Sets Off Spark, and Cuomo Fans Flame," *New York Times*, January 30, 1992.

102. "Bush Jarred in First Primary, Tsongas Wins Democratic Vote," *New York Times*, February 19, 1992. See also "Write In; Cuomo Aides Dissect the Campaign that Wasn't," *New York Times*, February 20, 1992.

103. "Albany Plan Would Ease Prisoner Rise," *New York Times*, March 13, 1992.

104. "Clinton Is Victor in New York with 41% of Democratic Vote," *New York Times*, April 8, 1992.

105. "Prosecutor Cites Problems in Crown Heights Inquiry," *New York Times*, April 15, 1992.

106. "Cuomo May Not Speak at the Convention," *New York Times*, May 27, 1992.

107. "Quayle Attacks New York as Home of Liberal Failure," *New York Times*, June 16, 1992.

108. "Cuomo Turnabout: Now He Will Nominate Clinton," *New York Times*, July 7, 1992.

109. Ibid.

110. "CBS Adds Hour for Cuomo," *New York Times*, July 14, 1992.

111. All quotations from the speech are taken from the C-Span text and link, http://www.c-span.org/video/?27121-1/democratic-convention-nomination-speech.

112. "CBS Awake at Cuomo's Rousing Alarm," *Washington Post*, July 18, 1992.

113. Ibid.

114. Paul J. Quirk and Jon K. Dalager, "The Election: A 'New Democrat' and a New Kind of Presidential Campaign," in Michael Nelson, ed., *The Elections of 1992*, New York: Congressional Quarterly, 1993, 77.

115. "Justice Cuomo?" *New York Times*, April 4, 1993.

116. "Mario Cuomo: Keeping the Faith," *New York Magazine*, April 6, 1998.

117. George Stephanopoulos, *All Too Human: A Political Education*, Boston: Little, Brown, 1999, 172.

118. Ibid. Stephanopoulos's full account runs from page 166 to page 174 in *All Too Human*.

119. "Book Tells of 'Courtship' to Get Cuomo on High Court," *New York Times*, March 8, 1999.
120. Ibid.
121. "Trump, in a Federal Lawsuit, Seeks to Block Indian Casinos," *New York Times*, May 4, 1993.
122. The measure would later be killed by Senate Republicans.
123. "Ousted Speaker in Albany Wins Case on Appeal," *New York Times*, June 25, 1993.
124. "Rethinking 42nd St. for Next Decade," *New York Times*, June 27, 1993.
125. "Peekskill Legislator to Seek Governor Nomination," *New York Times*, November 10, 1993.
126. "A Poll Shows Cuomo Rating Sliding Lower," *New York Times*, November 19, 1993.
127. "Outflanking GOP," *New York Times*, January 6, 1994.
128. "Pataki's Fundraising Outpaced Cuomo's in July, Reports Show," *New York Times*, August 13, 1994.
129. "Cuomo Announces He Will Run Again, Despite Low Polls," *New York Times*, January 8, 1994.
130. "In Cuomo Strategy, Black Voters Are Vital in the Struggle for Survival," *New York Times*, October 4, 1994.
131. Butts's disappointment in the outcome of the 1994 race was evident in his fond recollections of Cuomo. "I think that Mario Cuomo was an outstanding politician, a man sensitive to the needs of all human beings, and deeply committed to justice and fairness, particularly for the working class American," Butts told me when asked of his opinion of Cuomo. "He was a good man, a masterful politician, a great governor." Author's telephone interview with the Reverend Dr. Calvin Butts, III, June 9, 2016.
132. "As State Split, High Turnout Upstate Elected Pataki and Reflected Change," *New York Times*, November 10, 1994.
133. "Pataki Defeats Cuomo in Race Called at the Wire," *Washington Post*, November 9, 1994. See also "GOP Celebrates Its Sweep to Power," *New York Times*, November 10, 1994.
134. "A King among Democrats, Cuomo Loses in New York," *Philadelphia Inquirer*, November 9, 1994.
135. "In New York, Cuomo Loses to Once Obscure Challenger," *New York Times*, November 9, 1994.
136. "Governor, Philosophical, Concedes, and Soldiers On," *New York Times*, November 9, 1994.
137. "Cuomo, a Mystery in an Enigma in a Politician, and His Final Race," *New York Times*, November 13, 1994.
138. "The Turmoil of a Split Decision," *Washington Post*, December 21, 1991.
139. "A Political Legacy That's Steeped in the Bloodline," *Times Union*, February 7, 2011.

140. "At Funeral for Mario Cuomo, Praise for a Leader's Role as a Humanist," *New York Times*, January 6, 2015.

141. Stephanopoulos, 25.

EPILOGUE

1. My interview with Giordano Maddalena, Mario Cuomo's first cousin, took place on the afternoon of Friday, July 13, 2012, at her home in Tramonti, Italy. Subsequent interviews were conducted on July 26, 2013, in Tramonti and Nocera Superiore. The interviews were facilitated by my research assistant and interpreter, Angels Miralda.

2. Andrea was born in Brooklyn and later returned to Italy for a time before once again settling in the United States.

3. Author's interview with Gigi Mauro, Nocera Superiore, July 26, 2013.

4. Author's interview with Rosaria (Rosy) Cuomo, July 26, 2013, in Nocera Superiore.

5. "Italy's Cuomos Claim Mario as Favorite Son," *New York Times*, January 1, 1983.

6. "Mafia Planned to Kill Mario Cuomo during Italy Trip as New York Governor," *Guardian*, March 11, 2016.

7. Ibid.

8. Ibid.

9. "The Powell Decision: Worries," *New York Times*, November 9, 1995.

10. FBI letter to author, November 19, 2015, signed David M. Hardy, Section Chief, Record/Information Dissemination Section\0 Records Management Division, Federal Bureau of Investigation.

11. Isaac Kramnick, ed., *The Federalist Papers*, New York: Penguin Books, 1987, 414.

Bibliography

Archives

Biblioteca Nazionale Centrale di Roma, Rome, Italy
Biblioteca di Studi Meridionali Giustino Fortunato, Rome, Italy
Eagleton Institute of Politics, Center on the American Governor,
    Rutgers University
Comune di Nocera Superiore, Nocera Superiore, Italy
Comune di Tramonti, Tramonti, Italy
Istituto Gramsci, Rome, Italy
Library of Congress, Washington, DC
Ministero Degli Affari Esteri, Rome, Italy
New York State Archives, Albany, New York

Libraries

Biblioteca Nazionale di Napoli, Naples, Italy
Biblioteca di Storia Moderna e Contemporanea, Rome, Italy
Lauinger Library, Georgetown University, Washington, DC
Library of Congress, Washington, DC
New York Public Library, New York, New York
New York State Library, Albany, NY
Seeley G. Mudd Manuscript Library, Princeton University
St. John's University Library

Newspapers and Magazines

Amsterdam News
The Atlantic
Chicago Tribune

Golden State Report
Lakeland Ledger
Los Angeles Times
Le Monde
National Review
The New Yorker
New York Daily News
New York Magazine
New York Newsday
New York Observer
New York Post
New York Review of Books
New York Times
Prep Shadow (St. John's University)
Il Progresso Italo-Americano
Red Owl (St. John's University)
La Repubblica
Res Gestae (St. John's University)
Sarasota Herald Tribune
The Torch (St. John's University)
Washington Post
The Village Voice
Vincentian (St. John's University)

I N T E R V I E W S

Anonymous New York State Official
Gerald Benjamin
Rev. Dr. Calvin Butts, III
Rosaria (Rosy) Cuomo
Dr. Nicholas D'Arienzo
Elizabeth Drew
Joseph Grandmaison
Giordano Maddalena
Joseph Mattone
Gigi Mauro
Ray Scheppach
Peter Quinn

A R T I C L E S

Ambar, Saladin. "The Rise of the Sunbelt Governors: Conservative
    Outsiders in the White House." *Presidential Studies Quarterly*,
    Mar. 2014.
Hall, Stuart. "Gramsci's Relevance to the Analysis of Racism and
    Ethnicity." United Nations Educational, Scientific, and Cultural
    Organization, 1 Aug. 1985.

B O O K S

Axelrod, David. *Believer: My Forty Years in Politics*. Penguin Press, 2015.

Baer, Kenneth S. *Reinventing Democrats: The Politics of Liberalism from Reagan to Clinton*. UP of Kansas, 2000.

Benjamin, Gerald, editor. *The Oxford Handbook of New York State Government and Politics*. Oxford UP, 2012.

Black, Conrad. *Franklin Delano Roosevelt: Champion of Freedom*. Public Affairs, 2003.

Brinkley, Douglas, editor. *The Reagan Diaries*. Harper Collins, 2007.

Busch, Andrew E. *Reagan's Victory: The Presidential Election of 1980 and the Rise of the Right*. UP of Kansas, 2005.

Cannon, Lou. *Governor Reagan: His Rise to Power*. Public Affairs, 2003.

Clarke, Thurston. *Ask Not: The Inauguration of John F. Kennedy and the Speech that Changed America*. Penguin, 2004.

Clinton, Bill. *My Life*. Alfred A. Knopf, 2004.

Cohen, Marty, et al. *The Party Decides: Presidential Nominations Before and After Reform*. U of Chicago P, 2008.

Colby, Peter W., editor. *New York State Today: Politics, Government, Public Policy*. State U of New York P, 1985.

Cuomo, Andrew M. *All Things Possible: Setbacks and Success in Politics and Life*. HarperCollins, 2014.

Cuomo, Mario. *Diaries of Mario M. Cuomo: The Campaign for Governor*. Random House, 1984.

——. *Forest Hills Diary: The Crisis of Low-Income Housing*. Random House, 1974.

——. *More Than Words: The Speeches of Mario Cuomo*. St. Martin's Press, 1993.

Dickie, John. *Darkest Italy: The Nation and Stereotypes of the Mezzogiorno, 1860–1900*. St. Martin's Press, 1999.

Freidel, Frank. *Roosevelt: A Rendezvous with Destiny*. Boston: Little, Brown, 1990.

Gabaccia, Donna, and Vicki Ruiz, editors. *American Dreaming, Global Realities: Rethinking US Immigration History*. U of Illinois P, 2006.

Gillon, Steven M. *The Pact: Bill Clinton, Newt Gingrich, and the Rivalry that Defined a Generation*. Oxford UP, 2008.

Glazer Nathan, and Daniel Patrick Moynihan. *Beyond the Melting Pot: The Negroes, Puerto Ricans, Jews, Italians, and Irish of New York City*. MIT P, 1976.

Jacobson, Matthew Frye. *Whiteness of a Different Color: European Immigrants and the Alchemy of Race*. Harvard UP, 1998.

Gimpel, James G. *National Elections and the Autonomy of American State Party Systems*. U of Pittsburgh P, 1996.

Jeffers, H. Paul. *The Napoleon of New York: Mayor Fiorello LaGuardia*. John Wiley and Sons, 2002.

Katznelson, Ira. *City Trenches: Urban Politics and the Patterning of Class in the United States*. U of Chicago P, 1981.

————. *When Affirmative Action Was White: An Untold History of Racial Inequality in Twentieth Century America.* W. W. Norton, 2006.

Kramnick, Isaac, editor. *The Federalist Papers.* Penguin Books, 1987.

Kramnick, Isaac, and Theodore Lowi, editors. *American Political Thought.* W. W. Norton, 2009.

Locke John. *A Letter Concerning Toleration: Latin and English Texts.* Edited by Mario Montuori, M. Nijhoff, 1963.

Lyttelton, Adrian. *Liberal and Fascist Italy.* Oxford UP, 2002.

McElvaine, Robert S. *Mario Cuomo: A Biography.* Charles Scribner's Sons, 1988.

McWilliams, Wilson Carey. *Redeeming Democracy in America.* Edited by Patrick J. Deneen and Susan J. McWilliams, UP of Kansas, 2011.

Massey, Douglas S., and Nancy Denton. *American Apartheid: Segregation and the Making of the Underclass.* Harvard UP, 1993.

Miroff, Bruce. *The Liberals' Moment: The McGovern Insurgency and the Identity Crisis of the Democratic Party.* UP of Kansas, 2007.

Moynihan, Daniel Patrick. *Daniel Patrick Moynihan: A Portrait in Letters of an American Visionary.* Edited by Steven R. Weisman, Public Affairs, 2010.

Nelson, Michael, editor. *The Elections of 1984.* Congressional Quarterly Press, 1985.

————, editor. *The Elections of 1992.* Congressional Quarterly Press, 1993.

Official Proceedings of the 1984 Democratic National Convention. Democratic National Committee, 1984.

Public Papers of Mario M. Cuomo, 1985. State of New York, 1989.

Renshon, Stanley A., editor. *The Clinton Presidency: Campaigning, Governing, and the Psychology of Leadership.* Westview Press, 1995.

Rosen, Hy. *From Rocky to Pataki: Character and Caricatures in New York Politics.* Syracuse UP, 1998.

Sennett, Richard. *The Fall of Public Man.* W. W. Norton, 1976.

Shrum, Robert. *No Excuses: Confessions of a Serial Campaigner.* Simon and Schuster, 2007.

Snayerson, Michael. *The Contender: Andrew Cuomo.* Twelve, 2015.

Soffer, Jonathan. *Ed Koch and the Rebuilding of New York City.* Columbia UP, 2010.

Stephanopoulos, George. *All too Human: A Political Education.* Little, Brown, 1999.

Stonecash, Jeffrey M., et al., editors. *Governing New York State.* State U of New York P, 1994.

Tichenor, Daniel J. *Dividing Lines: The Politics of Immigration Control in America.* Princeton UP, 2002.

de Chardin, Pierre Teilhard. *The Divine Milieu.* Harper Perennial, 1960.

Underwood, James E., and William J. Daniels. *Governor Rockefeller in New York.* Greenwood Press, 1982.

Viteritti, Joseph P., editor. *Summer in the City: John Lindsay, New York, and the American Dream.* Johns Hopkins UP, 2014.

Williams, Mason B. *City of Ambition: FDR, La Guardia, and the Making of Modern New York.* W. W. Norton, 2014.

Willits, Greg, and Jennifer Willits. *The Catholics Next Door: Adventures in Imperfect Living.* Servant Books, 2012.

Wills, Garry. *Under God: The Classic Work on Religion and Politics.* Simon and Schuster, 1990.

Index